Donated

In Memory of

Bonnie C. Henzel

ALSO BY DARRA GOLDSTEIN

The Georgian Feast
A Taste of Russia

The Vegetarian Hearth

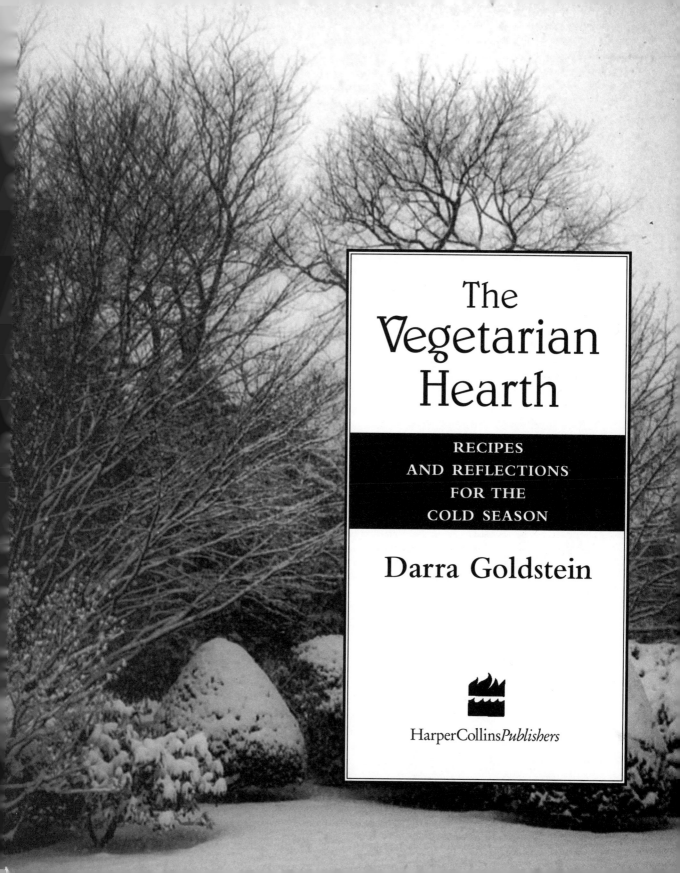

The Vegetarian Hearth

RECIPES AND REFLECTIONS FOR THE COLD SEASON

Darra Goldstein

HarperCollins*Publishers*

HarperCollins books may be purchased for educational, business, or sales promotional use.
For information please write: Special Markets Department, HarperCollins Publishers, Inc.,
10 East 53rd Street, New York, NY 10022.

FIRST EDITION

Designed by BTD/Beth Tondreau

Library of Congress Cataloging-in-Publication Data

Goldstein, Darra.
 The vegetarian hearth : recipes and reflections for the cold season / Darra Goldstein. — 1st ed.
  p.   cm.
 Includes bibliographical references and index.
 ISBN 0-06-018760-3
 1. Vegetarian cookery.   I. Title.
 TX837.G64   1996
 641.5'636—dc20   96-9012

96 97 98 99 00 ❖/RRD 10 9 8 7 6 5 4 3 2 1

For Jared Haft Goldstein
(1952–1991)

Rosemary and rue keep
Seeming and savour all winter long.

—WILLIAM SHAKESPEARE, *The Winter's Tale*

Contents

Acknowledgments

This book has carried me far beyond the sites of my previous culinary investigations, Russia and the Republic of Georgia, and I have my visionary editor, Susan Friedland, to thank for encouraging me to branch out gastronomically. The book found its proper home thanks to the astute efforts of my agent, Susan Lescher, who over the years has also become a treasured friend. I have benefited from the expertise and support of many others: Lisa and Lou Ekus and Merrilyn Lewis, whose enthusiasm for my work is unflagging; Mary Lou and Bob Heiss of Northampton's Coffee Gallery, who have kept my winter larder so amply filled; Jeanne Lemlin, who generously welcomed me into the vegetarian world; my friends in Williamstown, especially Ilona Bell, Eva Grudin, Deborah Rothschild, and Jane Denitz Smith, who have limitless patience with my obsessions; and my colleagues at Williams, who take pleasure in my culinary work. My parents, Irving and Helen Haft Goldstein, never fail to provide crucial help with my projects, cheerfully researching esoteric points and answering late-night queries about the chemical compositions of food. Bill Collins introduced me to West Virginia's buckwheat culture and provided valuable information about the local buckwheat cakes. Thanks are also due Nadya Shokhen and Volodya Tokarev for that wonderful mid-winter picnic near Abramtsevo, and Anna Fels for imagining a hearth in the heat of midsummer. Most of all I want to thank my family: my daughter, Leila, for proudly adding "vegetarian" to her five-year-old's vocabulary; and my husband, Dean Crawford, for enduring my singlemindedness as well as bushels of rutabagas. Without his guidance, fine palate, and editorial expertise this book could not have been written.

Introduction

I must have been five when I first sensed the deep pleasures and secret excitement that cold weather brings. It is a memory seasoned with the imagination's magical ability to transport. Sitting before the fire by my father's side, I was sounding out the long words in the heavy volume on his lap. At my father's encouragement, I had chosen a book from *his* library, a room suffused with lamplight more luminous than any photograph could capture. I no longer know what compelled me to pull John Greenleaf Whittier's *Snow-Bound: A Winter Idyl* from the shelf, but long before Disney took over my childhood, Whittier carried me into another kingdom:

> And, where the drift was deepest, made
> A tunnel walled and overlaid
> With dazzling crystal: we had read
> Of rare Aladdin's wondrous cave,
> And to our own his name we gave . . .

In Whittier's wintry landscape, prosaic clothesline posts turned into "tall and sheeted ghosts." The well was no cistern, but a pagoda with a Chinese roof, "And even the long sweep, high aloof,/In its slant splendor, seemed to tell/Of Pisa's leaning miracle." That evening, the cold world outside became suddenly enticing to me, while our small domestic scene gained a new, roofless dimension. *Snow-Bound* celebrates the pleasures of the hearth and home as Whittier recalls his childhood, describing with nostalgia the cider simmering by the fire, the roasting apples sputtering as they bake, the baskets filled with lately gathered nuts. Though my five-year-old palate had not yet learned to appreciate mulled cider, Whittier's verses encouraged my first winter reveries, even as they fostered my reading.

At the word "idyl" others may be inclined to picture sunny meadows and bubbling brooks, but for me it still evokes the cold season. If the world seems inert, it is because we are privy only to the surface of things: the real mystery resides below. Under ice lies running water, while bulbs gather energy under ground. Extreme cold is harsh, but it is also highly sensual; we gain new awareness of our bodies as our extremities tingle and we feel—even see—each breath. Sensations are distilled to a peak of intensity, like that of the *Eiswein* I tasted when I grew older. This coveted ice wine can be produced only after grapes have endured three days of hard frosts. Shriveled and dull on the outside, the frozen grapes yield minute quantities of extraordinarily sweet juice, which ferments into a rare and delectable wine. Frost may tinge vegetables brown, but in recompense it adds sweetness to artichokes, brussels sprouts, and turnips. Similarly intense are the dried fruits of winter: apricots, figs, raisins, and dates reward with sugar and energy at every bite.

Cold-weather passions remained with me as I grew, and as I progressed from hot chocolate to mulled cider to mulled wine and hot toddies. When it came time to study abroad, I chose Helsinki, Stockholm, and Moscow over Paris or Rome. I found that the lush, Tolstoyan rye fields of late summer appealed to me less than winter's snowy expanses. I also came to appreciate the cold as a prerequisite for getting warm, reveling in the abandon of each layer shed, luxuriating in the warmth that slowly overcomes the body, enjoying a langorousness that is all the more welcome for the muscular tautness it replaces.

Some years ago, recognizing my delight in the pleasures of the cold and their aftermath, a Russian friend suggested that we picnic in below-zero weather, and our impromptu lunch in a birch grove proved to be one of the best meals of my life, even though we remained standing up. Part of my pleasure, I must admit, derived from the excitement of the illicit journey we had just accomplished, traveling undetected from Moscow to a small village several hours to the north, successfully eluding the authorities and the threat of detainment for defying regulations. But there was more to my elation than a spy-versus-spy sort of triumph. The setting was spectacular, dazzlingly white from the birch trunks and snow, with a stillness broken only by trees crackling from the cold. We pressed together, our fingers freed from mittens for eating, groping giddily, our appetites aroused by the weather. Nadya's carefully packed basket revealed thermoses of hot tea and freshly baked pies stuffed with mushrooms and onions. The mushrooms recalled an earlier adventure, a fall day when we quoted plangent lines from Pushkin while foraging for mushrooms and berries beneath wet leaves and rotting stumps. We'd eaten a good part of our bounty for supper that night, but the remaining mushrooms we had salted and layered in crocks with black currant leaves, peppercorns, dill, and cloves. And here they were again, a kind of miracle of recollection by taste and smell. Mixed with golden slices of onion and encased in tender dough, the mushrooms tasted like the essence of the earth. By the time we savored the last bites of pie and emptied the thermoses of tea, I felt quite toasty (aided, no doubt, by the vodka we'd had the foresight to bring along).

Over the years, well-meaning friends, knowing of my interest in food, have tried to convince me to travel to more auspicious climates where diets aren't constrained by such severe seasonal limitations. Yet I find myself returning again and again to the north. The truth is, I eat lavishly wherever I go. Of course it helps that I have developed a fondness for such generally scorned vegetables as the rutabaga. But the discovery of white salsify and black scorzonera in Stockholm's market is as exciting to me as encountering a new chile pepper in Mexico City. More important, I recognize that cold weather provokes something beyond my appetite, stimulating thoughts not only of sustenance, but of nurture as well. Al fresco meals on a hot summer's night may be divine, but they lack the comforts of food consumed in front of a hearth fire as winds rage outside and frost ices the windows. Perhaps more than elsewhere, people in cold climates know the importance of a sustaining meal. And because the cold season revolves around customs and rituals, it is a time for shared gatherings.

Turning indoors means not only self-reflection, but also closer communion with family and friends. Whether we choose to look backward in memory or forward in dreamings, we muse together.

It's not that I want to remain in hibernation, dreaming in my winter den indefinitely. I look forward to warm weather like anyone else, eagerly awaiting spring and summer with their glorious bloomings—first the snowdrops and crocuses, then the daffodils and tulips with the rhubarb and early sweet peas not far behind; when tomatoes are no longer mere wintertime visions, like so many sugarplums dancing in my head, and I gather them with abandon from the garden. But inevitably, come late August, with the first hint of a chill in the air, I tire of pagan summer pleasures and find myself thinking about cold-weather delights. I think of the spicy smells of the season—ginger, cloves, nutmeg, and cardamom—and of aromatic cheeses tinted green with sage. The cold season represents a special kind of warmth, comfort, and indulgence. For me, winter's meditative appeal with its impulse toward spiritual replenishment offers a necessary balance to the wantonness of summer. From the unchecked revelry of *A Midsummer Night's Dream* I move to the contemplation of *The Winter's Tale.*

Accompanying this inward turning of my psyche is an actual movement inside, as we stow the grill and focus on the hearth. Baked squash and roasted chestnuts celebrate the onset of the frosty season just as asparagus heralds the coming of spring; only the seclusion of the indoors engages the concentration, encouraging us to create a lush and warm environment. Here is our opportunity to praise the essential, earthy flavors of winter vegetables, too often overshadowed by their splashier summer cousins.

Although the cuisines of cold climates take particular advantage of winter's gifts, the recipes in this book are not limited to foods from the north. Instead, I offer hearty foods from throughout the nontropical world. We may seldom think of Italy or France when we consider bleak weather, but most Mediterranean countries contain regions where special cold-weather delicacies are enjoyed. Thus the high plains of Turkey's Anatolia, the mountains of Lombardy, and the rugged shores of Brittany all offer lusty dishes suitable for winter entertaining. A thick lentil soup from Turkey, aromatic with dried mint, is every bit as gratifying on a blustery day—and less predictable—than a standard vegetable soup.

Where useful, I have used ingredients such as citrus fruits and nuts that are commonly available in our stores throughout the winter, even though they originate in warmer climes. Nevertheless, many of my recipes feature root vegetables, but the tastiness of their preparation should dispel any lingering prejudice that they might be bland or boring.

Too many vegetarians rue the passing of summer, finding the lack of ripe tomatoes and fresh herbs an impediment to a satisfying meal. Rather than mourning the loss of dazzling Mediterranean possibilities, we should give cold weather a chance, recognizing winter as a culinary season in its own right, one that offers ample gustatory rewards. Few pleasures are more satisfying than coming in from the cold to a warm house filled with the aromas of freshly baked bread and slowly simmered soups, or the earthy smell of oven-roasted vegetables. Winter need not be a time of gastronomic deprivation, a season to be weathered, a culinary gap to be endured year after year. The cold season can and ought to be an opportunity to luxuriate in the comforts of hearth and home.

May this book pique your spirit as well as your palate. Let them not languish in winter!

The Winter Pantry

IF, AS T. S. ELIOT WROTE, "Home is where one starts from," then it is also the place to which we return again and again, for security and provisioning, or simply for reasons of nostalgia. Metonymically, home is represented by the hearth, where ritual meals reflect a belief in the power of the domestic sphere. This power is also tangibly expressed by food supplies in the pantry, or larder, which represents the innermost core of the home. It is telling that in Homer's *Odyssey,* Penelope holds the keys to the storeroom and keeps the home fires burning until her husband returns. She is a heroine not only by dint of her unflagging loyalty and cleverness, but also because she successfully controls the household provisions. When Odysseus learns that her suitors have abused the hospitality of his home, he slaughters them. Yet, arguably, *The Odyssey* is less about Odysseus's exploits than about the importance of coming home—and of having a home to return to. Had Penelope not remained loyal, her husband's twenty-year voyage and mythic struggles would have been for naught. We lionize Odysseus's perseverance, courage, and resourcefulness in the context of his admirable goal: getting home again.

The ancient Romans also recognized the importance of the household. In their world, domestic gods called penates protected the storerooms, their name deriving from *penus,* the archaic word for larder or cupboard, a sacred place in classical mythology. The Romans certainly understood the meaningful connection between home fires and domestic provisioning: they called the inner sanctum of the temple of Vesta, keeper of the hearth for the entire city of Rome, by this name. Penates residing in Vesta's temple watched over the food supplies there. With time, their presence extended to regular households, where they worked together with other minor divinities, the *lares,* to safeguard house and home.

The larder demanded protection. Each year, months of effort went into putting up food supplies to keep the family fed from harvest to harvest. More than any other part of the home, the larder represented plenitude and security. Today, as we hasten toward the twenty-first century, it is hard to imagine the importance of keeping a larder full—we have little need to be self-sufficient when it is so much easier to run to the store for ready-made food. At one time, however, every respectable household had a larder, sometimes several, and our forebears made a distinction between a proper larder and what we generally call a pantry today. Medieval English country houses used an "undercroft," a cellarlike story beneath the living area of the house, for storing dried goods and wines; this space later evolved into separate preparation and storage rooms within the house itself. By Elizabethan times, the great houses contained several larders. A wet larder was used for pickling vegetables or salting fish and meat. The dry larder epitomized abundance. Filled to bursting with baskets of seeds and grains, burlap sacks of potatoes, barrels of cider, tubs of brined cucumbers, crocks of tutti-frutti, and jars of jams and preserves, this room was conveniently located off the kitchen, so that provisions could be fetched at a moment's notice. Here, wicker creels filled with bread dangled in the air; bunches of herbs hung from the rafters to dry. Large cones of sugar were also suspended from the ceiling at a safe distance from ants.

Houses of the well-to-do also contained an elaborate network of larders, including a separate game larder constructed away from the house to shield the residents from unpleasant smells. In the still-house fruits were distilled into liqueurs and cordials, or boiled down into jellies, preserves, conserves, and syrups. Often a special pastry pantry held a large trough and marble slab for rolling out dough. Wealthy turn-of-the-century houses in America typically had two pantries, one by the kitchen for food and equipment, the other a butler's pantry for serving. The butler's pantry was originally used for washing dishes and uncorking wine (the word "butler" derives from the Old French *bouteillier* or "bottle bearer"). Here, too, was the narrow zone in which the worlds of mistress and man collided, where the woman of the house met the butler or chief steward in his domain to go over the day's requirements.

This system began to change in mid-nineteenth-century England, when ever greater numbers of shops appeared to serve the populace. With the availability and convenience of store-bought foods, larders began to disappear, particularly the specialized ones. And as the number of household servants declined, the need for separate rooms for food preparation became less clear. These trends were accelerated in America by the work of Catherine Beecher, who believed that with rational planning, the American woman could dispense with servants altogether. Along with her sister Harriet Beecher Stowe, Beecher published in 1869 *The American Woman's Home,* a guide to "the principles of domestic science." She proselytized for both self-sufficiency and Christian ethics, convinced that the two went hand-in-hand. Beecher aimed to help the American woman along the path of self-sufficiency by providing plans for an efficient kitchen; in fact, her designs are striking for their modernity. She proposes streamlined countertops for work surfaces, with built-in shelves and storage bins for staple items underneath, making a separate pantry less crucial, if not obsolete. In the decades that followed the publication of her book, her ideas on the rational use of space and household economy were furthered by the burgeoning women's movement. Domestic reformers like Charlotte Perkins Gilman sought to liberate women entirely from their daily chores by advocating communal kitchens in special feminist residential hotels. Others, like Christine Frederick, felt that women belonged in their own kitchens. Frederick's 1919 book, *Household Engineering,* introduced industrial, production-line techniques into the home as a way of making the household more efficient. Her ideal kitchen was a large, open room with built-in cabinets instead of a separate pantry, providing more convenient and effective storage space. The cabinets could be stocked with the packaged foods that were becoming increasingly available. Today's "living kitchen" is in fact a clear extension of these early ideas for a self-contained and self-sufficient room, only now the perfect kitchen encompasses not just cooking functions, but all sorts of other purposes, from homework to R & R.

Interestingly, however, with the rise in warehouse stores and shopping clubs, people have begun stockpiling again, buying staple items in bulk, in large boxes and cans. And it's not just a matter of economy. For too long, the food industry had the American public convinced that convenience foods were the wave of the future: 1950s TV dinners evolved into today's microwavable meals. While the convenience of these prepared foods is indisputable, few now pretend that they are tasty, and the latest nutrition reports reveal many of them as quite unwholesome. Pared-down packaging may be sleek, but it suggests the opposite of plenty: there is something terribly stingy about meals-for-one. The truth is that we still crave the impression of abundance, the promise of a shared meal. And a full larder pledges both.

What does the ideal pantry or larder look like, and where should it be located? The best position is on the north side of the house, separated by at least a door from the steamy kitchen, in order to keep food as cool as possible. In warmer climates, tiles line the larder walls to keep foods crisp and dry, while small windows provide ventilation. Turkey's foremost culinary authority, Nevin Halici, gives a wonderful description of a traditional larder in Sille, a town not far from the city of Konya. A special wooden or stone shelf lines one side of the room, with indentations for large amphoras of bulgur, vermicelli, chickpeas, lentils, and beans. Onions and potatoes crowd in the spaces between the earthenware vessels. Another wall is given over to branches of oleaster, or wild olive, from which bunches of grapes or other fruits are hung for winter storage. Against a third wall stands a cupboard with jars for cheese, yogurt, and butter. Melons hang from the rafters, as do baskets of sundry foods. Mortar and pestle, rolling pin, and dough trough are all part of the standard larder equipment.

Except perhaps for the oleaster branches, this Turkish larder does not seem especially foreign. For, even though the larder as a physical space has all but disappeared in twentieth-century life, as an idea it remains fixed in our minds, conjuring up images of comfort and secret wishes fulfilled. We imagine a fantasyland of sparkling glasses and stirring smells, a Cockaigne of shimmering fruit preserves and brandies, of sugar cones and fruitcakes seasoning in whiskey or rum. Large oaken tubs overflow with sawdust or sand, concealing buried carrots, turnips, cabbages, and beets; the pungent aroma of vinegary brine lures us on. We stumble upon carefully stashed holiday goodies—tins of cookies and honeycakes, peppernut dough mellowing in the cool air, plum pudding ripening in cheesecloth. Home-brewed beer and dandelion wine magically ferment, while garlands of dried herbs cascade from above. Balls of cheese hang to ripen from the rafters, garlic dangles from the joists. All is essential, nothing overly processed. All is potential, offering visions of enticing meals to come: A cool, dark room capturing summer in its depths seems all the more special for its secret profusion in the dark days of winter. The pantry is a place apart, a fantastic realm from which bounty emanates. It is also sacred, a tribute to labor and to the good earth.

Historically, the astute housewife was aware of the power of the store-room and used it to her advantage. A well-stocked larder represented a source of pride, an emblem of efficiency, a symbol of domestic prowess. By embodying plenty, the larder offered the promise not only of hospitality, but also the more crucial appeasement of hunger through motherly or wifely love. In this regard a full larder continues to represent the fecundity of the home. This association with fruitfulness as a female characteristic is especially evident in Russian, where the noun for larder, *kladovaia,* carries a feminine ending. Also implicit in the Russian word is the idea of a treasure, or *klad,* and indeed, in nineteenth-century Russian literature, male characters seem to be more than ordinarily aroused by the hidden aspect of the larder and its tacit promise of a treasure that they can win by entry. The larder titillates them nearly as much as a woman does, and so the secrets of the larder come to be equated with the secrets of the womb. In Nikolai Gogol's "Old-World Landowners," Afanasy Ivanovich is fully aware of the larder as the dark recesses of the home, essential to its productivity. He—and his appetite—are continually stimulated by the sight of the servant girls running in and out the door. Gogol plays on the implicit connection between the sites of prolifigacy by relating that "the larder continually revealed and hid its interior," a display that quickly arouses Afanasy Ivanovich, who urgently calls for his wife to bring him something to eat.

The darker side of the larder's allure is revealed in Mikhail Saltykov-Shchedrin's novel *The Golovlevs,* where the family matriarch, Arina Petrovna, wields her power over the larder so perversely that she ultimately destroys her family. Although her children are grown, they insist on returning home, hoping for handouts, unable to resist the myth of home as a haven where physical sustenance is automatically and unconditionally provided. Nourishment becomes the book's prevailing metaphor, a gastronomic conceit that chronicles the family's dyspepsia and eventual demise. Although the Golovlev storerooms are filled to bursting and new produce is continually being toted in, Arina Petrovna refuses to allow any of the fresh goods to be eaten until the spoiled ones have been used up. One son dies of starvation. Another, Judas, seizes power and ultimately betrays his mother by withholding food from her. Succeeding generations of Golovlevs have found a convenient way to attain and wield power; they recognize that at the heart of authority lies the ability to eat. Capriciously, even maliciously, they desire to control the behavior of others, sometimes to the point of risking their survival. The family is dysfunctional to its very core. Even though the Golovlev tables are lavishly set and their larders full, no real nourishment takes place; eating is merely an empty extension of power. *The Golovlevs* chillingly demonstrates that the larder is much more than a room filled with provisions. It is also a highly emotional construct, critical to our psychological well-being.

As a place apart, the larder demands a special conception of space and time. The provisioner must think not only about ordering and rotating the goods on shelves, but also about regulating their distribution so that they will last until the next harvest or, at the least, sustain the family throughout the winter. In his culinary memoir, *Delights & Prejudices,* James Beard recalls his mother's efforts to stock up for winter. For four months, from June to October, she canned steadily to fill the cellar. By the end of each season one hundred or more jars of jam had emerged from her large brass preserving kettle. She put up apples, corn, prunes, pears, and plums and made pickles. She also laid down stores of wines, flour, sugar, and canned luxury goods. Not unlike Gogol's archetypical matron from a century before, Mrs. Beard took pride in preparing more than was needed, in order always to have delicacies on hand.

If this labor and profusion now seem outmoded, we need only examine our own contemporary habits to find that the idea of the plentiful pantry is still with us. Although we rarely have the luxury of a separate room, we approximate its riches through intricate cabinetry, whose doors accordion out to display myriad foods at a single glance. The illuminated riches of refrigerator and freezer similarly entice. What has changed for most of us is the ease with which we can reprovision. No longer must we be fully self-reliant. Shops are never too far away, nor roads so impassable that the mail-order deliveries cannot get through. The individuality of home-bottled tomato or mushroom ketchup has given way to generic store-bought brands; preserving and salting have been replaced by safety-sealed packages. Few of us take the time to gather mushrooms, berries, or wild edibles from forest and field to put up for long storage. Nor do we shred endless heads of cabbage for sauerkraut or painstakingly pick out sunflower seeds for toasting. There is no need to bake fifty pies at a time as insurance against lean times to come. And yet, in its state of unabashed preparedness, a larder still betokens a family's resource-fullness.

Keeping even a few homemade products on hand can increase our sense of preparedness and worth. In our hectic lives, winter preserves are especially convenient, for we can bottle foods at our leisure, without racing to capture the summer harvest at its peak of freshness. The winter pantry does not aim to recall summer's bounty, but to delight with the earthy produce of winter. Gingered pears, savory onions, and tart cranberries all provide a complex counterpoint to root-vegetable sweetness. And besides, simply by opening the cupboard door to rows of gleaming jars, we can bask in the splendor of our labors, a source of light in this season of darkness.

Spicy Winter Crudités

Jerusalem Artichoke Pickles

Onion Jam

Cranberry Chutney

Ginger Pear Preserves

Apple Marmalade

Glacéed Kumquats

Spicy Winter Crudités

Why wait for summer's baby vegetables to make a beautiful crudité platter, when you can serve marinated winter vegetables that don't require a dip? This vegetable medley is crisp and lively with spice. Try adding other vegetables for different color and flavor, such as julienned rutabaga or shredded cabbage.

- 1 red onion, peeled, sliced, and separated into rings
- 1 green bell pepper, cored, seeded, and cut into strips
- 1 red or yellow bell pepper, cored, seeded, and cut into strips
- 1 turnip, peeled and thinly sliced, each slice halved
- 2 cups cauliflower florets
- 2 cups broccoli florets
- 1 cup baby carrots, trimmed
- ½ cup thinly sliced radishes
- 2 tablespoons salt
- 10 cups cold water

Marinade

> 1 yellow onion, peeled and finely chopped
> ⅛ teaspoon saffron threads
> ⅛ teaspoon turmeric
> ¼ teaspoon ground cumin
> ½ teaspoon freshly ground black pepper
> ¼ teaspoon paprika
> 1 teaspoon cayenne
> 1¾ teaspoons salt
> 1½ cups olive oil

Place the prepared vegetables in a large bowl, sprinkle them with the 2 tablespoons of salt, and add the cold water. Leave to soak for 24 hours at cool room temperature.

The next day, drain and rinse the vegetables. Prepare the marinade by simmering the onion, spices, and salt in the olive oil for 10 minutes.

Spread the vegetables in a 9 x 13-inch dish. Pour the hot marinade over them. Cool to room temperature, then refrigerate for 48 hours, stirring periodically to coat all of the vegetables with the oil. Transfer to a decorative bowl to serve, either cold or at room temperature.

Serves 12.

Jerusalem Artichoke Pickles

These excellent pickles add a welcome crunch in winter. The longer they marinate, the zestier they will be.

1 medium red onion, peeled and thinly sliced
2 large garlic cloves, peeled and minced
1½ cups extra-light olive oil
1 cup cider vinegar
2 teaspoons kosher salt
4 whole black peppercorns
¾ pound Jerusalem artichokes, well scrubbed
2 small hot red peppers
¼ teaspoon dill seed

Place the onion, garlic, oil, vinegar, salt, and peppercorns in a medium saucepan. Bring to a boil and simmer, uncovered, for 15 minutes. Just before the pickling liquid is ready, slice the artichokes and place them in a clean 1-quart jar. Pour the hot liquid over the artichokes. Add the red peppers and dill seed to the jar and seal.

Allow the pickles to cool to room temperature, then refrigerate for at least 48 hours before serving. Serve cold or at room temperature.

Makes 1 quart.

Onion Jam

Trendy restaurants claim to have discovered onion jam, but the Russians have known it for centuries as *vzvar*, a thick, sweet-and-sour vegetable confit. Try this delicious condiment with plain roasted vegetables, atop a tofu burger, or as an accompaniment to a potato or rutabaga casserole. It keeps well in the refrigerator.

2 pounds yellow onions, peeled and chopped
2 tablespoons olive oil
½ cup lightly packed light brown sugar
½ cup port
¼ cup red wine vinegar
⅛ teaspoon salt
¼ teaspoon freshly ground black pepper
  Dash of cayenne
1 teaspoon Dijon mustard
2 to 4 tablespoons honey (depending on the sweetness of
  the onions)

In a large skillet cook the onions in the olive oil until softened, 12 to 15 minutes. Stir in the remaining ingredients and simmer the mixture until thickened, about 75 minutes. Serve at room temperature.

Makes about 3 cups.

Cranberry Chutney

After Thanksgiving, the cranberry is too often forgotten, only occasionally making a guest appearance in batter breads or muffins. This pungent chutney celebrates the cranberry and is an exciting change from the standard sweet mango preserve.

12 ounces fresh cranberries (about 3 cups)
 1 red onion, peeled and finely chopped (1 cup)
 1 apple, peeled, cored, and chopped
 1 cup finely chopped green bell pepper
 1 cup finely chopped dried apricots
 ½ cup golden raisins
 2 teaspoons grated orange rind
 ½ cup freshly squeezed orange juice
 1 teaspoon grated lemon rind
 ¼ cup freshly squeezed lemon juice
 2 tablespoons minced peeled fresh gingerroot
 1¼ cups firmly packed light brown sugar
 1 cup sugar
 1½ cups cider vinegar
 ½ teaspoon salt
   Freshly ground white pepper
 ⅛ teaspoon dry mustard
   Pinch of ground allspice

Mix all of the ingredients together in a large, heavy saucepan. Bring to a boil and simmer, uncovered, stirring occasionally, for about 1 hour, until thick and syrupy. Pour into containers and chill before serving. The chutney tastes best after mellowing for at least a couple of days in the refrigerator. It keeps well.

Makes 2 pints.

Ginger Pear Preserves

When gingersnaps, gingerbread, and ginger preserves fill the air with wonderful smells, they quickly enliven a housebound day. These preserves are lovely on toast and make a special holiday gift.

1½ pounds Bosc pears (3 large), peeled, cored, and finely chopped
1½ ounces fresh gingerroot (about a 3-inch knob), peeled and finely chopped
1½ pounds sugar (3¾ cups)
½ cup freshly squeezed lemon juice
2 teaspoons grated lemon rind

Place all of the ingredients in a large, wide pan, stirring to mix well. Simmer slowly until the preserve is thick and amber-colored, skimming the froth from the surface and stirring occasionally. This will take about 2 hours; the mixture should register 220°F on a candy thermometer. (The preserve can cook unattended for about an hour and a half, but be sure to watch it carefully during the last half hour so that it doesn't burn or become too thick.)

Pour into sterilized jars and seal. Process in a hot water bath or store in the refrigerator.

Makes 2 pints.

Apple Marmalade

In *The Seasonal Hearth,* Adelaide Hechtlinger reprints a recipe for Apple Marmalade from the October 1884 issue of *Household* magazine: "Take green fruit, sour, equal quantities of apples and sugar, cook the apples (a peck before they are cored) with a little water, and two lemons. When thoroughly cooked then sift, add sugar, boil fifteen minutes and can. This is delicious; much bettter than the ripe fruit, and it looks clearer, too. Common sour apples that are juicy, or crab apples, are the best for this. Try it." Try it I did. Here is my version, which yields a sweet jam with translucent apple slices that shimmer on toast.

> 2 pounds tart apples, peeled, cored, and sliced (about 6 cups)
> 2 pounds sugar (4½ cups)
>   Grated rind and juice of 2 lemons (½ cup juice)
> 1¼ cups water

Mix together the apples, sugar, lemon rind, juice, and water in a heavy, wide-bottomed saucepan. Bring to a boil, skimming any froth that rises to the surface. Cook for 20 to 25 minutes, until a candy thermometer registers 220°F.

Pour into sterilized jars and seal. Process in a hot water bath or store in the refrigerator.

Makes 3 pints.

NOTE: This jam makes a delicious topping for pancakes or ice cream.

Glacéed Kumquats

I love the sour tang of kumquats and their diminutive shape. Candying the fruit turns them deep gold in color and extends their regrettably short season. They make a lovely holiday bonbon.

  2 cups plus 3 tablespoons sugar
1½ cups water
  ½ teaspoon cream of tartar
  ½ pound kumquats (about 2 cups)

In a large saucepan dissolve the 2 cups sugar in the water over medium heat. Add the cream of tartar and boil gently for about 10 minutes, until a syrup forms.

Pierce the kumquats lengthwise with a skewer and add them to the syrup. Simmer until tender, about 30 minutes. Drain well and remove from skewers. (The syrup can be reserved for another use.)

Preheat the oven to 250°F. Place the kumquats on a baking sheet lined with a double thickness of paper towels. Dry in the oven for 75 minutes, turning a couple of times and moving them to dry areas of the paper toweling.

Place the 3 tablespoons sugar in a bowl and dredge the kumquats in it. Store them in the refrigerator in an airtight container lined with wax paper, with additional wax paper between the layers.

Makes about 2 dozen kumquats.

1

Beverages

Hot drinks are enjoyed wherever cold weather reigns, providing a necessary antidote to seasonal chills. William Cowper, the poet who gave us the adage "Variety's the very spice of life," appealingly describes the virtues of a warm drink:

Now stir the fire, and close the shutters fast,
Let fall the curtains, wheel the sofa round,
And, while the bubbling and loud-hissing urn
Throws up a steamy column, and the cups,
That cheer but not inebriate, wait on each,
So let us welcome peaceful evening in.

—WILLIAM COWPER, "THE WINTER EVENING"

We should reconsider the pleasures of such bracing beverages as hot toddies and mulled wine, which renew the spirit even as they fortify the body. In Russia, Cowper's hissing urn finds its counterpart in the samovar, whose brisk steaming has come to symbolize Russian country life. A hot samovar promised tea at a moment's notice; on the street, vendors sold cups full of *sbiten'*, an ancient meadlike beverage mulled with honey and spices. In Germany, winter cheer means a mugful of *Glühwein*, red wine flavored with spices, while Sweden's colder climate calls for *glögg*, spiced wine enriched with aquavit and port. As Cowper reminds us, however, the best cold-weather drinks need not inebriate to restore: a cup of hot chocolate spells instant comfort, as do mulled cider and *slemp*, a Dutch specialty made with hot milk, saffron, and tea.

The earliest winter drinks were heated by stirring with a red-hot poker from the fire. Today, the preparation of hot drinks is far simpler, if less dramatic. The following sampler is ideal for entertaining, inclement weather, or simply when you need some soothing.

Mulled Cider

Cranberry Quaff

Hot Chocolate

Hot Spiced Milk *(Slemp)*

Glögg

Mulled Wine

Dean's Hot Buttered Rum

Hot Rum Toddy

Hot Apple Toddy

Hot Plum Brandy *(Šumadijski čaj)*

SEE ALSO:

Flaming Punch *(Krambambuli* or *Khzhonka)* (page 285)

Mulled Cider

Each year I eagerly await the fall apple harvest, less for the crisp fruits at the local farmers' stands than for the first pressing of cider, which I enjoy straight and cold. My love affair with the drink continues as the seasons change, but once the temperature drops I heat the cider with sugar and spices for a warming libation.

- 1 quart apple cider
- 2 tablespoons light brown sugar
- 8 whole cloves
- 4 whole allspice berries
- Two 3-inch cinnamon sticks
- Peel of ½ orange, removed in a continuous spiral

In a medium saucepan heat the cider with the brown sugar, spices, and orange peel just to the boiling point. Turn off the heat and leave the cider to stand for 1 hour before serving. Serve hot. Reheat if necessary.

Serves 4.

VARIATION: For a hearty, old-fashioned mulled cider, 15 minutes before serving place four unpeeled crab or lady apples in an ovenproof dish and bake at 350°F for 15 minutes. When the cider is ready, drop one hot baked apple into each mug of liquid. The apples will split open and add an intense apple flavor to the drink.

Cranberry Quaff

This ruby drink, tart yet sweet on the tongue, is loaded with vitamin C, just the thing to ward off cold-weather contagions.

One 12-ounce package fresh cranberries
3 cups water
½ cup sugar
½ cup freshly squeezed orange juice
1 tablespoon freshly squeezed lemon juice

In a large saucepan bring the cranberries and water to a boil. Cook over medium heat for 5 minutes, or until the cranberries burst.

Force the berries and their juice through a food mill into a bowl, then strain the juice into a clean saucepan. (If you want a clear drink without any seeds, pour it through a fine strainer lined with cheesecloth.)

Add the sugar to the cranberry juice and heat for a few minutes until it dissolves. Stir in the orange and lemon juices and serve.

Serves 4.

NOTES: If you do not have a food mill, use a colander lined with a double layer of cheesecloth, pressing down on the cranberry pulp with a wooden spoon to extract as much juice as possible. Proceed as directed above.

This drink keeps well in the refrigerator and may be reheated.

Hot Chocolate

Genuine hot chocolate is the stuff of childhood memories, of coming indoors after skating or sledding, noses red and fingers frozen, and clamoring for this warming drink. It takes only minutes longer to make hot chocolate from scratch than to boil water for a mix, and what a difference in taste! Here is my daughter's favorite hot chocolate, which turns out rich and sweet. For an added indulgence, spoon a dollop of whipped cream onto each mugful.

    4 ounces (4 squares) semisweet chocolate
    ¼ cup water
    6 tablespoons light brown sugar
       Pinch of salt
    1 quart milk
    2 teaspoons pure vanilla extract

In a large saucepan over low heat mix the chocolate, water, brown sugar, and salt, whisking constantly until the chocolate melts. Gradually stir in the milk and continue to heat until very hot. Do not allow the milk to boil. Just before serving, stir in the vanilla. Pour into mugs and serve.

Serves 4.

VARIATION: For an adult pleaser, mix equal portions of prepared hot chocolate and strong hot coffee.

Hot Spiced Milk *(Slemp)*

This pale yellow drink, subtly infused with saffron, is a healthy alternative to the holiday excess of eggnog. *Slemp* is an old-fashioned beverage once fashionable at Christmas and New Year's in the Netherlands, where it was served at open houses. Vendors also set up *slemp* stands along Amsterdam's canals so that skaters could stop for a pick-me-up. It is elegant enough to offer in your finest punch cups but also makes a comforting dram before bed. The saffron, cinnamon, cloves, and tea reflect the active Dutch presence in the East Indies. For proper flavor, be sure to use high-quality saffron.

    1 **quart milk**
    ¼ **cup sugar**
One **6-inch cinnamon stick**
    3 **whole cloves**
       Peel of 1 lemon, removed in a continuous spiral
    ⅛ **teaspoon saffron threads**
    1 **tablespoon strong brewed black tea**
       Freshly grated nutmeg (optional)

In a medium saucepan place the milk, sugar, cinnamon, cloves, lemon peel, and saffron. Bring the mixture to a boil, then remove from the heat and stir in the tea. Allow to steep for 15 minutes, then strain into cups to serve warm, topped with freshly grated nutmeg, if desired.

Serves 4 to 6.

Glögg

Winter cheer is synonymous with hot drinks, and those made with alcohol are especially fortifying. One of my favorite drinks of the season is *glögg,* a Swedish mulled wine. Swedes celebrate the holidays with lavish buffets that invariably feature a kettle of this hot wine, its steam condensing on the windows and shimmering in the candlelight to create an air of magic.

There are many ways to prepare *glögg,* with vermouth, sauternes, juice, tea, or even water added to the spiced wine. I like the traditional combination of red wine, aquavit, and port, which makes the drink like liquid ruby. For dramatic effect, the *glögg* may be ignited, using sugar cubes soaked in spirits, but it tastes just as good ladled straight from the pot.

1 bottle (750 ml) fruity red wine (such as a Bordeaux)
⅓ cup plain aquavit or vodka
⅓ cup ruby port
Two 3-inch cinnamon sticks
8 whole cloves
½ teaspoon cardamom seed (removed from about 16 whole pods)
One 4-inch knob of fresh gingerroot, peeled
¼ cup firmly packed dark brown sugar
⅓ cup whole blanched almonds
⅓ cup raisins

In a medium saucepan mix together the wine, spirits, port, cinnamon sticks, cloves, cardamom seed, and gingerroot. Cover and refrigerate overnight.

About 30 minutes before serving, remove the wine mixture from the refrigerator and stir in the brown sugar. Warm over low heat, stirring for a few minutes until the sugar melts. Simmer gently for about 20 minutes.

Meanwhile, preheat the oven to 350°F. Place the almonds on a cookie sheet and toast them in the oven until golden, about 10 minutes.

Divide the toasted almonds and raisins among four heatproof mugs. When the *glögg* is thoroughly heated, strain into the mugs and serve.

Serves 4.

Mulled Wine

Germans enjoy a simpler spiced wine, appropriately called *Glühwein,* or "Glow Wine." To make 4 servings, mix 1 bottle (750 ml) fruity red wine in a saucepan with 2 tablespoons sugar, two 2-inch cinnamon sticks, 2 whole allspice berries, and 1 tangerine stuck with 6 whole cloves (a couple of slices of orange or lemon may be substituted for the tangerine). Bring to a simmer and cook gently for 20 minutes. Strain into mugs and serve.

Dean's Hot Buttered Rum

This simple drink is my favorite nightcap, though I'm not sure whether I most appreciate its soothing warmth or my husband's ministrations. It takes him only 5 minutes to prepare.

    1   jigger (1 ounce) dark rum (or more, to taste)
    1   tablespoon light brown sugar or pure maple syrup
    2   teaspoons freshly squeezed lemon juice
    1   cup boiling water
    1   teaspoon unsalted butter (optional)
    1   cinnamon stick

Mix together the rum, sugar, and lemon juice in a heatproof mug. Add the boiling water and the butter, stirring with the cinnamon stick. Serve immediately.

Serves 1.

Hot Rum Toddy

A hot toddy is more potent than hot buttered rum. For 1 serving, mix 2 jiggers (2 ounces) rum with ½ cup boiling water in a mug. Stir in 1 teaspoon sugar. Float a thin slice of lemon in the drink and grate a little nutmeg on top.

Toddies may also be made using brandy, whiskey, or gin in place of the rum.

Hot Apple Toddy

This recipe, similar to a wassail bowl but flavored with rum and cognac instead of ale, is adapted from Ted Saucier's *Bottoms Up!*, a somewhat licentious compilation of drink recipes from famous restaurants and imbibers. The Rabbit Club of Philadelphia was known for this luscious drink, which you can try at home if you have a roaring fire and plenty of time. Since most of us have neither, I offer the recipe less out of practicality than as a curiosity. It does, however, accurately reflect the time-honored practice of heating drinks indirectly, which allows flavors to blend in a way that modern direct heating can't quite duplicate. The Rabbit Club would put the ingredients for the toddy together at seven o'clock in the morning, then leave the crock to heat by the fire until luncheon at one o'clock.

12 Winesap or pippin apples
12 sugar cubes
 2 bottles (750 ml each) light rum
 1 bottle (750 ml) cognac
 2 quarts boiling water

Preheat the oven to 350°F. Place the apples in a lightly greased, shallow baking dish. Do not peel or core them. Set one cube of sugar on top of each apple. Bake until the apples are tender but still hold their shape, 30 to 60 minutes, depending on the texture of the apples.

Place the baked apples in a large earthenware crock and add the rum, cognac, and boiling water. Keep the crock close to an open fire, pouring the contents back and forth into another container from time to time to mix well, taking care not to bruise or break the apples. The longer the crock stands before the fire, the better. Make sure that the mixture does not boil.

Serve in small glasses.

Serves 50.

Hot Plum Brandy *(Šumadijski čaj)*

This deceptively named *čaj* or "tea," a Serbian specialty from a famous plum-growing region, is actually quite potent. It is slightly tricky to make, but its rich, fruity flavor is due reward.

1½ **cups plum brandy** *(slivovitz)*
1¼ **cups water**
⅓ **cup sugar**

Heat the brandy and water in a medium saucepan. The mixture should be very hot, but do not allow it to boil.

While the brandy is heating, in another saucepan stir the sugar constantly over low heat for about 15 minutes until it caramelizes to a light amber color, being careful not to let it burn.

As soon as the sugar has caramelized, pour about ¼ cup of the hot brandy mixture into the pan, whisking rapidly. The sugar will seize up slightly into a sticky mass; continue to whisk the mixture over low heat until the sugar melts again, gradually adding the rest of the liquid.

Serve hot in small punch cups.

Serves 6.

VARIATION: For those with a sweet tooth, the sugar may be increased to ½ cup to make a drink like a hot liqueur.

2

Appetizers

The key to successful cold-weather entertaining lies in greeting guests with warm food, which makes them feel coddled even as it takes the edge off their chill. No matter how beautifully arrayed raw vegetables and dips may be, they simply can't satisfy the body's need for stoking. Denizens of cold climates have long understood the soothing benefit of hot foods at the ready: the Swedish smorgasbord and Russian *zakuska* table are designed to pamper and fortify guests when they come in from the cold. Though I rarely have the leisure to provide a host of appetizers, I try always to offer something hot for nibbling. Here is a sampling of wintertime starters, which are also well suited for afternoon snacking following an excursion outdoors.

Warm Hummus

Sicilian Olives

Roasted Red Pepper and Cheese Pockets

Cheese Baked in Grape Leaves

Pear and Brie Croustades

Roasted Potatoes with *Rouille*

Roasted Chestnuts

Spicy Squash Turnovers *(Oshkovok somsa)*

Georgian Vegetable Torte

SEE ALSO:

Brandied Onions (page 152)

Chickpea Fritters *(Panelle)* (page 287)

Puffed Cheese Ring *(Gougère)* (page 68)

Spicy Winter Crudités (page 8)

Warm Hummus

The best hummus I ever tasted was at the Tuğra Restaurant in Istanbul's Čirağan Palace Hotel, where Vedat Başaran offers a menu of historic dishes from the Ottoman Empire. This recipe is inspired by the warm hummus he serves, richly textured with nuts and tingling with hot sauce.

½ pound dried chickpeas
¼ teaspoon baking soda
1 tablespoon finely chopped walnuts
1 tablespoon pine nuts
¼ cup tahini
2 tablespoons water
¼ cup freshly squeezed lemon juice
2 large garlic cloves, put through a garlic press
½ teaspoon salt
   Freshly ground white pepper

   Hot pepper sauce

Soak the chickpeas with the baking soda in water to cover overnight. The next day, drain and cover them with fresh water. Bring to a boil and simmer until the beans are very soft, about 45 minutes.

While the beans are cooking, toast the nuts in a skillet over very low heat, being careful not to let them burn. (Start with the walnuts, then add the pine nuts, which take less time to toast.) Set aside.

In a medium bowl, beat the tahini with the water until smooth. When the chickpeas are done, drain them and puree in a food processor fitted with the steel blade. Mix the puree with the tahini. Stir in the lemon juice, garlic, salt, and pepper.

Stir in the nuts. Serve the hummus warm, mounded on plates and drizzled with hot sauce.

Makes about 2 cups hummus, serving 8.

Sicilian Olives

Even olives can get dressed for winter. In eastern Sicily they are heated gently with garlic and coated with vinegar to bring out their flavor. This savory method is described in *Sicilia e le isole in Bocca (A Taste of Sicily and the Islands)*, a charming book on Sicilian food by Antonio Cardella.

1   heaping cup black brine-cured olives, such as Kalamata, rinsed
1   large garlic clove, peeled and minced (or more, to taste)
3   tablespoons olive oil
1   tablespoon red wine vinegar
    Pinch of dried marjoram

In a small saucepan heat the olives and the garlic in the olive oil over medium heat, stirring occasionally, until the garlic just begins to turn golden, about 3 minutes. Do not let it burn. Stir in the vinegar and marjoram. Turn out into a bowl and leave to cool slightly before serving, to develop their flavor and avoid burns.

Serves 4.

NOTE: Since the flavor of the olives improves as they marinate, you can prepare them ahead of time and store them in the refrigerator. Reheat gently to serve.

VARIATION: For flame-roasted olives, pit the olives and thread them on skewers. Roast over an open flame in the fireplace until sizzling.

Roasted Red Pepper and Cheese Pockets

B y varying the type of cheese in this simple appetizer, you can adapt the peppers to any number of culinary styles. Try Italian fontina for a subtle taste or Greek feta for more assertive flavor. I like to drizzle the peppers with a spicy herb- and pepper-infused oil from Provence. If you use plain olive oil, you may want to sprinkle the peppers with a pinch of dried herbs, such as oregano or rosemary.

4   red bell peppers, halved, cored, and seeded
½   pound Italian fontina cheese, cut into 16 strips
2   tablespoons aromatic olive oil
    Salt

Preheat the broiler. Place the pepper halves skin side up on a broiling pan. Broil close to the heat for about 5 minutes, until the skin is charred all over. Put the peppers in a paper bag and close it tightly. Leave them to cool, then peel.

Reduce the oven temperature to 400°F. Lightly brush a baking dish with olive oil.

Place two strips of cheese in each pepper half and fold the edges of the pepper around the cheese to enclose it completely. Lay the peppers in the dish seam side down. Drizzle with the olive oil and sprinkle with a little salt.

Bake for 15 minutes, until the cheese is bubbly. Serve hot.

Serves 4 to 8.

Cheese Baked in Grape Leaves

The idea for this recipe comes from Holly Garrison's *Periyali Cookbook,* where grape leaves are stuffed with *manouri,* a Greek ricottalike cheese. Here I've filled the packets with Sonoma Dry Jack cheese, whose mellow flavor and creamy texture work wonderfully with the briny leaves.

One 8-ounce jar grape leaves
2 tablespoons olive oil
8 ounces Sonoma Dry Jack cheese, rind removed,
    cut into 1-inch squares

Bring a large kettle of water to a boil. Remove the grape leaves from the jar and blanch them in the boiling water for 2 minutes. Rinse and drain.

Brush a 9 x 13-inch baking dish with some of the olive oil. Preheat the oven to 350°F.

Take a grape leaf and place it vein side up on a work surface. With a sharp knife remove the stem. Place a square of cheese on the leaf just above the notch where the stem was removed. Fold up the bottom of the leaf onto the cheese, then fold in the sides to enclose it. Roll the cheese up in the rest of the leaf.

Place the stuffed leaves in a single layer in the baking dish and brush with the remaining olive oil. Bake for 12 to 15 minutes, until the cheese has melted. Serve hot.

Makes about 2 dozen stuffed leaves.

NOTE: If you can't find Dry Jack cheese locally, it is available from the Williams-Sonoma mail-order catalog. Or experiment with another favorite cheese.

Pear and Brie Croustades

These elegant appetizers disappear quickly.

2 tablespoons unsalted butter, melted
12 pieces white sandwich bread
1 ripe Bosc pear, peeled, halved lengthwise, and cored
6 ounces Brie, rind removed, cut into 24 small pieces
Freshly ground black pepper

24 small sprigs of watercress

Preheat the oven to 375°F. Brush the twenty-four cups of a mini-muffin pan with half of the butter.

With a rolling pin, flatten each slice of bread. Cut out two 2½-inch rounds from each slice, avoiding the crust. Fit each round into a muffin cup and brush with the remaining butter. Bake for 10 to 12 minutes, until crisp and lightly browned. Increase the oven temperature to 400°F.

Cut each pear half in half again lengthwise, then slice into ¼-inch pieces. Place one piece of pear in each croustade. Top the pears with the cheese and grind a little black pepper over them. Bake for 6 to 8 minutes, until the cheese is bubbly.

Remove from the oven and decorate each croustade with a watercress sprig. Serve immediately.

Makes 2 dozen croustades.

Roasted Potatoes with Rouille

Rouille is a thick, spicy garlic sauce from Provence. It tastes quite wonderful served over roasted potatoes, and if you use a combination of Yellow Finn and purple potatoes, the golden *rouille* is beautifully set off. The intensity of the sauce can be controlled by using smaller or larger cloves of garlic, but be sure that whatever follows this appetizer is hearty enough to stand up to it.

1 pound yellow or purple potatoes, scrubbed and
   cut into chunks
1 tablespoon olive oil

Rouille
4 garlic cloves, peeled and chopped
½ teaspoon salt
½ cup fresh bread crumbs
   Water
½ teaspoon cayenne
½ cup olive oil

Preheat the oven to 450°F. Place the potatoes in a baking dish and brush with 1 tablespoon of olive oil. Roast them for 20 to 25 minutes, stirring once or twice, until they are tender but still firm.

To make the *rouille,* pound the garlic and salt with a mortar and pestle. Moisten the bread crumbs with a little water and squeeze to make a paste. Work this paste into the pounded garlic. Add the cayenne. Gradually beat in the olive oil to form a thick sauce. (If your mortar is not large enough to hold the olive oil, the garlic and bread crumb mixture may be transferred to the bowl of a food processor fitted with the steel blade. Gradually add the olive oil through the feed tube.)

Serve the hot potatoes drizzled with some of the *rouille.*

Serves 4 to 6.

NOTE: The *rouille* may be made ahead of time and held in the refrigerator. Bring to room temperature before serving.

Roasted Chestnuts

Sometimes the simplest things are the best. New Yorkers have long been able to indulge in the freshly roasted chestnuts hawked by street vendors, but the rest of us need not feel deprived: we can enjoy them at home. The nuts taste best when tinged with smoke from a fire, but they are delightful even when prepared in a conventional oven. On a cold night, roasted chestnuts make a much more interesting party appetizer than mixed nuts. They're also great for snacking.

1 pound fresh chestnuts

With a sharp knife cut a deep X on the flat side of each chestnut. Place them to roast on the hearth near a hot fire for about 15 minutes, until the flaps of each X split open. The nuts will be dark brown and look burned in places. Peel them and eat while still hot.

Serves 4.

NOTE: If you do not have a fireplace, the chestnuts may be cut as directed above and roasted in a 425°F oven for about 15 minutes.

Spicy Squash Turnovers *(Oshkovok somsa)*

These appetizing little pies from Uzbekistan are related to Indian samosas, except that they are baked instead of deep-fried. If you have squash on hand but are tired of serving it mashed or baked, try cooking it into this zesty filling.

Dough

1½	cups unbleached white flour
1½	teaspoons salt
½	cup warm water
1	tablespoon sour cream

Filling

2	tablespoons vegetable oil
1	large onion, peeled and finely chopped
1	pound butternut squash, peeled and grated
½	teaspoon salt
¼	teaspoon freshly ground black pepper
¼	teaspoon ground cumin
⅛	teaspoon cayenne
1	egg, lightly beaten

To make the dough, measure the flour and salt out onto a floured surface, making a mound with a well in the center. Carefully add the water and mix into a ball. Knead the dough briefly until it is pliable, then shape it into a ball and leave to rest at room temperature under an overturned bowl for 1 hour.

Roll the dough out into a 12-inch square. Brush with the sour cream, then roll up like a jelly roll. Cover tightly with plastic wrap and refrigerate overnight.

For the filling, in a large skillet heat 1 tablespoon of the oil and sauté the onion until soft, about 10 minutes. Add the grated squash along with the remaining tablespoon of oil. Stir in the salt, pepper, cumin, and cayenne. Cook the mixture, stirring, over medium heat until it is thick, about 10 minutes.

Preheat the oven to 350°F. Lightly grease a baking sheet.

To make the turnovers, divide the dough into eight pieces and roll out each piece into a 5-inch square. Place about 2 tablespoons of filling on half of each square, then bring the edges of the dough over the filling to form a triangle. Seal tightly.

Place the turnovers on the baking sheet and brush with the beaten egg. Bake for 20 minutes, until lightly browned. Serve warm.

Makes 8 turnovers, serving 4.

Georgian Vegetable Torte

This fresh-tasting salad of raw and cooked vegetables comes from the Republic of Georgia, where it is served on special occasions. The vegetables are enhanced with an aromatic walnut dressing and layered in a colorful mound. Thanks go to Diana Johnson for describing the sumptuous torte she remembered from Kutaisi.

¾ **pound waxy potatoes**
½ **pound beets (2 medium)**
1 **large carrot, peeled**
3 **scallions, trimmed**
½ **cucumber, peeled and seeded**

Dressing
½ **cup walnuts**
3 **garlic cloves, peeled and chopped**
½ **teaspoon salt**
¼ **teaspoon ground coriander seed**
⅛ **teaspoon cayenne**
½ **cup chopped parsley**
2 **teaspoons red wine vinegar**
¼ **cup hot water**

   Salt for sprinkling
¼ **cup chopped fresh coriander (cilantro)**

Boil the unpeeled potatoes in salted water until just tender, 25 to 35 minutes, depending on size. Cool, peel, and dice.

In a separate pan boil the unpeeled beets in salted water until just tender, about 25 minutes. Cool and peel. Grate the beets coarsely.

Grate the carrot coarsely, finely chop the scallions, and dice the cucumber.

To prepare the dressing, place the walnuts, garlic, salt, ground coriander, cayenne, and parsley in the bowl of a food processor fitted with the steel blade. Pulse until the walnuts are ground. Add the vinegar and water and continue to pulse until a moist paste is formed. You will have about ½ cup of dressing.

On a large, round serving platter place a layer of diced potatoes, salt them lightly, and dab with about 2 tablespoons of the dressing. Cover the potatoes with a layer of grated carrots to within 1 inch of the edges, so that a border of potatoes remains visible. Salt lightly. Top the carrots with 2 more tablespoons of the dressing. Next add a layer of grated beets, once again salting them lightly and leaving a border around the edges so that some carrots are visible. Spread on 2 more tablespoons of dressing, then layer with the finely chopped scallions, leaving a border of beets. Add the remaining dressing, then top with the diced cucumber, making sure that some scallions show around the edges. Salt lightly.

Cover the salad with plastic wrap and refrigerate for 2 to 4 hours to allow the flavors to blend. Bring to room temperature before serving, garnished with chopped fresh coriander.

Serves 8.

3

Soups

Winter is a time for soup. A stockpot sputtering cheerfully on the back burner adds moisture to the dry air, condensing as steam on the windows and creating coziness.

The soups I offer here are mainly made from scratch, but I've also included two recipes for basic stocks that are just right for the winter pantry. Since most soups improve upon standing, they can be prepared at leisure and then reheated. These cold-weather soups are not dainty broths for the fainthearted. Instead, they announce themselves and their marvelous ability to revive and restore at the coldest of times. Served with nothing more than a loaf of crusty bread, hot soup is the star of casual winter dining.

Cabbage Pie Soup

Roasted Vegetable Broth

Butternut Squash and Apple Puree

Roasted Chestnut Soup

Almond Soup *(Sopa de Almendras)*

Turkish Lentil Soup

Mushroom and Barley Soup

Mushroom Broth

Parsnip, Potato, and Spinach Chowder

Red Bean Soup

Yellow Pea Soup

Winter Fruit Soup

Rose Hip Soup

SEE ALSO:

Vegetarian Borshch (page 218)

Cabbage Pie Soup

Yes, cabbage pie soup is an odd name, but there's no better description for this wonderful dish, as lush as any French onion soup and not at all plebeian. This recipe is based on my memory of a meal I tasted one snowy weekend in northern Finland, when even my hearty hosts stayed close by the fire. Broth alone could not have satisfied on such a blustery evening, but when poured over a slice of flaky cabbage pie, the soup turned sweet and filling. For ease of preparation, the broth can be prepared well ahead (it freezes nicely), as can the dough. And for a simple supper, the cabbage pie is excellent on its own.

Dough

- 2 cups unbleached white flour
- ½ pound (2 sticks) unsalted butter, cut into small pieces
- 1 cup sour cream

Filling

- 4 tablespoons unsalted butter
- 1 small head of white cabbage (about 2½ pounds), tough outer leaves removed, cored, and coarsely grated
- 1 cup water
- 2 teaspoons salt
- 6 tablespoons sugar
- 2 tablespoons cider vinegar
- Freshly ground white pepper

- 1 egg, beaten
- 1 quart hot Roasted Vegetable Broth (recipe follows)

To prepare the dough, place the flour and butter in the bowl of a food processor fitted with the steel blade and pulse until the mixture resembles fine cornmeal. Add the sour cream and pulse until the dough is just blended and begins to pull away from the sides of the bowl.

Shape the dough into two balls, wrap each in wax paper, and refrigerate for at least 1 hour.

To make the filling, melt the butter in a large skillet. Add the cabbage, stirring to coat it well. Stir in the remaining filling ingredients. Cook, covered, over medium-low heat until the cabbage softens, about 20 minutes. Cook, uncovered, for 10 minutes more, stirring occasionally, until the liquid has evaporated.

Preheat the oven to 425°F.

On a floured board roll out one ball of dough into a rectangle about 12 x 15 inches. Fit it into a 9 x 13-inch baking dish. Spoon the cabbage filling evenly over the dough. Roll out a second crust and lay it over the filling, turning the edges under. Brush with the beaten egg. Bake until crisp and brown, 25 to 30 minutes. Cut into large squares.

Taste the broth for seasoning. It will probably need a little salt.

Use wide, flat soup plates. Place a square of pie in the bottom of each, then pour broth over. Serve at once.

Serves 8.

Roasted Vegetable Broth

1 large onion, unpeeled and quartered

6 garlic cloves, unpeeled and left whole

2 leeks, including 1 inch of the greens, sliced lengthwise and rinsed well

4 large carrots, unpeeled and halved

1 parsnip, peeled and halved

1 small turnip, peeled and quartered

1 fennel bulb, trimmed and quartered

½ pound button mushrooms, wiped and left whole

1 tablespoon olive oil

1 cup water or dry white wine plus 2 quarts water

1 large handful of parsley sprigs (1 ounce)

½ pound cabbage, coarsely chopped (about half of a medium head)

1 bay leaf

1½ teaspoons black peppercorns
¼ teaspoon dried savory
½ teaspoon salt (or more, to taste)

Preheat the oven to 400°F.

Place the onion, garlic, leeks, carrots, parsnip, turnip, fennel, and mushrooms in a large roasting pan and drizzle with the olive oil. Roast the vegetables, stirring two or three times, until browned, about 45 minutes. Transfer them to a large stockpot. Deglaze the roasting pan with 1 cup of water or wine, scraping up all the browned bits clinging to the pan. Pour this liquid into the pot with the vegetables.

Add the 2 quarts water, the parsley, cabbage, bay leaf, peppercorns, and savory. Bring to a boil, then simmer the stock for 1½ hours.

Strain the stock, pressing down on the vegetables. Season to taste with salt.

Makes 2 quarts.

NOTE: You can vary the mix of vegetables depending on what you have on hand. If you want a pale stock for another recipe, peel the onion first; leaving the skin on produces a mahogany-colored broth.

Butternut Squash and Apple Puree

T o capture the essence of the harvest, try this beautiful soup.

1 large onion, peeled and chopped
3 garlic cloves, peeled and finely chopped
4 tablespoons unsalted butter
2 pounds butternut squash, peeled, seeded,
   and cut into 2-inch pieces
¾ pound tart apples, such as Jonathan or Winesap, peeled,
   cored, and coarsely chopped (see Note)
1 cup coarse fresh white bread crumbs
2 cups apple cider
4 cups Roasted Vegetable Broth (page 44) or vegetable stock
2 teaspoons salt
½ teaspoon freshly ground white pepper
¼ teaspoon dried marjoram
   Dash of allspice

In a stockpot, sauté the onion and garlic in the butter until soft, 10 to 12 minutes. Add the remaining ingredients. Simmer the soup, uncovered, for 45 minutes, or until the squash is tender. Puree the soup in batches in a food processor and reheat.

Serves 8.

N O T E : If tart local apples are unavailable, Granny Smiths may be used.

Roasted Chestnut Soup

Most chestnut soups rely on copious amounts of butter and cream for an elegant presentation. This version brings out the natural sweetness of the chestnuts by roasting them first, so no further dressing is needed. Served simply with a loaf of crusty bread, this thick soup makes a heartening rustic meal. It is also sophisticated enough to serve as a first course at your best dinner party.

1¼   pounds fresh chestnuts
2   large carrots, peeled and chopped
2   medium onions, peeled and chopped
1   large leek, including 2 inches of green, well rinsed
      and chopped
2   large garlic cloves, peeled and minced
2   tablespoons olive oil
2   teaspoons salt
2   cups dry white wine
2   quarts water
      Generous pinch of ground allspice
      Freshly ground black pepper
2   tablespoons Madeira

   Minced parsley

Preheat the oven to 425°F.

With a sharp knife cut a deep X in the flat side of each chestnut. Spread the nuts on a baking sheet and roast for about 15 minutes, until the cut flaps have split open. Peel the chestnuts while they are still warm.

In a large stockpot cook the carrots, onions, leek, and garlic in the olive oil, covered, over low heat for 10 to 12 minutes, until soft. Stir in the salt, wine, and water. Simmer for 1½ hours.

Strain the stock, reserving the vegetables. Return 6 cups of the stock to the pot. Add the reserved vegetables and the peeled chestnuts. Simmer for 20 minutes, or until the chestnuts are soft.

Force the soup, in batches, through a food mill, or purée it in a food processor. (If you use a food processor you may need to strain the soup through a sieve to make sure that no chunks of chestnut remain.) Return the smooth puree to a clean pan. Stir in the allspice, pepper, and Madeira. Taste for seasoning. Serve hot, garnished with parsley.

Serves 8.

NOTE: This makes a very thick soup; it may be thinned with a little vegetable broth, if desired.

Almond Soup *(Sopa de Almendras)*

The simple components of this excellent Spanish soup hardly hint at its rich, slightly exotic flavor. A specialty of Granada, it has become a cold-weather favorite at our house.

8   ounces whole blanched almonds (about 1½ cups)
¼   cup olive oil
6   garlic cloves, peeled and minced
2   cups cut-up crusty, day-old white bread (cut in 1-inch cubes)
2   tablespoons minced parsley
⅛   teaspoon saffron threads
    Scant ½ teaspoon salt
    Freshly ground white pepper
4   cups boiling water

Toasted slivered almonds

In a skillet fry the whole almonds in the olive oil over medium-low heat until they begin to turn color, about 3 minutes. Stir in the garlic, bread cubes, and parsley. Crumble in the saffron threads and add the salt and pepper. Continue to fry until the almonds and bread are golden, about 2 minutes longer.

Place the almond mixture in the bowl of a food processor fitted with the steel blade. Process until the mixture forms a fine, moist paste that sticks to the sides of the bowl.

Scrape the almond paste into a large saucepan. Gradually whisk in the boiling water. Simmer 5 minutes. Serve hot, garnished with toasted slivered almonds.

Serves 4 to 6.

Turkish Lentil Soup

Given to me by Nevin Halici, Turkey's great food scholar and national treasure, this spicy, aromatic soup is guaranteed to perk up the bleakest winter day. Although it keeps well, the soup will be zestiest if served shortly after preparation.

¼ cup dried chickpeas
⅓ cup bulgur
½ cup (heaping) green lentils
6 cups water
1 medium onion, peeled and thinly sliced
1½ teaspoons cayenne
1 teaspoon salt
1 tablespoon ground coriander seed
1 tablespoon unsalted butter
½ teaspoon dried mint

Soak the chickpeas in water to cover overnight.

The next day, drain the chickpeas and place them in a stockpot along with the bulgur, lentils, and water. Bring to a boil, then simmer the soup, partially covered, for 45 minutes.

Stir in the onion, 1 teaspoon of the cayenne, and the salt. Cook 15 minutes longer. Add the coriander and simmer for 5 more minutes.

Melt the butter and add to it the remaining ½ teaspoon cayenne and the dried mint. Pour the soup into a tureen and pour the butter mixture on top. Serve immediately.

Serves 4.

Mushroom and Barley Soup

Here is a hearty, healthy soup that is popular throughout Russia and Central Europe. If you make the mushroom broth ahead of time, the soup can be ready in a little over an hour. It is not at all necessary to add sour cream, but even the tiniest dab turns the soup wonderfully creamy and mellow.

2   medium onions, peeled and chopped
3   large garlic cloves, peeled and minced
1   tablespoon olive oil
6   cups Mushroom Broth (recipe follows)
2   large potatoes (1 pound), peeled and coarsely chopped
2   medium carrots, peeled and cut into rounds
2   bay leaves
1   teaspoon salt
    Freshly ground black pepper
½   cup barley
2   tablespoons unsalted butter or olive oil
1   pound white mushrooms, trimmed and sliced
2   to 3 teaspoons freshly squeezed lemon juice
1   tablespoon snipped fresh dill

    Sour cream (optional)

In a large stockpot sauté the onions and garlic in the olive oil until soft, 12 to 15 minutes. Add the mushroom broth to the pot, along with the potatoes, carrots, bay leaves, salt, pepper to taste, and barley. Simmer, covered, for 1 hour.

Sauté the mushrooms in the butter or olive oil for about 5 minutes, until they begin to give off liquid, then add them to the soup along with any pan juices. Simmer 10 minutes more.

Just before serving, stir in the lemon juice and snipped dill. Taste for seasoning. Serve hot, with a dab of sour cream for each bowl, if desired.

Serves 8.

Mushroom Broth

By using different mushrooms you can vary the flavor of this broth. I like a mix of shiitake, oyster, and portobello; cultivated white mushrooms will yield a milder flavor. Use this broth whenever a robust soup base is called for. It freezes well.

1½ to 2 ounces dried mushrooms
10 cups water
 1 large onion, peeled and chopped
 2 garlic cloves, peeled and chopped
 1 pound mixed fresh mushrooms, wiped and coarsely chopped
 1 tablespoon olive oil
 ¾ teaspoon black peppercorns
 ½ teaspoon salt

Soak the dried mushrooms in 2 cups of the water for about 30 minutes.

Meanwhile, in a large stockpot cook the onion, garlic, and fresh mushrooms in the olive oil over medium heat until softened, about 10 minutes.

Add the dried mushrooms to the stockpot along with their soaking liquid, the peppercorns, and the salt. Pour in the remaining 8 cups of water. Simmer the broth, covered, for 1 hour.

Strain the broth, pressing down on the vegetables.

Makes about 2 quarts.

Parsnip, Potato, and Spinach Chowder

arsnips are poetic—elegant and sweeping like lines of good verse. The name of Russia's great poet Boris Pasternak translates literally as "parsnip." And just as poetry transforms the mundane, parsnips can transform an everyday soup into a lyrical meal. Thanks to the parsnips' sweetness, this soup tastes far richer than it is, and the emerald spinach provides a lovely foil for the broth's milky whiteness.

1 medium onion, peeled and finely chopped
1 small garlic clove, peeled and minced
2 tablespoons unsalted butter
4 medium parsnips (1 pound), peeled and cut into 1-inch cubes
2 large potatoes (1 pound), peeled and cut into 1-inch cubes
4 cups water
¾ teaspoon salt
2 cups tightly packed fresh spinach
2 cups milk
  Freshly ground white pepper
  Dash of cayenne
2 scallions, finely chopped
1 tablespoon minced parsley
1 tablespoon minced fresh dill

In a stockpot sauté the onion and garlic in the butter until soft, 8 to 10 minutes. Add the parsnips and potatoes, stir to coat them, then continue to cook for 3 minutes. Add the water and salt and simmer, covered, until the vegetables are tender, 20 to 30 minutes.

Wash the spinach thoroughly and remove any coarse stems. Cut it into thin strips.

Add the milk, pepper, cayenne, scallions, spinach, and parsley to the soup. Simmer 10 minutes more. Just before serving, stir in the dill.

Serves 6.

Red Bean Soup

This soup is an Americanized version of *Lobios chorba,* a specialty of the Republic of Georgia that is thick with kidney beans and fresh herbs. Simple to prepare, it needs only a loaf of bread to make a satisfying meal.

½ pound dried small red beans (1½ cups)
2 quarts water
1 bay leaf
2 medium onions, peeled and chopped
1 large carrot, peeled and thinly sliced
2 leeks, white part only, well rinsed and thinly sliced
3 garlic cloves, peeled and minced
1 small jalapeño pepper, finely chopped
2 tablespoons olive oil
1¼ teaspoons salt
    Freshly ground black pepper
⅓ cup each minced celery leaf, parsley, and fresh dill

Soak the beans overnight in water to cover. The next day, drain them and place in a stockpot with the water and the bay leaf. Bring to a boil and simmer until the beans are tender, about 1 hour.

Meanwhile, in a skillet sauté the onions, carrot, leeks, garlic, and jalapeño in the olive oil until soft, about 15 minutes.

When the beans are ready, stir in the cooked vegetables, the salt, and pepper to taste. Simmer for 15 minutes. Stir in the minced herbs and simmer for 5 minutes more. Taste for seasoning and serve hot.

Serves 4 to 6.

VARIATION: To make *Lobios chorba,* use kidney beans instead of small red beans. Add ⅓ cup minced fresh coriander (cilantro) and 1 tablespoon red wine vinegar to the soup along with the celery, parsley, and dill. Do not simmer the extra 5 minutes, but serve right away.

Yellow Pea Soup

Yellow pea soup for supper is a Thursday night tradition throughout Scandinavia, where it is often followed by small pancakes with jam. I find this meatless version plenty satisfying with nothing more than bread and a small salad. Whole yellow peas are available at specialty stores; split peas may be substituted to make a thicker soup that is more like a puree. This recipe can be easily halved, but it's so good that it makes sense to cook up a potful.

1	pound whole dried yellow peas (see Note)
10	cups water
4	whole peppercorns
4	allspice berries
1	medium onion, peeled and finely chopped
2	large leeks, well rinsed and thinly sliced, white and pale green parts only
1	large carrot, peeled and diced
2	medium potatoes, peeled and diced
½	celery root (about 8 ounces), peeled and diced
2	teaspoons salt
½	teaspoon dried marjoram
½	teaspoon dried thyme
½	teaspoon ground ginger
	Freshly ground black pepper

Soak the yellow peas overnight in 8 cups (2 quarts) of water. Do not drain. The next day, add the remaining 2 cups of water, the peppercorns, allspice, onion, and leeks. Bring to a boil and simmer, covered, for 1 hour. Stir in the carrot, potatoes, celery root, and seasonings, and simmer for 1 hour more, until the peas are tender. Serve hot.

Serves 8.

NOTE: To substitute split peas, do not soak them overnight. Place the peas in the water along with the remaining ingredients. Bring to a boil and simmer the soup for 1 to 1½ hours, until the peas are tender.

Winter Fruit Soup

When the weather turns raw Scandinavians often enjoy this sweet soup for breakfast. Shimmering with the rich colors of autumn, it also makes a soothing lunch, or a novel first course at dinner.

¼	pound each dried apricots, prunes, and pears (about ¾ cup of each)
3	cups plus ¼ cup cold water
2	cups apple juice
2	tablespoons freshly squeezed lemon juice
½	cup sugar
One	3-inch cinnamon stick
2	tablespoons currants
3¾	teaspoons potato starch

Cut the dried apricots and prunes in half; quarter the pears. Place them in a stockpot with the 3 cups of cold water. Leave to soak for 30 minutes.

Stir in the apple juice, lemon juice, sugar, cinnamon stick, and currants. Bring the mixture to a boil, skimming off any foam that rises to the surface. Simmer, uncovered, for 10 minutes.

Dissolve the potato starch in the remaining ¼ cup water. Stir into the soup and simmer 5 minutes more.

Serve hot.

Serves 4.

Rose Hip Soup

Here is another interesting fruit soup from Scandinavia, this one bursting with vitamin C. In late summer, fresh rose hips are used to create
a beautiful, rose-colored soup. Although this version with dried rose
hips is less stunning, it still makes a wonderful wintertime tonic, especially
when topped with the traditional garnish of almonds and whipped cream.

4 ounces dried rose hips (1½ cups)
6 cups cold water
   Peel of 1 lemon, removed in a continuous spiral
6 tablespoons sugar
4 teaspoons potato starch
2 tablespoons freshly squeezed lemon juice
2 tablespoons sweet red wine or port

Chopped blanched almonds (optional)
Whipped cream (optional)

Soak the rose hips overnight in the cold water. The next day, simmer the
mixture with the lemon peel for 1 to 1½ hours. Strain the soup and measure
the liquid, adding enough water to make 4 cups. Pour into a clean pot and
bring to a simmer. Stir in the sugar.

Dissolve the potato starch in the lemon juice and add to the soup. Cook
for 2 or 3 minutes, until the sugar has dissolved and the soup is thickened.
Stir in the wine. Serve hot, garnished with almonds and whipped cream, if
desired.

Serves 4.

4

Eggs
and
Cheese

With our current concern for healthful eating, eggs and cheese are sometimes perceived as extravagances, no longer part of a sensible daily diet. Interestingly, though, both enjoy some repute as aphrodisiacs: eggs as the perfect symbol of fertility and regeneration; cheese for its sensuality. By combining the two, who knows what heights can be reached in the dark days of winter?

The recipes in this chapter are admittedly some of the richest in an otherwise moderate collection. However, their delectability can't be denied. So why not save them as treats for those days when you need a special indulgence?

Cornmeal Soufflé

Grits Soufflé

Stilton Bread Pudding

Spanish Omelet *(Tortilla de patatas)*

Basque-Style Scrambled Eggs *(Pipérade)*

Welsh Rabbit

Raclette

Puffed Cheese Ring *(Gougère)*

   Spinach and Watercress Puree

Cornmeal Soufflé

I confess to a passion for pesto, even in the depths of winter. Luckily, a delicious pesto can be made from fresh parsley, with just a touch of dried basil to add complexity to wintry sauces and stews. Here, pesto stars in a lush soufflé inspired by a recipe in *Vegetarian Pleasures,* the first of Jeanne Lemlin's wonderful cookbooks.

Parsley Pesto

- 1 cup tightly packed parsley leaves
- 1 garlic clove, peeled
- 2 tablespoons chopped walnuts
- ½ teaspoon dried basil
- ½ teaspoon salt
- ½ cup olive oil

Soufflé Batter

- ½ cup yellow cornmeal
- ½ cup cold water
- 2 cups milk
- 4 tablespoons unsalted butter
- ½ teaspoon salt
- 3 eggs, separated
- 4 ounces fontina cheese, grated
- ¼ cup grated Parmesan cheese
- 6 generous tablespoons parsley pesto

Preheat the oven to 375°F, placing a rack in the lower third of the oven. Grease a 1½-quart soufflé dish.

First, make the pesto. Place the parsley, garlic, walnuts, basil, and salt in the bowl of a food processor and pulse until the nuts are ground. With the motor running, slowly pour in the olive oil through the feed tube and process until blended. (These proportions will yield a little less than 1 cup of pesto.)

To prepare the batter, in a medium saucepan mix together the cornmeal and cold water, then gradually add the milk, stirring constantly. Cook over medium heat, stirring, until the mixture thickens, about 5 minutes. Stir in the butter and salt, then turn out into a bowl.

Beat in the egg yolks one at a time, then add the fontina and Parmesan cheeses.

In a separate bowl whip the egg whites until stiff but not dry.

Spoon the egg whites and the pesto onto the cornmeal batter, then carefully fold them in, making sure not to overmix. Scrape the batter into the prepared dish and bake for 35 to 40 minutes, or until the soufflé is no longer wobbly in the center. Serve immediately.

Serves 4.

Grits Soufflé

With all the hoopla about regional American cooking, it is amazing to me that grits have not been more widely celebrated. This Southern favorite—coarsely ground dried hominy—is not only deeply American, but also delicious. Good as they are as a breakfast porridge or side dish, I like to make my grits the star at suppertime by adding onions, garlic, cheese, and eggs. This casserole is unexpectedly light, thanks to the extra water used for cooking the grits and the egg whites beaten in before baking.

1 cup grits (preferably stone-ground white)
2½ cups water
1½ cups grated sharp Cheddar cheese
1 teaspoon salt
Freshly ground black pepper
Dash of cayenne
1 medium onion, peeled and finely chopped
2 large garlic cloves, peeled and minced
2 tablespoons unsalted butter
3 eggs, separated

Preheat the oven to 350°F. Lightly grease a 1½-quart soufflé dish.

Bring the grits and water to a boil in a medium saucepan, then simmer, covered, for about 10 minutes, until the liquid is absorbed. Stir in the cheese, salt, pepper, and cayenne, and set aside to cool slightly.

Meanwhile, sauté the onion and garlic in the butter for 5 to 8 minutes, until soft. Stir the onion mixture into the grits. Beat in the egg yolks.

Whip the egg whites until they form soft peaks, then fold into the grits. Gently turn the mixture into the prepared dish. Bake for 45 to 50 minutes, until lightly browned. Serve hot.

Serves 6 to 8.

Stilton Bread Pudding

A blend of Stilton cheese and tawny port, this pudding should dispel the notion that English food is bland.

  6 cups cubed stale crusty white bread (in ½-inch cubes)
  ½ pound Stilton cheese, crumbled (about 2 cups)
2½ cups milk
  ½ cup port
  3 large eggs, lightly beaten
  1 tablespoon Dijon mustard
1½ teaspoons salt
    Freshly ground black pepper

Butter a 2-quart soufflé dish. Place a layer of bread cubes on the bottom of the dish, then cover with some crumbled cheese. Continue layering until all of the bread cubes and cheese have been used.

In a large pitcher mix together the remaining ingredients and pour over the bread and cheese. Cover the dish with aluminum foil and chill the pudding overnight in the refrigerator.

The next day, place the casserole in the oven and turn the temperature to 350°F. Bake the pudding, uncovered, for 65 to 75 minutes, until firm and brown. Serve hot.

Serves 4.

Spanish Omelet *(Tortilla de patatas)*

Unlike its Mexican counterpart, the Spanish *tortilla* is an omelet, similar to an Italian frittata. This beautiful golden disk is bursting with potatoes and onions.

¼ cup olive oil plus more if necessary
1 medium onion, peeled and finely chopped
1 garlic clove, peeled and minced
2 cups diced peeled raw potato (2 large potatoes)
½ teaspoon salt
 Freshly ground black pepper
4 eggs, beaten

Heat the oil in a 10-inch skillet. Sauté the onion and garlic in the oil until golden, 10 to 12 minutes. Add the potatoes and cook 8 to 10 minutes longer, until they are just tender. Season with salt and pepper. With a slotted spoon remove the vegetables from the oil and add them to the beaten eggs.

There should be about 2 tablespoons of oil left in the skillet; add a bit more oil if necessary. Pour the egg mixture into the oil and cook it over medium heat for about 5 minutes, until the bottom is set and nicely browned. Carefully loosen the omelet with a spatula. Place a large plate over the skillet and invert the skillet so that the cooked side of the omelet comes out right side up on the plate. Carefully slide the omelet back into the pan to cook on the other side. Cook 1 to 2 minutes longer, until the omelet is golden. Slide out onto a plate and serve hot or at room temperature, cut into wedges.

Serves 4 to 6.

Basque-Style Scrambled Eggs *(Pipérade)*

These delightfully spicy eggs are equally appealing for supper or brunch. The eggs look best when they are still moist and in large pieces, so be sure to use a gentle hand when scrambling them.

2 medium onions, peeled and finely chopped
3 garlic cloves, peeled and minced
1 green bell pepper, cored, seeded, and diced
1 red bell pepper, cored, seeded, and diced
4 tablespoons olive oil
One 28-ounce can tomatoes, drained and coarsely chopped
1 teaspoon salt
¼ teaspoon freshly ground black pepper
⅛ teaspoon cayenne
¼ teaspoon dried thyme
8 large eggs

1 tablespoon finely chopped parsley

In a large skillet sauté the onions, garlic, and peppers in the olive oil until softened, about 10 minutes. Stir in the tomatoes, ½ teaspoon of the salt, and the pepper, cayenne, and thyme. Continue to cook for 15 minutes over medium heat, until the mixture has thickened.

Beat the eggs and season them with the remaining ½ teaspoon of salt. Add them to the pan with the vegetable mixture. Cook over medium-high heat for 3 to 4 minutes, stirring the eggs occasionally with a spatula to scramble them. Try not to break them up too much. Turn the mixture out onto a platter while the eggs are still moist. Serve hot, garnished with parsley.

Serves 6.

Welsh Rabbit

What's in a name? Apparently a lot, considering the century-old debate over the proper appellation for this old English dish. Some food writers insist that the real name is "rarebit," a distortion of "rearbit" or postprandial savory; others are just as vehement about "rabbit," said to denote a playful substitute for meat. I belong to the latter camp, as this rich cheese dish needs no fancying up either in name or ingredients. The earliest form of Welsh rabbit was cheese simply melted at an open fire, then scraped over toast.

The original Welsh rabbit has spawned an endless number of variations, each more fanciful than the next. In *The Complete Book of Cheese*, Bob Brown offers "Sixty-Five Sizzling Rabbits," including a Succotash Rabbit and Ginger Ale Rabbit. He also gives recipes for a Blushing Bunny and a Rum Tum Tiddy, two variations for which Americans are responsible but should not necessarily be proud. Although not usually a food purist, here I'm adamant about plain cheese and ale: Welsh rabbit is wonderful precisely for its intensity of flavor. The only concession I make is to substitute Pickapeppa sauce for the traditional anchovy-based Worcestershire.

We no longer feel free to enjoy Welsh rabbit as often as Samuel Johnson once did, but for an occasional indulgence, there is hardly a more satisfying dish. Easy to prepare, the success of the rabbit depends largely on the quality of the cheese: a good, sharp farmhouse Cheddar should be used rather than a generic supermarket brand. Also keep in mind that time and tide and Welsh rabbit wait for no man: once the rabbit is served it should be eaten immediately, before it hardens on the plate. (It can, however, be held over simmering water for 10 to 15 minutes before serving.)

1   tablespoon salted butter
¼   teaspoon dry mustard
½   cup ale (measured so that the clear liquid comes up to
      the ½-cup mark, with the foam extending above)
2   egg yolks
¾   pound sharp Cheddar, grated
¼   teaspoon salt
1   teaspoon Pickapeppa sauce

Hot toast

In a double boiler over simmering water whisk the butter with the dry mustard until it melts. Stir in the ale and the egg yolks, mixing well, and heat until warm. Gradually add the grated cheese, a couple of tablespoonfuls at a time, stirring constantly with the whisk in one direction only and adding more cheese only after the previous amount has been incorporated. Do not allow the mixture to boil. The mixing will take about 10 minutes. Stir in the salt and Pickapeppa sauce and pour over slices of hot toast.

Serves 4.

VARIATIONS: For a Golden Buck, poach an egg and serve it on top of the cheese toast. For an Irish Rabbit, add about ⅓ cup finely chopped dill pickles to the cheese before serving. The rabbit is also delicious poured over sliced tart apples.

Raclette

As a child, I was enamored with the story of Heidi, the orphaned Swiss girl who had to trudge up a mountain in the middle of summer wearing layers of heavy clothes. Heidi's life seemed magical to me, at least when she went to live with her grandfather. At their first shared meal, her grandfather melted cheese before the fire, toasting it until golden and soft as butter. I reveled in Heidi's contentment, and when, a decade later, I found myself in the kind of Swiss village where Heidi might have lived, I eagerly tasted my childhood dream. I've been a devotee of raclette ever since.

What could be simpler than melted cheese and potatoes, with tart pickles and onions providing zest? The secret of raclette lies in the excellent melting properties of the cheese produced in the canton of Valais (*raclette* means "scraper" in French), as well as in the actively shared meal, as friends gather around the hearth and take turns scraping the melting cheese. Because a large piece of cheese is easiest to handle, raclette makes perfect winter party fare.

> **One 10-pound half wheel of raclette cheese**
> **Freshly boiled potatoes**
> **Gherkins**
> **Pickled onions**

Make a hot fire in the fireplace. Place one heatproof plate per person in a low oven to warm. Have ready an oven mitt, wide tongs, and a large knife, as well as wicker plate holders (such as those used to hold picnic paper plates) for serving.

Wearing the oven mitt and using tongs, hold the cheese on edge next to the fire, with the cut side vertical and perpendicular to the flames. When the cheese begins to bubble and melt, quickly scrape one portion onto a heated plate. Serve immediately with hot boiled potatoes, gherkins, and pickled onions. Repeat the scraping as often as necessary, one serving at a time.

Count on 4 to 6 ounces of cheese per person.

Puffed Cheese Ring *(Gougère)*

This classic French dish is made from cream puff paste mixed with cheese. Spoonfuls of the batter, arranged in a ring, bake into a beautiful golden crown that is satisfying enough to serve for supper or brunch. Although *gougère* is often presented with a creamy filling in the center of the ring, I like to offer the accompaniment on the side so that the bread doesn't get soggy. An emerald puree of spinach and watercress complements the *gougère* nicely.

½ cup milk
3 tablespoons unsalted butter
   Scant ¼ teaspoon salt
⅛ teaspoon freshly ground white pepper
¾ cup all-purpose flour
4 eggs, at room temperature
¾ cup (3 ounces) diced plus 2 tablespoons
   grated Gruyère cheese

Spinach and Watercress Puree (optional; recipe follows)

Preheat the oven to 425°F. Lightly grease a baking sheet.

In a medium saucepan bring the milk and butter to a boil. Stir in the salt, pepper, and flour and stir briskly for about 1 minute, until the mixture comes away from the sides of the pan. Remove from the heat.

Beat in three of the eggs, one at a time, until the batter is smooth and shiny. Stir in the diced cheese.

On the prepared baking sheet spoon large tablespoons of the batter into a 9-inch ring, making sure that all of the puffs are touching. Leave 2 inches open in the center of the ring. Brush with the remaining egg, lightly beaten, and sprinkle with the grated cheese.

Bake at 425°F for 10 minutes, then reduce the heat to 400°F and bake for 15 minutes more, until puffed and golden. Serve warm or at room temperature, with a vegetable puree on the side, if desired.

Serves 6.

VARIATION: You can make individual puffs for appetizers. Simply place heaping tablespoons of the batter an inch apart on the baking sheet and bake for about 15 minutes instead of 25.

Spinach and Watercress Puree

2   bunches fresh spinach (about 1¼ pounds),
     coarse stems removed
1   bunch watercress (4 to 6 ounces), coarse stems removed
1   small garlic clove, peeled
4   tablespoons unsalted butter, cut into pieces and softened
⅛   teaspoon salt

Rinse the spinach and watercress well to remove any grit, then transfer them, with water still clinging to the leaves, to a large pan. Cook, covered, over medium heat until just wilted, about 5 minutes.

Drain the leaves well and place them in the bowl of a food processor fitted with the steel blade. Put the garlic through a press and add it to the spinach and watercress. Add the butter and salt and process to a smooth puree. Serve immediately.

Serves 4 to 6.

Shrovetide Festivities

COME FEBRUARY, WINTER SEEMS too long, daylight too scant. Doctors today advocate sitting under special lamps to beat the blues, but in older times, the prescription was simpler: just celebrate. Where solstice celebrations invoked the powers of light, late-winter festivities heralded the imminence of spring. Ritually burying winter until the next year, people indulged in a last burst of merriment before agricultural labors had to begin once again. Late February and March, with their hints of warmth and damp promise of spring, offer a fine time for gaiety.

Following the establishment of Christianity, the annual merrymaking commonly became known as carnival, from the Latin *carne levare,* "to throw away meat." Although its etymology reflects the religious intent underlying the festivities, carnival itself seems highly sacrilegious in its creation of a topsy-turvy world where masquerades, revelries, and excess are the order of the day. During Lent, no meat is allowed, and observant Christians avoid dairy products, too. People have justified pre-Lenten indulgence as a way to store extra calories for the upcoming lean forty days, not unlike bears preparing for hibernation. The French call their celebration *Mardi Gras* or "Fat Tuesday," the Russians, *Maslenitsa* or "Butter Week"; the English popularly refer to their day of penance, Shrove Tuesday, as "Pancake Tuesday." No matter where it is celebrated, the carnival season, or Shrovetide, is a communal holiday that brings people together. In the past, entire towns would take sides in competitions like races and tug-of-wars. Shrovetide was also a time for affirming familial bonds, a custom possibly dating from the Roman February festival of Parentalia, when deceased relatives, especially parents, were honored with food at their graves. The Romans similarly appeased the *lares,* the gods of the household, with prepared foods at this season.

Food is essential to carnival celebrations wherever they occur, and more often than not, some sort of pancake—round in the image of the sun—is traditional. The French eat crêpes, the Russians, *bliny,* the English, griddle cakes. Crêpes, waffles, and beignets are traditional Mardi Gras fare in France; so popular are beignets in New Orleans that they have been adopted for year-round enjoyment there. Alsatian peasants believed that beignets had magical powers: they could ward off an invasion of summer mosquitoes, or make hens more productive. For this reason hens generally received the first puffy pancake. Crêpes, too, were considered a source of good luck and magical power. Nineteenth-century shepherds and neatherds in Poitou would hang a crêpe in a high tree, attach bouquets of heather and laurel to the tree, then dance around it. Some village families kept a carnival crêpe from year to year as a *porte-bonheur,* placing it on top of the highest cupboard in the house. Many refused to allow cooked crêpes to be taken out of the house, lest good luck leave along with them. Crêpe-making proved a good test for marriage. In Alsace on *Jungfrauen Fassnacht,* young village men would accompany marriageable girls to the local inn to taste the crêpes they had prepared. Badly made pancakes were nailed to the door of the town hall for all to see, to the public shame of the maker. So beloved are carnival pancakes in France that virtually every region has its own specialty, including beignets made with acacia flowers, or clotted cream, or cheese. I can't decide whether I'd rather indulge in *fantaisies bourguignonnes,* rich with butter, rum, and orange flower water, or yeasty *merveilles périgourdines,* flavored with anise.

Russians consider blini the most ancient Slavic food, prepared by their pagan ancestors in celebration of the sun. The stuff of lore in Russian literature and life, blini to this day are eaten in enormous quantities, though current consumption is paltry compared to the nineteenth century, when gourmands regularly finished off two or three dozen pancakes at a time. This voraciousness alarmed Anton Chekhov. A practicing physician as well as a writer, Chekhov frequently saw the dangers of overindulgence firsthand. In his satirical sketch "On Human Frailty [A Butter Week Theme for a Sermon]" he describes in mouthwatering detail the preparation of blini for a certain Semyon Podtykin. Podtykin can barely contain his impatience for the meal. The table is set with several sorts of vodkas and wine; bowls of garnishes cry out for the pancakes. The reader shares Podtykin's sweet anticipation: we can almost taste the piping hot blini and feel the lushness of sour cream and butter on our palates. But just as Podtykin is about to take his first bite, he keels over from a heart attack. He is left unfulfilled, along with the reader.

Each day of Butter Week had its own name and its own particular rituals. On "Gourmand Wednesday," mothers invited their married daughters and sons-in-law for blini; the young couple was expected to reciprocate on "Mother-in-Law's Friday." The carnival proper began on "Revelry Thursday," when everything—eating, drinking, dancing, and singing—was taken to extremes. Saturday, known as "Kissing Day," was awaited with especial eagerness by the village boys, who were allowed to visit any girl celebrating her first Butter Week as a bride. The newlywed girls would bring each guest a beer, then receive three kisses in return. These girls kissed a lot: newlywed couples were expected to kiss publicly during Butter Week, a ritual known as "salting mushrooms" for Lent, a way of making the upcoming fast savory. An even livelier practice was the communal kissing that involved most of the young people in a village. Dressed up in finery for the occasion, boys and girls lined up in rows on either side of the village's main street and began to kiss one another, a sport that could last for up to an hour. Interestingly, despite the free-for-all, this mass kissing was not seen as shameless. It gave the unmarried an opportunity for the kind of sexual release enjoyed by those who had married during the wedding season, which ran from Epiphany (January 6) until Butter Week.

Even more greatly anticipated than kissing, however, was sledding on ice, the favorite Butter Week pastime in Russia. Elaborately constructed wooden ice slides became popular in the eighteenth century. They stood quite high, often with multiple launching platforms that could take up an entire city block. Water was repeatedly poured down the projecting slides until it froze into a thick sheet of ice, which provided free entertainment for the populace. Sledders went down singly on toboggans, or sometimes several people joined hands and skied down the slides in a row on specially designed skis made of leather. To avoid collisions, several lanes operated at once, but a sense of danger only heightened the exhilaration of the sport. According to the French writer Théophile Gautier, who visited St. Petersburg in 1858, Russian slides had become the rage of Paris around the time of Waterloo. They also turned out to be the precursors of roller coasters, although ironically enough, when mechanized roller coasters were introduced to Russia, they received the cognomen "American slides."

Other Butter Week amusements included the building and sacking of ice forts at the river, when the attacking team was punished with a dunk in the icy water. Victor and vanquished alike would then troop home for steaming pancakes. Individual and mass fistfights were also staged. One late seventeenth-century visitor to Russia considered the fighting demonic, claiming that during Butter Week, more than one hundred people were killed. But it took another century before the Orthodox Church curtailed the fighting by decreeing that henceforth Butter Week would last only eight days instead of the original fourteen.

Troika races were another highlight of the season. In an early form of drag racing, the troikas—three horses decorated for the occasion with fancy harnesses, shaft-bows, and bells—were hitched to sleighs and sent careening down city streets. Horses in St. Petersburg would often race several abreast along the frozen Neva River. One legendary Butter Week spectacle followed Peter the Great's signing of the Neustadt Treaty in 1722. On "Revelry Thursday," a triumphant procession of nearly one hundred sleighs drawn by pigs, goats, and sheep entered Moscow's Kremlin gates, guided by revelers in masks and disguises. The sleighs were followed by dozens of boats and ships pulled on runners and sleds, with the figure of Neptune at their head. Sixteen horses drew a three-masted, eighty-eight cannon ship fitted with the latest in maritime technology. The Tsar himself sat at the helm, dressed as a naval captain and pretending to steer the ship as it moved. The royal suite was followed by masqueraders dressed up as animals from Aesop's fables. Catherine the Great later continued the raucous Butter Week traditions by celebrating her coronation with a city-wide masquerade that lasted for three days.

At the end of Butter Week, a straw scarecrow—*maslenitsa* personified—was carried out of town in procession and burned in the fields to bury winter symbolically and fete the sun, thereby ensuring fertility. Like the personification of winter as an old man, *maslenitsa* had human features. Legend tells that she was born in the far north to Father Frost. Once, at the harshest and saddest time of year, a villager noticed her hiding behind a huge snowdrift. She appeared as a beautiful girl, and since the man felt sorry for her, he asked the villagers to warm and cheer her up. But when *maslenitsa* arrived in the village, she was no longer the frail beauty the man had seen, but a hefty dame with fat cheeks, sly eyes, and a deep guffaw. She warmed the man's blood and made him forget all about winter, grabbing him by the hands and twirling him around until he fainted. Russians personify the lustiness of their holiday in *maslenitsa* as they bid her goodbye for another year.

English villagers ritually saw winter out in the form of Jack O'Lent, an effigy made of wood or straw and dressed in old clothing. On Ash Wednesday Jack O'Lent was carried through town, giving the villagers a final opportunity to kick, hit, and generally rough him up. Then, in this battered condition, he was burned. A similar burial is enacted in France on Ash Wednesday, when Carnival, in the form of a wildly dressed comic figure, is pulled to pieces. Symbolically, this burial represents not only the death of winter, but also the end of the carnival season's high times and good living, for the rigors of the Lenten fast lie just ahead. Whatever shape the effigy of winter takes, when it is burned the sun is released from winter's imprisonment, and light is finally liberated.

Marked by fairs, sports, and games condoning rowdiness and wild behavior, Shrovetide was the most popular festival in England after Christmas. At Eton, the schoolboys annually justified their increased consumption of ale by dedicating verses to Bacchus, whom they associated with Shrovetide. Westminster School in London developed official regulations for the game of Tossing the Pancake, in which the school cook tossed out a pancake for the boys to catch, encouraging a rowdy free-for-all like a rugby scrimmage. Village games often began as one-on-one competitions but soon spread to encompass entire communities, when mass contests of football and shuttlecock, great tug-of-wars, fisticuffs, and cock-fights were staged. Pancakes apparently were not the only objects tossed: the English also enjoyed throwing cocks and even dogs. The Reformers and Puritans had tried to curtail these competitions, just as they had put an end to Christmas revelries, but the popularity of the games enabled them to persist until the twentieth century. Only the threat of personal injury lawsuits finally caused the government to outlaw them as a public nuisance.

Happily, no attempts were ever made to curtail eating, even overeating. Depending on the region, different foods were enjoyed throughout the week preceding Lent. In the southwest people went "Lent-crocking" for shrovings or gifts of pancakes, or simply for the ingredients or the money to make them for Shrove Tuesday. Collops were considered good luck on Monday, fritters on Wednesday. I would have liked to spend the Saturday before Lent in Lincolnshire, where people filled up on eggs and a special crumbly frying pan pudding baked a bit thicker than pancakes. The day was variously known as "Egg Saturday" or "Brusting Saturday," from an old form of "bursting."

But the food that most substantiates the carnival season is pancakes, whether tossed in contest or less aggressively. In England, Shrove pancakes were originally baked in a long-handled copper pan over a hot fire, which in some regions was fueled by tinder-dry Christmas greenery. Pancakes were often prepared to the ringing of church bells. Residents of Gloucestershire claim that their Shrove Tuesday bells chime "pan-on, pan-on," calling people to eat, as much as to worship. "Pancake bells" resounded throughout England like a call to indulgence. When they ring in the town of Olney, Buckinghamshire, women still dash out of their houses, frying pans in hand, and race to the church, all the while tossing pancakes. Whoever reaches the church first wins this strange competition, which has endured since the fifteenth century.

Just before Lent, rich cakes also appear in various guises throughout Europe. In Sweden, the traditional Shrovetide treat is *semlor,* luscious buns filled to bursting with whipped cream and almond paste. Because they eat so many of these buns on Shrove Tuesday, the Swedes jocularly refer to the holiday as "Seven-Meals-a Day." Danes prepare *fastelavnsboller* for their Shrovetide celebrations. Children would rise before dawn and scurry to their parents' bedroom to beat the sheets with wooden switches, crying "Give us buns! Give us buns!" Shrovetide buns would miraculously appear from underneath the covers, where the parents had taken care not only to hide them but also to keep from squashing them. Some families hung the buns on strings from a chandelier, then set the chandelier spinning. Each player tried to get a bite of bun; whoever did, won the bun as a reward.

The Viennese enjoy *Faschingskrapfen,* or jelly doughnuts, as they waltz their way through the carnival season of Fasching, which begins the day after Epiphany and continues until Shrove Tuesday. Similar doughnuts, *Fastnachten,* are enjoyed in Germany and Switzerland. The Pennsylvania Dutch brought the term *Fastnacht* to America, where the buns represent the original American doughnuts, minus the hole. These buns were filled with jam. The food historian William Woys Weaver reports that they were often broken up and dropped into hot coffee for a breakfast of *coffeebrockle.*

Though carnival is still celebrated with abandon in such cities as Rio de Janeiro and New Orleans, the significance behind the annual revelry has largely been lost. The festivities may be spirited, and the costumes elaborate, but ultimately the celebration has been divested of its original, symbolic meaning. Cockthrows and dog tosses now seem like barbaric games of the past, as do village-wide demonstrations of fisticuffs. What has endured, though, is the pancake, in its many delicious forms of griddle cakes, crêpes, fritters, beignets, and doughnuts. The vitality of the pancake—like the Christmas wassail bowl—demonstrates just how enduring culinary customs are. True, we no longer believe that eating pancakes safeguards us from hunger in the year ahead; nor do we accept that in imitating the sun, pancakes symbolize our survival. And for that we can be grateful. But even if pancake eating is today no more than an indulgence, devoid of any higher meaning, we still clamor for them. We want to bid winter a lush, sweet farewell. As a communal holiday, Shrovetide once affirmed the necessary bonds that enabled families and villages to function harmoniously. So when we sit down to share pancakes with family and friends, we share in an age-old ritual. With each taste of pancake, we partake of community, enabling us to experience the warm spirit of winter, even if we no longer feel entirely free to eat to our heart's content.

Russian Butter Week Pancakes *(Fine Blini and Buckwheat Blini)*
    Fine Blini
    Buckwheat Blini
Sweet Buckwheat Crêpes *(Crêpes de blé noir)*
New Orleans Rice Fritters *(Calas)*
Shrovetide Buns *(Semlor)*
    Almond Paste

Russian Butter Week Pancakes (*Bliny*)

The epitome of luxury and plenty, blini are one of Russia's great contributions to world cuisine. The early twentieth-century writer Alexander Kuprin explains the significance of these pancakes in Russian life: "Symbol of the sun, of beautiful days, of good harvests, of harmonious marriages and healthy children . . . The *blin* is round, like the bounteous sun. The *blin* is golden and hot, like the all-warming sun, the *blin* is slathered with melted butter, reminding us of sacrifices once offered to powerful stone idols."

As solar symbols, blini are especially enjoyed during Butter Week, when the pallid light of winter begins to transform itself into springtime's rejuvenating sun. And what would blini be without butter? Their sponginess is calculated to soak up as much as possible. Connoisseurs disagree over whether the melted butter should be drizzled over the pancakes or used for dipping. Vladimir Nabokov, ever the arbiter of proper usage, unequivocally states that the blini must be dipped into butter. And we know that Chichikov, Nikolai Gogol's hero from *Dead Souls,* rolled his blini up three at a time before dipping them in melted butter; and he easily polished off nearly a dozen at one go.

Blini come in many varieties. Thicker and puffier than French crêpes, they are lighter than American pancakes. I offer two recipes here, the first for wheat-flour blini (called *krasnye,* or "fine," in Russian), the second for buckwheat pancakes. The wheat-flour blini are especially elegant and were once the most expensive to prepare, yet I remain partial to the more traditional buckwheat pancakes with their earthier flavor and slightly more porous texture.

The rising times given here are flexible, since several slow risings make the blini light. The batter practically prepares itself; cooking the pancakes takes some practice, though. Experienced Russian cooks know that "the first *blin* is always a lump." You might even find that the first three or four pancakes you make look decidedly imperfect, but they'll still taste good, and you'll soon get the hang of it. Results will be best if you cook the blini in a crêpe pan or small cast-iron skillet that has been well greased with clarified butter or vegetable oil. Russian cooks use a halved raw potato to swab the skillet with butter in between pancakes.

Fine Blini

2½ teaspoons active dry yeast
2 teaspoons sugar
¾ teaspoon salt
3 cups all-purpose flour
3 cups lukewarm milk plus up to ½ cup more if necessary
3 egg yolks
3 tablespoons unsalted butter, melted and cooled
2 egg whites
½ cup heavy cream

Clarified butter or vegetable oil for cooking
Choice of garnishes (see Notes)

Mix the yeast, sugar, salt, and flour together in a large bowl. Stir in 3 cups of the milk. Cover and leave to rise until bubbly, 1½ to 2 hours.

Stir in the egg yolks and butter, mixing well. Cover again and leave to rise for another 1 to 2 hours.

Beat the egg whites until stiff but not dry. Whip the cream until it forms soft peaks. Fold the egg whites and cream into the batter. Check the batter. It should be the consistency of heavy cream. If it is too thick, gently add up to ½ cup more lukewarm milk. Cover and let rise for 30 minutes.

Heat one or more crêpe pans or small skillets, preferably cast-iron. Brush with clarified butter or vegetable oil.

Take about 2 tablespoons of batter from the top and pour it onto a hot pan, swirling to make a pancake that is about 5 inches in diameter. Cook over medium heat until bubbles appear on the surface and the underside is brown, approximately 1 minute. Turn and cook briefly on the other side (the second side should not be as brown). Repeat this procedure for each pancake, greasing the skillet beforehand.

Serve immediately, with a choice of garnishes.

Serves 6.

NOTES: Blini taste best hot from the pan, but they can be held briefly by piling them in a heated, deep dish covered with a linen towel.

The traditional accompaniment to blini would be smoked fish or caviar, which adds a salty counterpoint and interesting texture to the rich, tender pancakes. Sautéed wild mushrooms, onions, or scallions; cooked buckwheat groats; and chopped hard-boiled eggs also make excellent garnishes. So does sour cream. And if you haven't eaten your fill of blini for supper, you can always have some with jam for dessert.

Leftover blini may be filled with minced vegetables or cheese, folded into envelopes, and sautéed in butter or oil until brown. These are known as *blinchiki,* and they make an excellent supper.

Buckwheat Blini

2½ teaspoons active dry yeast
1 teaspoon sugar
½ teaspoon salt
1 cup buckwheat flour
2 cups lukewarm milk
1¼ cups all-purpose flour
¼ cup sour cream
3 eggs, separated
2 tablespoons unsalted butter, melted (optional)
½ cup heavy cream

Clarified butter or vegetable oil for cooking
Choice of garnishes

Mix the yeast, sugar, salt, and buckwheat flour together in a large bowl. Stir in the milk. Cover and leave to rise until bubbly, 1 to 1½ hours.

Stir in the all-purpose flour, the sour cream, egg yolks, and butter (if adding it), mixing well. Cover again and leave to rise for 2 hours.

Beat the egg whites until stiff but not dry. Whip the cream until it forms soft peaks. Fold the egg whites and cream into the batter. Cover and let rise for 30 minutes.

Heat one or more crêpe pans or small skillets, preferably cast-iron. Brush with clarified butter or vegetable oil.

Take about 2 tablespoons of batter from the top and pour it onto a hot pan, swirling to make a pancake that is about 5 inches in diameter. Cook over medium heat until bubbles appear on the surface and the underside is brown, approximately 1 minute. Turn and cook briefly on the other side (the second side should not be as brown). Repeat this procedure for each pancake, greasing the skillet beforehand.

Serve immediately, with a choice of garnishes.

Serves 6.

Sweet Buckwheat Crêpes *(Crêpes de blé noir)*

These delicate French pancakes are thinner and crisper than Russian *bliny*. The batter benefits from an overnight rest in the refrigerator, but if you are pressed for time, it can sit for just 2 to 3 hours before baking.

1 cup buckwheat flour
Pinch of salt
¼ cup sugar
¾ cup milk
¼ cup water
3 eggs, lightly beaten
4 tablespoons unsalted butter, melted
¼ teaspoon ground cinnamon
2 teaspoons rum
½ teaspoon orange flower water

Clarified butter or vegetable oil for cooking
Sugar or jam

In a medium bowl mix together the buckwheat flour, salt, sugar, milk, and water. Beat in the eggs and the butter, then add the cinnamon, rum, and orange flower water, mixing well. Cover the bowl and refrigerate the batter overnight.

To cook, grease a well-seasoned crêpe pan or 8-inch cast-iron skillet with clarified butter or vegetable oil. Heat the pan well, then pour on 2 to 3 table-spoons of the batter, swirling it over the bottom of the pan to cover it. Cook over medium heat until bubbles appear on the surface and the underside is lightly browned, about 1 minute. Turn the crêpe and cook briefly on the other side.

Fold the pancake in quarters and serve warm with sugar or jam. Repeat with the remaining batter.

Serves 4 to 6.

NOTE: As with *bliny,* the first crêpe often turns out badly, so don't despair.

VARIATION: To make savory crêpes, omit the sugar, cinnamon, rum, and orange flower water. Cook the pancakes as directed above, but before folding each one sprinkle it with a couple tablespoons of grated Gruyère cheese, or some sautéed minced mushrooms and shallots. Fold and leave on the pan for about 30 seconds, until the cheese melts or the filling is heated through. Serve plain or with a light béchamel sauce.

New Orleans Rice Fritters *(Calas)*

One of the glories of nineteenth-century Creole cuisine, *calas* have all but disappeared from modern life. They once were hawked through the streets of New Orleans by colorful vendors singing a lively refrain. Along with beignets, these fritters enhanced the Mardi Gras season. They should be served piping hot, lavishly sprinkled with sugar or cane syrup and accompanied by a steaming cup of *café au lait*.

   4   cups water plus 2 tablespoons lukewarm water
   ¼   teaspoon salt
   1   cup raw rice
   2½ teaspoons active dry yeast
   4   eggs, well beaten, at room temperature
   ½   cup sugar
   1   cup all-purpose flour
   1   teaspoon ground cinnamon
   1   teaspoon ground nutmeg

       Vegetable oil for frying
       Confectioners' sugar or cane syrup

The evening before you plan to make the fritters, bring 4 cups of the water and the salt to a boil in a large pan. Add the rice and simmer, uncovered, until the rice is soft and the water has been absorbed, about 25 minutes. Transfer the rice to a bowl and mash it, then allow it to cool to lukewarm.

Dissolve the yeast in the remaining 2 tablespoons of lukewarm water. Stir into the rice. Cover the bowl and leave at room temperature overnight.

The next day, beat the eggs into the rice mixture, then stir in the sugar, flour, cinnamon, and nutmeg. Leave to rise for 15 minutes.

Put the batter in the refrigerator to chill for at least 1 hour before frying.

Heat 3 inches of vegetable oil in a deep-fat fryer or deep pan to 350°F. Drop the batter by tablespoonfuls into the hot fat, being careful not to crowd the fritters. Fry until golden, about 3 to 4 minutes, turning once. Drain on paper toweling. Serve hot with plenty of sugar or cane syrup.

Serves 10 to 12.

Shrovetide Buns *(Semlor)*

Each year the Swedes look forward to *Semmeldags* or Simnel time, when bakeries throughout the country display these rich buns. *Semlor* are related to the old English simnel buns, deriving from the Latin *simila,* a fine wheat flour which also lent its name to "semolina." Only the best ingredients were used for pre-Lenten baking.

Swedish folklore tells that the first *semlor* were created several hundred years ago by a baker's apprentice trying to avoid the customary flogging meted out at the beginning of Lent by his harsh master, who believed that the boy would benefit from a taste of the whip. The apprentice begged his master not to whip him, promising anything in return. "Fine," agreed the baker. "If you can make a bun that is better and tastier than any other, I will not whip you." Predictably, the boy created a masterpiece, the *semla* that has come down in history, legend, and song; and in so doing, he not only avoided a flogging but won the baker's daughter, and the bakery, too.

Semlor are traditionally served in a shallow bowl of hot milk, which is how I like them best. Most Swedes today simply eat them plain, with coffee. Either way, they're a treat.

Dough

2½ teaspoons active dry yeast

¼ cup lukewarm water

1 cup lukewarm milk

½ cup (1 stick) unsalted butter, melted and cooled

1 egg, lightly beaten, at room temperature

½ cup sugar

½ teaspoon ground cinnamon

½ teaspoon salt

4 to 4½ cups all-purpose flour

1 lightly beaten egg
  Almond Paste (recipe follows; see Note)

½ cup heavy cream, whipped
  Confectioners' sugar
  Hot milk (optional)

Dissolve the yeast in the water and leave to proof for 10 minutes, until bubbly. Stir in the milk, melted butter, egg, sugar, cinnamon, salt, and 3½ cups of the flour. Beat well. Gradually add enough flour to form a soft dough. Turn out onto a floured board and knead until the dough is smooth and elastic, about 10 minutes.

Place the dough in a large greased bowl, turning to grease the top. Cover and leave to rise until doubled, about 1½ hours.

Divide the dough into twelve pieces. Shape each piece into a bun and place on a lightly greased baking sheet. Cover the buns and leave them to rise until puffy, about 45 minutes.

Preheat the oven to 400°F. Brush the buns with the beaten egg. Bake for 10 to 12 minutes, until nicely browned. Cool on a rack.

To serve, cut the buns in half horizontally with a sharp knife. Spread a heaping tablespoon of almond paste on the bottom half of each bun, then add a generous dollop of whipped cream. Replace the top of the bun and dust it with confectioners' sugar. If desired, place the buns in shallow soup bowls and pour some hot milk around them. Serve with forks.

Makes 12 buns.

Almond Paste

1 cup blanched whole almonds
1 teaspoon almond extract
2 cups confectioners' sugar
2 egg whites, lightly beaten

Grind the almonds until fine in a nut grinder or food processor. Transfer to a bowl and stir in the almond extract and confectioners' sugar. Mix in the egg whites with a fork to form a solid mass.

> **NOTE:** Commercially produced almond paste may be substituted for homemade, though the texture of the homemade is lighter and the flavor less cloyingly sweet.

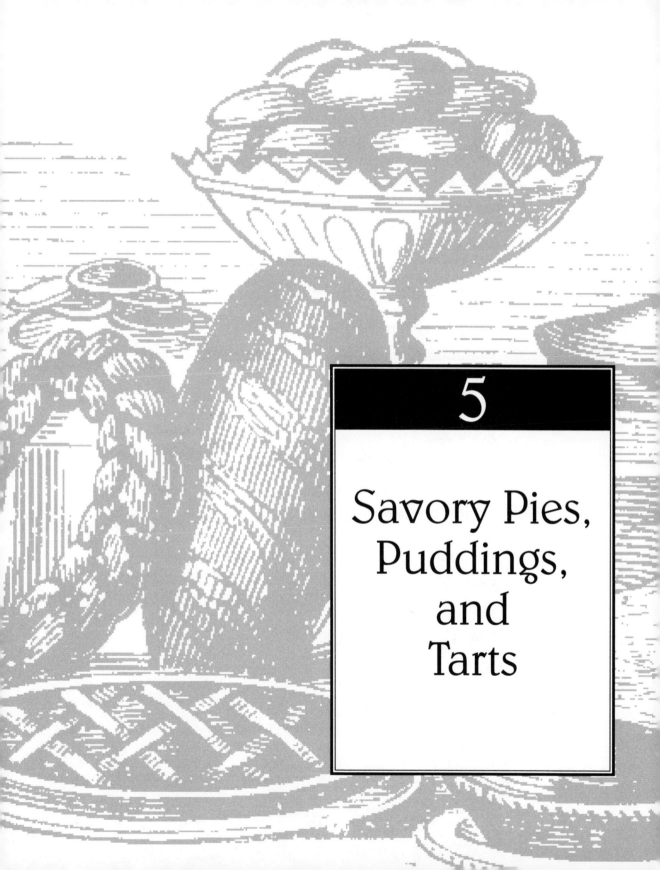

5

Savory Pies,
Puddings,
and
Tarts

Pies and tarts come in a panoply of shapes and sizes, which is part of their appeal. Turnovers provide individual pockets of dough to enclose chopped vegetables, while a single large, crusty envelope creates a dramatic coulibiac. Or you may prefer to expose the filling's wanton beauty and turn it into a savory tart. Puddings are more genteel, though no less satisfying. Airy or firm, smooth or chunky in texture, vegetable puddings are really the grown-up cousins of our childhood comfort foods. What follows is an eclectic choice of savory treats representing not only a variety of shapes and sizes, but also of cultures.

Green Olive Turnovers *(Yeşil zeytinli börek)*

Mushroom Coulibiac

White Bean and Potato Pie

Onion Pie

Potato Kugel

Sweet Potato and Clementine Pudding

Carrot and Parsnip Pudding

Roasted Red Pepper Tart

SEE ALSO:

Carrot Pie *(Pirog s morkov'iu)* (page 222)

Georgian Cheese Bread *(Khachapuri)* (page 248)

Stilton Bread Pudding (page 62)

Green Olive Turnovers *(Yeşil zeytinli börek)*

These meal-sized turnovers, like tangy calzone, are a regional specialty of Gaziantep, Turkey, near the Syrian border. They make excellent lunch or picnic fare. This recipe is adapted from *Samples of Turkish Cuisine* by Ayşe Baysal, a professor at Hacettepe University in Ankara, who works to promote the nutritive qualities of Turkish food.

Dough

- 2½ teaspoons active dry yeast
- ¼ cup lukewarm water
- 1 teaspoon sugar
- 2 teaspoons salt
- 1½ cups plain yogurt, at room temperature
- ½ cup olive oil
- 4½ to 5 cups unbleached white flour

Filling

- 2 medium onions, peeled and finely chopped (2 cups)
- 1 tablespoon olive oil
- 4 teaspoons tomato paste
- 3 cups coarsely chopped green Spanish pimiento-stuffed olives (one 15-ounce jar, drained)
- ½ cup finely chopped walnuts
- ½ teaspoon freshly ground black pepper
- ½ teaspoon cayenne
- 1 cup minced parsley

Proof the yeast in the water for 10 minutes, until bubbly. Stir in the sugar, salt, yogurt, olive oil, and enough flour to make a soft dough. Turn out onto a floured surface and knead until smooth and elastic, about 10 minutes. Place the dough in a lightly greased bowl and turn to grease the top. Cover with plastic wrap and leave to rise until doubled in bulk, 1 to 1½ hours.

In a large skillet sauté the onions in the olive oil until soft, about 10 minutes. Stir in the remaining filling ingredients and mix well. Remove the pan from the heat and set aside.

To make the turnovers, punch down the dough and divide it into twelve pieces. Roll out each piece ¼ inch thick into 5-inch rounds. Spoon a generous amount of olive filling (about ¼ cup) onto half of each round, then fold the dough over to enclose it. Seal the edges well and crimp with your fingers or a fork. Place the turnovers on lightly greased baking sheets and cover them with a towel. Leave to rise for about 20 minutes.

Preheat the oven to 350°F. Bake the turnovers for 30 minutes, until evenly browned. Serve warm.

Makes 12 turnovers, serving 6.

Mushroom Coulibiac

Coulibiac is the French term for a very old Russian pie, the *kulebiaka*. The envelope of dough may be puff pastry, yeast dough, or a rich short pastry (as in this recipe), the choice depending on the type of filling and the desired formality of presentation. This coulibiac emerges from the oven golden and crisp and makes a lovely centerpiece for a special meal.

Dough

1 cup all-purpose flour
½ teaspoon salt
1 teaspoon baking powder
½ cup (1 stick) unsalted butter, cut into pieces
¼ pound cream cheese, cut into pieces

Filling

1 medium onion, peeled and finely chopped
3 tablespoons unsalted butter or olive oil
1 pound mixed wild mushrooms, trimmed and finely chopped (see Note)
⅓ cup raw barley
⅔ cup water
Pinch plus 1 teaspoon salt

Freshly ground black pepper

3 tablespoons sour cream

2 tablespoons snipped fresh dill

1 egg yolk, lightly beaten

Place the flour, salt, and baking powder in the bowl of a food processor fitted with the steel blade. Add the butter and cream cheese and process, using the pulse motion, until the mixture resembles coarse meal. Turn out into a bowl and with your hands gently press the mixture until the dough sticks together and forms a ball. Do not overmix or the pastry will be tough.

Wrap the dough in wax paper and chill for at least 1 hour before using.

In a large skillet sauté the onion in 2 tablespoons of the butter or oil until it begins to turn golden, 8 to 10 minutes. Add the remaining tablespoon of butter or oil to the skillet along with the mushrooms and cook the mixture for 10 minutes more, stirring occasionally.

Meanwhile, in a small saucepan bring the barley, the water, and a pinch of salt to a boil. Cover and simmer for 15 minutes. The grains will still be chewy. Stir the cooked barley into the mushroom mixture. Add the remaining 1 teaspoon salt and the pepper, sour cream, and dill.

Preheat the oven to 400°F.

To assemble the pie, roll out the dough on a well-floured surface to a 10 x 14-inch rectangle. Trim the edges, saving the scraps to make decorative shapes for the top of the pie, if desired.

Mound the mushroom mixture lengthwise down the center of the dough. Bring the two long sides of the dough up to meet in the center over the filling, then fold up the two short sides to enclose it completely. Seal the edges with cold water.

Gently place the finished pie seam side down on an ungreased baking sheet. Brush all over with the beaten egg yolk and decorate the top, if desired. Bake for 20 minutes, until the pastry is crisp and nicely browned.

Allow to sit for 10 or 15 minutes before slicing.

Serves 6 to 8.

NOTE: Use any mushrooms you like for the filling. The coulibiac is also good with cultivated white mushrooms.

White Bean and Potato Pie

Except for the eggs, the ingredients in this recipe are standard for soup. One day, on a whim, I decided to turn them into a pie instead. The result is as decorative as it is delicious.

          2 cups dried navy beans
          5 cups water
          4 garlic cloves, peeled
          9 tablespoons olive oil
         2½ teaspoons salt
          2 medium onions, peeled and thinly sliced
          ½ pound russet potatoes, peeled and diced
          1 tablespoon tomato paste
          ¼ teaspoon red pepper flakes
             Freshly ground black pepper
          1 tablespoon fine dry bread crumbs
          ½ cup freshly grated Parmesan cheese
          3 eggs, lightly beaten
          1 tablespoon minced parsley

Place the beans in a stockpot with the water, the garlic cloves, 2 tablespoons of the oil, and 1 teaspoon of the salt. Bring to a boil and simmer, uncovered, for 1 hour, or until the water has been absorbed. Transfer the beans and garlic to the bowl of a food processor fitted with the metal blade and puree them.

While the beans are simmering, heat 6 tablespoons of the olive oil in a medium skillet. Add the onions and potatoes and cook over medium-low heat for 12 to 15 minutes, until the onions are golden and the potato tender. Stir in the tomato paste and pepper flakes. Season with black pepper and 1 teaspoon of the salt.

Lightly grease a 10-inch pie plate. Sprinkle it with the bread crumbs. Preheat the oven to 350°F.

Transfer the pureed beans to a bowl. Stir in the Parmesan cheese, the remaining ½ teaspoon of salt, and the remaining 1 tablespoon of olive oil.

Beat in the eggs. Scrape the mixture into the pie plate, smoothing the surface with a spatula.

Cover the beans with the onion and potato mixture, spreading it evenly over the top. Bake the pie for 35 to 40 minutes, until puffed and golden. Remove from the oven and sprinkle with the minced parsley. Serve warm.

Serves 8.

Onion Pie

The caramelized onions make this rustic pie delightfully mellow despite the pungent seasonings.

Crust

- 1½ cups all-purpose flour
- ½ teaspoon salt
- 6 tablespoons cold unsalted butter, in pieces
- 2 tablespoons vegetable shortening
- 5 to 6 tablespoons ice water

Filling

- 3 tablespoons olive oil
- 3 pounds yellow onions, peeled and thinly sliced
- 1 teaspoon salt
  Freshly ground black pepper
- 3 to 4 drops hot pepper sauce
- 2 teaspoons Dijon mustard
- ½ cup grated Gruyère or white Cheddar cheese
- ½ cup grated Parmesan cheese
- 3 eggs, lightly beaten

In a medium bowl mix together the flour and salt. Cut in the butter and shortening until the mixture resembles coarse meal. Add just enough water for the dough to hold together, being careful not to overmix. Wrap in wax paper and chill for 1 hour.

Preheat the oven to 450°F. Roll out the dough on a floured surface and carefully lift it into a 10-inch pie plate. Trim the edges and prick the dough all over with a fork.

Bake for 12 to 15 minutes, until golden. Cool on a rack.

To make the filling, heat the olive oil in a large skillet. Add the onions and cook over low heat, stirring occasionally, until they are soft and golden. This will take 45 to 50 minutes. Remove the pan from the heat.

Preheat the oven to 350°F.

Stir the salt, pepper, hot pepper sauce, mustard, and cheeses into the onions, mixing well. Stir in the eggs. Turn the mixture into the baked piecrust. Bake for 45 minutes, until puffed and golden.

Serves 6.

Potato Kugel

Although *kugel* is the Yiddish word for "cake," it is usually translated into English as "pudding." And, indeed, this dish can be either savory or sweet. Based on potatoes or noodles, *kugel* is a traditional Sabbath favorite in Eastern European Jewish cuisine. My favorite type is made with potatoes. Often matzo meal or flour is mixed into the batter, but I prefer to add milk to make the potatoes creamy.

    2   medium onions, peeled and finely chopped
    1   garlic clove, peeled and minced
    2   tablespoons unsalted butter
    3   pounds potatoes, peeled and coarsely grated
    1   small carrot, peeled and coarsely grated
    ¾   cup milk
    2   eggs, separated

1 teaspoon salt
¼ teaspoon freshly ground black pepper

Sauté the onions and garlic in the butter until golden, 10 to 12 minutes.

Preheat the oven to 375°F. Grease a 2½-quart gratin dish or shallow baking dish.

Place the grated potatoes in a dish towel and squeeze as much moisture from them as possible. Turn them into a large bowl and mix with the cooked onions, the carrot, milk, lightly beaten egg yolks, salt, and pepper.

Beat the egg whites until they form soft peaks and fold into the potato mixture. Spread the potatoes in the prepared dish. Bake for 75 minutes, until the top is crisp and the inside creamy. Serve hot.

Serves 8.

Sweet Potato and Clementine Pudding

Too often sweet potatoes are treated with so much sugar that they become cloyingly sweet. This pudding is an exception. Here, the citrusy tang of clementines heightens the essential flavor of the sweet potatoes, making the pudding just sweet enough to tempt you to come back for more.

2 pounds sweet potatoes
2 tablespoons unsalted butter
4 tablespoons light brown sugar
2 tablespoons dark rum
1 teaspoon grated lemon peel
¼ teaspoon ground cinnamon
¼ teaspoon ground nutmeg
  Generous pinch of ground cloves
¼ teaspoon salt
4 small seedless clementines, each about 2 inches in diameter, peeled and separated into segments (see Note)
2 tablespoons coarsely ground walnuts

Boil the sweet potatoes in salted water to cover until tender, then peel and mash them.

Preheat the oven to 350°F. Grease a 1½-quart soufflé dish.

Stir the butter, 3 tablespoons of the sugar, the rum, lemon peel, spices, and salt into the mashed potatoes, mixing well. Fold in the clementines. Turn the mixture into the soufflé dish.

Mix the remaining 1 tablespoon of sugar with the ground walnuts and sprinkle over the top. Bake for 30 minutes, until lightly browned and bubbly.

Serves 6.

NOTE: Tangerines may be substituted for the clementines. Cut the segments in half if they are large.

Carrot and Parsnip Pudding

For carrot lovers, here is a pudding that is as light as the airiest soufflé. Parsnips add a hint of sweetness, while the vivid orange color suggests the promise of spring.

6 medium carrots (1¼ pounds), peeled and cut into chunks
4 medium parsnips (1 pound), peeled and cut into chunks
1 small onion, peeled and finely chopped (½ cup)
2 tablespoons unsalted butter
2 tablespoons all-purpose flour
½ cup milk
2 eggs, lightly beaten
1 tablespoon freshly squeezed lemon juice
¼ teaspoon salt (or more, to taste)
   Freshly ground white pepper
   A few grindings of nutmeg

Cook the carrot and parsnip chunks in a large kettle of boiling, salted water until tender, about 25 minutes.

Meanwhile, sauté the onion in the butter until just golden, about 5 minutes. Set aside.

When the vegetables are done, drain them and puree in a food processor fitted with the steel blade.

Preheat the oven to 350°F. Lightly grease a 1½-quart soufflé dish.

Turn the puree out into a mixing bowl. Stir in the onions and the flour. Beat in the milk, eggs, lemon juice, and seasonings. Scrape the mixture into the prepared dish and bake for 45 minutes, until firm.

Serves 4 to 6.

Roasted Red Pepper Tart

A luxuriant tart with a creamy texture.

Crust

  1½ cups all-purpose flour
   ½ teaspoon salt
   6 tablespoons cold unsalted butter, in pieces
   2 tablespoons vegetable shortening
   5 to 6 tablespoons ice water

Filling

   2 medium onions, peeled and thinly sliced
   1 tablespoon unsalted butter
   2 large red bell peppers, quartered, stems and seeds removed
   1 cup grated Gruyère cheese
   1 teaspoon salt
     Freshly ground white pepper
   ⅛ teaspoon dried thyme
   3 eggs, lightly beaten
   1 cup heavy cream

In a medium bowl mix together the flour and salt. Cut in the butter and shortening until the mixture resembles coarse meal. Add just enough water for the dough to hold together, being careful not to overmix. Wrap in wax paper and chill for 1 hour.

Preheat the oven to 450°F. Roll out the dough on a floured surface to a round about 12 inches in diameter. Carefully lift the dough into an 11½-inch tart pan with a removable bottom. Trim the edges and prick the dough all over with a fork.

Bake for 12 to 15 minutes, until golden. Cool on a rack.

To make the filling, cook the onions in the butter over low heat until golden, 15 to 20 minutes.

Preheat the broiler. Place the quartered peppers skin side up on a broiling pan. Broil close to the heat for about 5 minutes, or until the skin is charred all over. Put the peppers in a paper bag and close it tightly. Leave them to cool, then peel them. Slice the peppers into thin strips.

Lower the oven temperature to 350°F.

To assemble the tart, sprinkle the cheese over the bottom of the cooled crust. Top with the onions, then strew the peppers decoratively over the onions. Season with the salt, pepper, and thyme. Add the eggs to the cream and pour over the vegetables. Bake for 45 minutes, until golden.

Serve warm.

Serves 8.

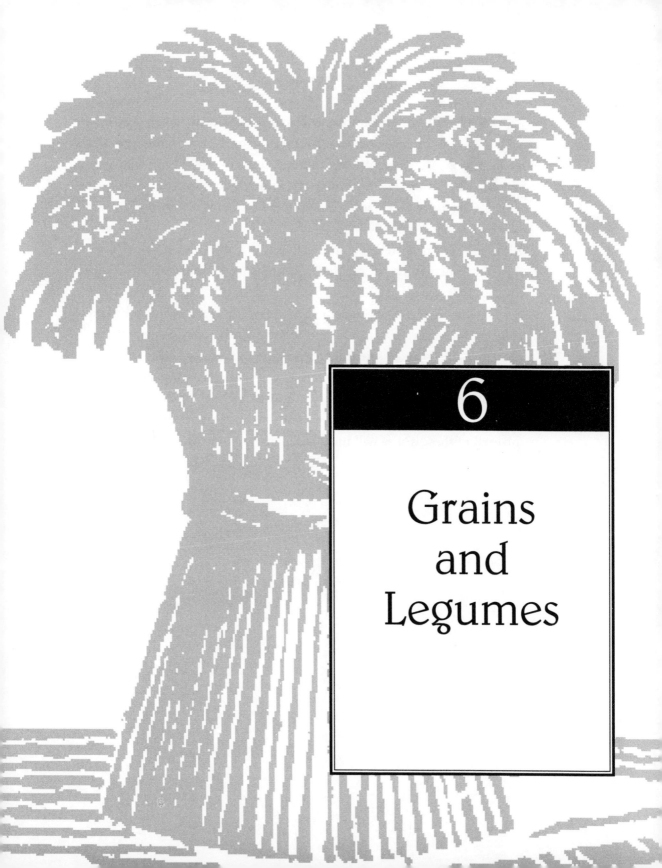

6

Grains
and
Legumes

Woolly mammoths still roamed the earth when wild grains began to appear. More and more grains sprouted as the Ice Age glaciers receded, until by 8000 B.C. wild grasses determined mankind's future: people in the fertile crescent between the Tigris and the Euphrates settled down to sow the seeds of civilization. Some 10,000 years later we are still enjoying grains. Although we are spared the arduous tasks of gathering and threshing, in the eating of grains we can feel continuity with our earliest civilized forebears.

Legumes are also an ancient food. Over the years wild pulses were cultivated into the beans, peas, and lentils we eat today as planters practiced an early form of scientific agriculture, repeatedly selecting the best seeds for the next year's crop. From the world's rich diversity of grains and legumes I could choose only a few to include in this chapter, but these recipes are among my favorites in the book. Nutritious and flavorful, each of these dishes will invigorate your cold-weather table.

Barley Pilaf

Hot and Spicy Bulgur

Maple Baked Beans

Black Bean Chili

Chickpeas with Chard

Curried Chickpeas and Onions

Lentils and Leeks

Barbecued Lentils

Millet Pancakes

Baked Millet with Winter Squash

Winter Holiday Pilaf *(Bairam plov)*

Barley Pilaf

Even after long cooking, barley retains its chewy bite. Here it stars in an excellent casserole.

- ½ cup pine nuts
- 4 tablespoons unsalted butter
- 8 scallions, trimmed and chopped, including greens
- 1½ cups raw pearl barley, rinsed and drained
- 3 cups vegetable broth
- ½ teaspoon salt
- Freshly ground black pepper
- ½ cup chopped parsley

In a large skillet cook the pine nuts in the butter over low heat until golden, 5 to 6 minutes, stirring occasionally. Watch the nuts closely, as they burn easily. Remove them from the pan with a slotted spoon and set aside. Add the chopped scallions and the barley to the butter remaining in the pan. Cook, stirring, over medium heat for 5 minutes, until the barley is toasted.

Preheat the oven to 350°F.

Heat the vegetable broth to boiling. Return the pine nuts to the skillet. Stir in the salt and add a liberal amount of black pepper. Stir in the parsley. Transfer the mixture to a 2-quart casserole. Pour the hot broth over the barley and cover.

Bake for 50 minutes, until the liquid has been absorbed. Stir before serving.

Serves 8.

Hot and Spicy Bulgur

This slightly searing, garlicky dish is hard to resist. To ensure that the grains remain chewy, I prefer not to boil the bulgur, but to soak and steam it before a brief simmering.

1 cup raw bulgur
6 tablespoons boiling water plus 1¾ cups water
1 teaspoon salt
2 tablespoons all-purpose flour
4 large garlic cloves, peeled and minced
3 tablespoons olive oil
1 tablespoon tomato paste
¾ teaspoon cayenne
½ cup minced parsley

Place the bulgur in the bowl of a food processor fitted with the metal blade and pour the boiling water over it. Cover the bowl and leave to rest for 10 minutes, then process until the grains are broken and sticky. Transfer to a mixing bowl. Stir in ¾ teaspoon of the salt, the flour, and ¼ cup of the remaining water.

Place the bulgur mixture in a steamer and steam over simmering water for 30 minutes.

Meanwhile, in a large saucepan sauté the garlic in the olive oil until just golden, 2 to 3 minutes. Stir in the tomato paste, cayenne, remaining ¼ teaspoon of salt and 1½ cups water. Cook gently for 5 minutes.

Scrape the steamed bulgur into the saucepan and stir to coat it with the sauce. Simmer, covered, for 5 minutes, then stir in the parsley and simmer 5 minutes more. Let the bulgur sit, covered, for 15 minutes before serving, or until all the liquid has been absorbed.

Serves 6.

Maple Baked Beans

These beans, baked slowly in the New England style, have a wonderful mapley sweetness. If you prefer more sauce, simply add additional liquid to the pot as the beans cook.

- 1 pound dried navy or pea beans
- ¼ teaspoon baking soda
- 4 cups water
- ¾ cup pure maple syrup
- 3 tablespoons molasses
- ½ cup canned crushed tomatoes
- 1½ teaspoons dry mustard
- ½ teaspoon ground ginger
- 1½ teaspoons salt
- ¼ teaspoon freshly ground black pepper
- ½ teaspoon dried thyme
- 1 small onion, peeled and chopped
- 2 garlic cloves, peeled
- 1 bay leaf

Soak the beans with the baking soda overnight in water to cover. The next day, drain them and cover with 4 cups of water. Bring to a boil and simmer until they are nearly tender, about 30 minutes. Drain, reserving the cooking liquid.

Preheat the oven to 250°F. Transfer the beans to a 3-quart casserole, preferably an earthenware bean pot.

In a medium bowl mix together the maple syrup, molasses, tomatoes, mustard, ginger, salt, pepper, and thyme. Pour over the beans, stirring to mix well. Stir in the chopped onion; tuck in the garlic cloves and bay leaf. Add about 1 cup of the reserved cooking liquid, or enough to cover the beans (feel free to add more if you like).

Cover the pot and bake for 5 to 6 hours, adding liquid as necessary so that the beans don't dry out.

Serves 6.

Black Bean Chili

Chili doesn't get much better than this spicy version with black beans. Cooked with tomatoes, the beans take on a beautiful mahogany color. Serve the chili plain or over boiled rice, and sprinkle with grated cheese if you like.

1	pound dried black beans
4	cups water
1	bay leaf
2	medium onions, peeled and chopped
4	large garlic cloves, peeled and minced
1	red bell pepper, cored, seeded, and finely chopped
1	tablespoon vegetable oil
One	28-ounce can tomatoes, coarsely chopped, including the juice
2	tablespoons tomato paste
1	tablespoon ground cumin
2	teaspoons paprika
½	teaspoon cayenne
4	teaspoons chili powder
1	teaspoon dried oregano
1½	teaspoons salt
	Freshly ground black pepper
1	tablespoon dark brown sugar

Grated Monterey Jack cheese (optional)

Soak the beans in water to cover overnight. The next day, drain them and place in a large stockpot with the 4 cups of water. Add the bay leaf and simmer for 25 to 30 minutes, until the beans are tender but still slightly chewy.

While the beans are simmering, slowly cook the onions, garlic, and red pepper in the oil for 12 to 15 minutes. Stir into the bean pot. Add the remaining ingredients except for the grated cheese and simmer, covered, for 1 hour. Serve hot, sprinkled with cheese, if desired.

Serves 6 to 8.

Chickpeas with Chard

This flavorful Armenian specialty pairs creamy chickpeas with slightly bitter chard, enhancing the combination with a hint of tomato. For a brightly colored dish, use red chard.

½ cup dried chickpeas
1½ cups water
1 small onion, peeled and finely chopped
¼ cup olive oil
1½ pounds Swiss chard, coarse stems removed,
leaves coarsely chopped (see Note)
2 tablespoons tomato paste
¾ teaspoon salt
Dash of cayenne
Freshly ground black pepper

Soak the chickpeas overnight in a stockpot in the 1½ cups water. The next day, bring the mixture to a boil and simmer until the chickpeas are barely tender, 35 to 40 minutes.

Meanwhile, sauté the onion in the olive oil for 8 to 10 minutes, until golden.

Bring a large kettle of water to a boil and blanch the chard leaves for 3 minutes. Drain.

When the chickpeas are ready, stir in the onion, the chard, the tomato paste, salt, and seasonings. Cook the mixture, covered, for 10 to 15 minutes, over low heat, until the chickpeas are tender. Serve hot.

Serves 4.

NOTE: Fresh spinach may be substituted for the chard. It will not need to be blanched. Boil the chickpeas until they are nearly tender, 45 to 50 minutes, then finish cooking them with the spinach as directed above for no more than 10 minutes.

Curried Chickpeas and Onions

Subtle curries are popular in Central Asia, where onions are abundant and sweet. This dish tastes best when freshly made, since the flavors tend to flatten with refrigeration.

1	cup (6 ounces) dried chickpeas
¼	teaspoon baking soda
3	cups water
2	pounds sweet onions (such as Vidalia, Walla Walla, or Maui), peeled and cut into eighths (see Note)
¼	cup olive oil
One	16-ounce can tomatoes
¼	teaspoon cayenne
½	teaspoon ground coriander
⅛	teaspoon ground cinnamon
¼	teaspoon turmeric
¼	teaspoon ground cumin
½	teaspoon salt
	Freshly ground black pepper

Soak the chickpeas with the baking soda overnight in water to cover. The next day, drain them and cover with the 3 cups water. Bring to a boil and cook over medium heat for about 15 minutes, or until they are barely tender. Drain, reserving the cooking liquid.

While the chickpeas are cooking, in a large pot sauté the onions in the olive oil until softened, 10 to 12 minutes. Drain the tomatoes, reserving the juice, and chop them coarsely. Add the tomatoes to the cooked onions.

Measure the reserved tomato juice and add enough of the cooking water from the chickpeas to make 1 to 1¼ cups. Add this liquid to the onion and tomato mixture. Stir in the remaining ingredients. Simmer for 30 minutes, until slightly thickened. Serve hot with rice or plenty of bread.

Serves 6 to 8.

NOTE: If sweet onions are unavailable, substitute red onions.

Lentils and Leeks

Hearty and delicious as well as nutritious, hot lentils and leeks are perfect cold-weather fare. This is my adaptation of a recipe developed by Ayşe Baysal for the Turkish Grain Board.

2   pounds leeks, well rinsed and sliced ½ inch thick,
        including some of the green part
2   large carrots, peeled and sliced ½ inch thick
¼   cup olive oil
2½ cups water
1   cup green lentils
1   tablespoon tomato paste
1   teaspoon sugar
1¼ teaspoons salt
    Freshly ground black pepper

In a large saucepan toss the leek and carrot slices with the olive oil. Cook over medium heat for 5 minutes, until the vegetables are lightly browned, then stir in the remaining ingredients. Cover the pan and simmer the mixture for 1 hour, until the lentils are tender and most of the liquid has been absorbed. To keep the leek slices intact, do not stir. Serve hot.

Serves 4 to 6.

Barbecued Lentils

These exciting lentils have a gingery tang. Be sure to use green lentils so that they retain their shape.

1 cup green lentils
3 cups water
9 tablespoons cider vinegar
1 small onion, peeled and quartered
¾ cup canned crushed tomatoes
3 tablespoons molasses
3 tablespoons dark brown sugar
1 tablespoon dry mustard
1½ teaspoons ground ginger
¼ teaspoon cayenne
½ teaspoon salt
Freshly ground black pepper

In a large saucepan bring the lentils, the water, 6 tablespoons of the vinegar, and the onion to a boil. Simmer for 20 minutes, then drain, reserving the liquid.

Preheat the oven to 250°F. In a medium bowl mix 1 cup of the reserved liquid with the remaining 3 tablespoons of vinegar and all of the other ingredients. Stir in the lentils, coating them well.

Transfer the lentils to a 2-quart casserole, preferably earthenware. Cover and bake for about 3 hours, or until most of the liquid has been absorbed. Serve hot.

Serves 6.

Millet Pancakes

Who says millet is just for the birds? For such a diminutive grain, it has surprisingly rich flavor, as revealed by these golden pancakes.

1 cup millet
2 cups milk
½ cup water
1 teaspoon salt
1 tablespoon sugar
⅓ cup farmer cheese (about 2 ounces)
1 egg, lightly beaten
2 tablespoons unsalted butter
1 tablespoon vegetable oil
2 tablespoons all-purpose flour

Sour cream (optional)

In a medium saucepan bring the millet, milk, water, and salt to a boil. Simmer, covered, for 20 minutes, until the liquid has been absorbed, then stir in the sugar, farmer cheese, and beaten egg. Allow the mixture to cool slightly.

In a large skillet heat the butter and oil. Shape the millet mixture into twelve cakes about 3 inches in diameter. Dredge them lightly in the flour. Place in the skillet and fry until golden and puffy, turning once, about 8 to 10 minutes in all. Serve immediately, topped with sour cream, if desired.

Makes 12 pancakes, serving 4.

Baked Millet with Winter Squash

Although sweetened millet porridge can be enjoyed for breakfast, this savory version has a homey suppertime appeal.

4 tablespoons unsalted butter
1 cup millet
8 ounces butternut squash, peeled and cut into ½-inch
    cubes (1½ cups)
2½ cups hot milk
1 teaspoon salt

Preheat the oven to 350°F. Lightly grease a 1½-quart casserole with a cover.

Melt the butter over low heat in a medium saucepan. Stir in the millet and squash cubes to coat. Add the hot milk and the salt, bring to a boil, and simmer, covered, for 5 minutes.

Transfer the millet mixture to the prepared casserole. Bake, covered, for 25 to 30 minutes, until the milk has been absorbed. Let stand for 10 minutes, then fluff with a fork. Serve hot.

Serves 6.

Winter Holiday Pilaf *(Bairam plov)*

U zbeks claim that their national cuisine boasts three hundred different kinds of pilaf, or *plov*. If so, then I probably won't live to taste them all—to my regret, since a well-made pilaf is one of the great rice dishes of the world. But I have feasted on at least one of the best, the fruit-laden pilaf offered here, a gift from Glenn and Asele Mack. Glenn has been studying Central Asian cuisine ever since he met Asele, whose relatives hail from Uzbekistan; he even worked for a time with an Uighur noodle master in Kazakhstan. Now back in Austin, Texas, Glenn and Asele hope to open a restaurant to introduce Americans to Central Asian food.

With its rich assortment of fresh and dried fruits, this pilaf is generally reserved for special occasions. Glenn and Asele were regaled with it in a small Kyrgyz village after a rigorous 15-hour bus ride over the Tian Shan Mountains. To make this dish accessible to Americans, I've taken a few liberties with the ingredients. Normally scarlet barberries would be used instead of lemon juice to add tartness and color (they're also prized for their high vitamin content). Uzbek cooks favor yellow carrots, which are somewhat less sweet than the orange. Their local black cumin seed is stronger than ours, and quince are readily available throughout Central Asia. But despite my modifications, this pilaf is a lavish way to regale guests, whether they've traveled 15 minutes by highway or 15 hours overland.

½ cup dried chickpeas
¼ cup light olive oil
1 small white onion, peeled and thinly sliced
½ pound carrots, peeled and julienned
1 small parsnip, peeled and julienned
1 quince, peeled, cored, and cut into 8 wedges (see Notes)
3 cups vegetable broth
2 teaspoons freshly squeezed lemon juice
¼ cup raisins
¼ cup dried apricots, halved
2 whole heads of garlic, unpeeled, ½ inch sliced from the tops
1½ teaspoons cumin seed
1 teaspoon ground cumin
½ teaspoon salt

Freshly ground black pepper
⅛ teaspoon paprika
Pinch of turmeric
1¼ cups raw rice
¼ cup finely chopped parsley
¼ cup finely chopped fresh coriander (cilantro)
Pomegranate seeds (optional)

Soak the chickpeas overnight in water to cover. Drain before using.

Heat the oil in a large wok. Add the onion and fry over medium-high heat for 1 to 2 minutes. Stir in the carrots and parsnip and cook, stirring occasionally, for 5 minutes more, until the vegetables are lightly browned. Place the quince, the drained chickpeas, 1½ cups of the vegetable broth, the lemon juice, raisins, and apricots on top of the vegetables. Submerge the heads of garlic in the broth in the center of the wok.

Bring the mixture to a boil, then stir in the cumin seed, ground cumin, salt, pepper, paprika, and turmeric. Pour the rice over the broth, then add the remaining 1½ cups broth. Cover the wok and cook over medium heat for 5 minutes. Remove the cover and stir the rice to coat each grain with broth, taking care not to disturb the fruits and vegetables at the bottom. Replace the cover and cook 10 minutes more. Then, with a chopstick make several holes in the rice to the bottom of the wok. Continue to cook the rice, covered, until it is tender and the liquid has been absorbed, 10 to 15 minutes longer.

Remove the garlic and set aside. Stir the pilaf gently to avoid mashing the quince. Transfer to a large platter and scatter the minced parsley, fresh coriander, and pomegranate seeds over the rice. Display the heads of garlic prominently on top and serve.

Serves 6.

NOTES: I have had success substituting a large Asian pear for the quince. Peel, core, and slice it into eight wedges. If neither quince nor Asian pears is available, try using a large, tart apple.

Pomegranate seeds freeze well. When the fruits are in season in the autumn, save the seeds, wrap them airtight, and store in the freezer for up to 6 months.

The traditional accompaniment to this pilaf is a plate of scallions and shredded radishes. I also like to serve flatbread on the side.

A World of Buckwheat

IN THE MAGICAL WORLD of Hans Christian Andersen, a weeping willow tells the tale of the vain and haughty buckwheat plant. One day, a storm threatens, and all the grains in the field—oats, corn, barley, and rye—bow down their heads in humility before the great power of Nature. All, that is, except buckwheat. As the other plants cower, buckwheat looks Heaven in the eye. Thunder and lightning envelop the field, but the buckwheat continues to stand upright and proud in its beautiful array of white blossoms. Soon the storm passes. The oats, corn, barley, and rye raise their heads to wave their stalks in the fresh breeze. The once-proud buckwheat, however, stands blackened and singed, for it has dared to defy Nature.

Yet it keeps cropping up, worldwide. Anyone who has seen a field of buckwheat in bloom can understand why Andersen attributes such pride to the plant. Shimmering like a sea of apple blossoms, buckwheat is especially magical on a moonlit night. Its sturdiness is cause for arrogance. But its taste, which Andersen overlooks, is buckwheat's proudest quality of all. The nutty flavor and nourishing warmth are appreciated in cold regions throughout the world. Even the great philosopher Kierkegaard reflected on its sensuousness:

> No pregnant woman can have stranger or more impatient desires than I. These desires concern sometimes the most trivial things, sometimes the most exalted, but they are equally imbued with the soul's momentary passion. At this moment I wish a bowl of buckwheat porridge. I remember from my school days that we always had this dish on Wednesdays. I remember how smooth and white it was when served, how the butter smiled at me, how

warm the porridge looked, how hungry I was, how impatient to be allowed to begin. Ah, such a dish of buckwheat porridge! I would give more than my birthright for it!

—SØREN KIERKEGAARD, "DIAPSALMATA," 1843

Although buckwheat has a long history of cultivation in North America, the plant finds little favor here. This disregard is puzzling, as well as relatively recent. A century ago, buckwheat was far more common in America, and even today, buckwheat cakes, or flapjacks, remain an integral part of the idealized American breakfast. "Long" stacks of griddle cakes are as much an American institution as pumpkin pie or pit barbecue, and they have been around longer than the United States themselves. *The Dictionary of American Regional English* reports that as early as 1772, a traveler to North America noted that "Buckwheat cakes . . . are likewise usual at Philadelphia and in other English colonies, especially in winter." In an 1820 letter to his daughter, John Pintard, founder of the New York Historical Society, confirms their popularity in the City of Brotherly Love: "Hasty pudding all winter long for supper, & buckwheat cakes, which came into vogue just before the revol[utionar]y war, for breakfast. In Philadelphia this article is or used to be considered such a treat, as to be served up for tea in large domestic parties, where they are always prepared the size of the griddle, and cut into quarters." A late eighteenth-century reporter for the *Worcester* (Massachusetts) *Gazette* found the pancakes in New England, as well; he was pleased that "danties [sic] of all sorts, too, are here . . . Pies, custards, cranb'ry tarts, and flapjacks." Over the next hundred years, the taste for flapjacks did not diminish; in fact, flapjacks were perceived by some as representative of American dining. In *American Society,* a two-volume study intended to acquaint English readers with American ways, the American diplomat George Makepeace Towle describes a typical American breakfast: "When you think you have finished your breakfast, a dish peculiarly American, if it is winter, makes its appearance. It is hard for the American to rise from his winter breakfast without his *buckwheat cakes.* They are eaten everywhere, and nothing could be nicer. They are made of the best buckwheat ground very finely; they are mixed and raised overnight, fried and brought smoking hot to the table; they are light and spongy, and are eaten with butter and treacle, or sugar-cane molasses." What is notable here is the emphasis on buckwheat. While pancakes may be prepared in any number of ways, most connoisseurs would agree with Towle that the best flapjacks are made with buckwheat, which lends a rich flavor and an appetizing umber hue to the batter.

The appeal of American buckwheat cakes was particularly strong among Americans abroad, who pined for their beloved breakfast food. From London, Benjamin Franklin wrote to his daughter to request the buckwheat flour he missed. Several well-known nineteeth-century writers evinced nothing less than devotion to American-style pancakes. Traveling through Europe, Mark Twain, in *A Tramp Abroad,* lamented the lack of a satisfying meal and indulged in visions of ". . . a great cup of American homemade coffee, with the cream a-froth on top, some real butter, firm and yellow and fresh, some smoking hot biscuits, a plate of hot buckwheat cakes, with transparent syrup . . ." James Fenimore Cooper treated his Parisian friends to homemade buckwheat cakes in the 1820s, while the foppish American artist James McNeill Whistler frequently served flapjacks at his sophisticated breakfast gatherings of London society. Meanwhile, at home in New York, Washington Irving fantasized about his dream breakfast: "Two dozen dainty slapjacks of buckwheat covered with a pitcher each of honey and treacle soaked by a hogshead of butter!"

The lavish treatment invariably accorded buckwheat flapjacks obviously heightened their appeal. And yet, even as buckwheat captured the American palate when ground into flour for pancakes, the foodstuff simultaneously suffered from a bad reputation as the fare of the poor. This contradiction makes the history of buckwheat in America particularly interesting. It's no accident that the word "buckwheat" and its derivations have accrued pejorative colloquial meanings. In certain parts of the country, for instance, a rustic or rube is known as a "buckwheater," an appellation that dates back to the nineteenth century when subsistence farmers would travel to town to barter or pay their bills with buckwheat rather than with money. The figure of a young country bumpkin entered mainstream American popular culture in the early years of television with the engaging character of Buckwheat, a mischievous member of the Little Rascals. Despite his mass appeal, Buckwheat stereotyped the rural black sharecropper in ways that make us uncomfortable today. Even in realms far removed from agriculture, the association of buckwheat with rural poverty remains. The seven-note system of harmony in primitive hymnody is commonly referred to as "buckwheat notes," in mockery of the shaped notes used instead of standard notation in the Bible Belt of the South. Finally, a quaint regionalism referring to the imminent birth of a baby is "buckwheat crop," most likely because buckwheat ripens so quickly.

How did buckwheat come to be such a colorful presence in American life, simultaneously adored and reviled? Strange as it may seem, a search for the answer takes us to the vast steppes and mountains of Central Asia, the birthplace of buckwheat. The two varieties of buckwheat most frequently cultivated today, *Fagopyrum esculentum* and *F. tataricum*, are both indigenous to that region; *F. esculentum* is generally considered to have the superior flavor, though *F. tataricum* is the hardier variety, thriving at an altitude of over 14,000 feet, even in poor soil. This hardiness makes buckwheat adaptable to rigorous climates throughout the world.

The progress of buckwheat from the remote reaches of Central Asia to the tables of eager American diners is fascinating to trace, for its journey to America represents the last leg of a culinary odyssey that began hundreds of years ago when merchants and caravans traversed the Silk Road from China through Central Asia to the West. Before its westward journey, however, buckwheat spread first to China, in all likelihood introduced by the nomadic tribe of Uighurs. From China, the plant traveled to Korea and Japan, and today buckwheat noodles are still greatly enjoyed throughout Asia. But in a twist of gastronomic irony, the peoples of Central Asia no longer include buckwheat in their diet. Instead, its culinary uses now characterize other highly diverse cuisines in both the East and the West. Before returning to the specific use of buckwheat in America, we can explore some of these culinary traditions.

In northern China, the first stopover for buckwheat from Central

Asia, the plant is called *qiáo mài*, which refers to a form of wheat. This term is actually a misnomer, because even though buckwheat is generally treated as a grain, it actually belongs to the same family of plants as rhubarb, the *Polygonaceae*. The groat that is made into porridge or ground into flour is technically an achene, the fruiting part of the plant. The importance of buckwheat to Chinese agriculture is evident from a twelfth-century report in which Ch'ang Ch'un, an emissary from China to the court of Genghis Khan in Central Asia, specifically notes that buckwheat was absent among the Mongols in Central Asia. From his report we can deduce that buckwheat was already in common use in China by that time. Additional documents from the late fourteenth century show that ritual sacrificial offerings to ancestors included buckwheat noodles. Throughout the intervening centuries, northern Chinese families prepared small, spaetzlelike noodles called *fenssu* by forcing dough made from buckwheat flour through holes in a device similar to a colander. Even into the first quarter of this century, over 90 percent of Chinese families were still purchasing buckwheat flour. Today, however, it is used only occasionally by the Tibeto-Burman peoples of China's western highlands to make noodles, dumplings, or thick pancakes. By contrast, in neighboring Tibet buckwheat remains a staple food. Not only are heavy pancakes prepared with buttermilk and buckwheat flour, but as Rinjing Dorje reports in *Food in Tibetan Life*, the fresh leaves of the plant are used to make an unusual salad that tastes like a cross between watercress and spinach.

Moving eastward from China, buckwheat was introduced to Japan, where the traditional buckwheat noodles, *soba*, are still considered to bring good luck. For this reason they are customarily served on New Year's Eve or offered as a housewarming present. The belief in their propitiousness may stem from the practice of Japanese goldsmiths who used buckwheat dough to collect the gold dust in their shops, thereby endowing the dough with auspicious properties. Or perhaps the length of the noodles promises a long life. The dried hulls of the groats are also put to good use in Japan, as a filler for pillows. Special shops sell the hulls, which are usually mixed with feathers to obtain the desired degree of firmness.

The introduction of buckwheat to the East by the nomadic tribes that ranged freely about Central Asia and China is not unexpected; it is the westward trek of the plant that offers the intriguing story. Most sources agree that invading Turks introduced buckwheat into Europe, probably in the thirteenth century. A few disputers argue that the Crusaders, rather than the Turks, carried the new foodstuff back to Europe. At any rate, the use of the word "buckwheat" in English was first recorded in 1548. The English word is usually considered a derivative of the Middle Dutch *boek-weit* or "beech wheat." This reference to the beech tree is actually quite apt, since the three-cornered buckwheat fruit (the groat) resembles the triangular beech nut. The English and Dutch words for buckwheat are noteworthy because they describe the image of the plant. As logical as this etymology seems, in most other languages a different rationale prevailed for naming the plant. The Turkish presence, or at least the association of buckwheat with the "Saracen" infidels, came to identify the plant throughout most of the Western world where it is used. Thus, in Spain buckwheat is *trigo sarraceno* (Saracen wheat), in Italy *saracena* (Saracen), and in France *sarrasin* (though Walloon dialect transformed the Old French *bucaille* into *beaucuit*, resulting in a neat verbal pun). Germans know the plant as *Heidenkraut* ("heathen plant"), Poles as *poganka* ("heathen"), and Czechs, similarly, as *pohanka*. Even the Finns refer to buckwheat as *tattari* (Tatar).

One odd piece does not quite fit into this neat linguistic puzzle. In Russia, the country today most closely associated with buckwheat, the standard term for the foodstuff is *grechnevaia kasha* ("Greek porridge") or simply *grechka,* from the root for "Greek." (Interestingly, rice received the "heathen" cognomen in Russia, where it was originally known as "Saracen millet.") Materials exist documenting the cultivation of buckwheat as a minor crop in the thirteenth and fourteenth centuries. Yet, strangely for a country that endured Mongol occupation for nearly two centuries (the thirteenth to fifteenth), buckwheat is not associated with the Turkic infidels, even though they left their mark elsewhere on the Russian culinary language. The Russian name for buckwheat probably derives instead from commerce with the Greek merchants who had important outposts in the Crimea and along the Black Sea coast, where they had contact with Turks. However, the fact that the first recorded use of *grechka* dates only to 1561 remains perplexing.

Despite the hazy etymology, it makes sense to dwell on Russia for a moment, since buckwheat is so crucial not only to the diet but also to the national identity. Numerous aphorisms reveal the significance of buckwheat porridge in Russian life; at the same time, these sayings reflect a certain ambivalence toward this staple food, at once the salvation and bane of a hungry population. The sentiment of "Buckwheat porridge is our dear mother" is countered by "Buckwheat porridge is our woe: you don't want to eat it, but you hate to throw it away." The reliance on buckwheat is evident in an ancient ritual surrounding the cooking of the groats. On New Year's Day, at exactly two o'clock in the morning, the oldest female member of the household was sent to the barn for groats, while the oldest male retrieved water from the river or well. These ingredients were placed on the table in separate containers, which were not to be touched until the stove was ready. When the stove heated up, the entire family sat down at the table, and the matriarch mixed the water with the groats, reciting a special incantation. Her conjuring related a charming story of some large and ruddy buckwheat groats that were invited to a royal feast in the holy city of Constantinople. The buckwheat consorted with princes and noblemen but after the feast loyally returned to Russia to enrich her humble homes. As the incantation ended, the family rose, and with a bow the housewife put the porridge into the stove. Then everyone sat down to wait. When the pot was removed from the stove, the nervousness was palpable: Was the pot full? If the porridge had spilled over the side, or if a crack had appeared in the earthenware pot, hardship loomed in the coming year. The crusty top was cut with a knife to reveal the steaming porridge within. If the groats were plump and ruddy, the year would be good, the harvest abundant. If, though, the groats were shriveled and white, trouble lay ahead. The lucky family sat down to enjoy a breakfast of *kasha,* but the unlucky family threw its porridge into the river.

Buckwheat groats represent more than just homely peasant fare, however. In her exhaustive book, *A Gift to Young Housewives,* Russia's famous nineteenth-century cookbook author, Elena Molokhovets, offers many ways to use buckwheat: in croutons and sausages, in stuffings and fritters, even in sweet puddings. And buckwheat flour forms the basis of the classic raised Russian pancakes or *bliny,* which when served with caviar constitute the most elegant fare. Although *bliny* may be mixed entirely from wheat flour, knowing cooks insist that the buckwheat flour gives the pancakes the desired plumpness and porousness that allows them to soak up copious amounts of butter.

The Russian use of buckwheat influenced cookery elsewhere. Russian Jews brought the porridge to North America, where it is called simply *"kasha."* Many Americans who swear by their buckwheat pancakes make absolutely no connection between the flour that gives the flapjacks excellent flavor and texture and the groats from which the flour is ground; for most Americans, *kasha* remains a foreign dish. Either homespun to the point of social embarrassment or utterly elegant, buckwheat elicits a strong response wherever it appears.

In France, the great chef Escoffier created a recipe for *Kache* of Buckwheat for Soups, made of buckwheat flour mixed to a paste with water, then baked, kneaded with butter, cut into rounds, and fried. This garnish, with its Russian name, implies elegance. Escoffier pays no attention to France's own buckwheat traditions, no doubt considering the use of buckwheat among the poor and provincial too lowly for his definitive work on *haute cuisine.* Nonetheless, Brittany's *crêpes de blé noir* are rightfully renowned. Folk poetry even compares the crêpe maker to a Greek hero for the finesse with which he is able to flip the pancakes. The buckwheat crêpes are often wrapped around grilled sardines or sausages or a pat of the fine local butter. Although *crêpes de blé noir* are still enjoyed today, other local buckwheat dishes have become less common, such as *far breton* or *noce,* boiled porridge containing dried fruits, and *kig ar fars,* buckwheat dumplings. Buckwheat beer is no longer brewed as it was in the eighteenth century, but buckwheat flour noodles, such as the Val d'Isère's *crozets,* remain regionally popular. Raised buckwheat pancakes called *bouriols* are still found on occasion, and travelers to Brittany can usually taste *Le Floron,* a three-grain bread that is traditionally marked with the Breton fleur-de-lys. Because buckwheat flour contains very little gluten, the addition of other grains is necessary for a good-textured loaf. (In *Le Grand Dictionnaire de Cuisine,* Alexandre Dumas complains that on its own, "bread made from buckwheat is the worst of all breads. The day after it has been baked it dries up, splits, crumbles, causes flatulence and is altogether detestable.")

Just as buckwheat readily took hold in Brittany's austere climate and poor soil, so it found favor elsewhere in areas of rugged terrain. A quick culinary tour through other European countries not usually associated with buckwheat reveals inventive uses of the plant wherever difficult agricultural conditions prevail. In Italy's northern province of Lombardy, for instance, buckwheat is used instead of cornmeal to make a hearty polenta, and this same sort of dish is found in Austria, in the mountainous region of Styria bordering Slovenia. Here, *Sterz,* a pudding made with cornmeal or buckwheat flour and served with cracklings, is still common. Across the border in Slovenia, buckwheat is used extensively to prepare breads, porridge, and a special buckwheat noodle dough that is made into a boiled dumpling filled with sweetened cheese.

Buckwheat's journey to North America brings us full circle, to that quintessential stack of flapjacks on the American breakfast table. Interestingly, the key players in this last leg of the journey proved to be the Dutch. The exact date of buckwheat's arrival in the Netherlands is unknown, but it is likely that agents of the Dutch West India Company, which had representatives throughout Central Asia, introduced the plant independently from the rest of Europe. In *The Sensible Cook,* the culinary historian Peter Rose describes how the Dutch used buckwheat to make *Jan in der Zak* ("John in the Bag"), an old-fashioned pudding similar to *far breton.* Buckwheat flour, raisins, and candied peel were combined, then poured into a cloth and suspended in water to boil until done. The pudding was dried in front of the fire and sliced before serving. Quite apart from this culinary usage, however, the Dutch recognized buckwheat as an important agricultural crop for both livestock forage and soil enrichment; its rapid maturation made it particularly well suited for crop rotation. Thus, when in 1624 the Dutch West India Company sponsored the voyage of the first thirty Dutch families to New Netherland (now New York), the organizers made sure that the colonists' provisions included buckwheat seed.

Documents from a 1625 expedition to New Netherland state that provisions for the early settlers included all sorts of seeds for planting. We know that buckwheat seed was among these provisions, since the record of the original purchase of Manhattan Island from the native Indians in 1626 states that buckwheat was already established in the new colony. The letter describing the purchase is reproduced in *The Sensible Cook: Dutch Foodways in the Old and the New World:* "[the colonists] sowed all their grain in the middle of May, and harvested it the middle of August. Thereof being samples of summer grain such as wheat, rye, barley, oats, buckwheat, canary seed, small beans and flax." But the Dutch did more than just introduce buckwheat to the New World; they also introduced their tradition of pancakes. The colonists added buckwheat to the usual wheat flour batter, and thus buckwheat flapjacks were born.

Buckwheat eventually spread throughout New York State, where it is still an important crop. Further to the south, less successful attempts were made to cultivate the plant. George Washington planted buckwheat at Mount Vernon as an ameliorator crop, but his initial enthusiasm palled when he discovered that the plant did not thrive in the Virginia climate. Following Washington's example, Thomas Jefferson also sowed buckwheat at his Virginia estate, Monticello. Jefferson grew buckwheat almost entirely for seed and as a green dressing in his crop rotation, noting in his *Farm Book* that it requires "strong land" and that its "produce is very precarious." The editors of his published notes comment that Jefferson "probably also grew enough [buckwheat] to make flour for table use." Although buckwheat is rarely planted in the American South today, it remains an important ingredient in Southern recipes, for pancakes particularly.

Some of the best pancakes are to be found in Preston County, West Virginia, where since 1941 the Kingwood Volunteer Fire Department has sponsored an annual buckwheat festival that always begins on the last Thursday of September. This four-day event features a lavish parade, agricultural exhibits, amusement rides, a turkey-calling contest, a 5K run, a horse show and antique car show, a country music gala, and contests in log rolling, ax throwing, chain-saw carving, tractor driving, bicycle decorating, and lamb dressing. But the main attraction is the all-you-can eat buckwheat cake dinner. The 1994 festival dished up over 16,000 dinners requiring 2 tons of buckwheat flour and 50 pounds of yeast. King Buckwheat and Queen Ceres—along with their attendant maids of honor, junior and senior princesses, children's court, Lady of Agriculture, and King and Lady Fireman—reign over the festivities.

The inhabitants of Preston County gladly celebrate buckwheat, acknowledging its important place in America's regional, populist cuisine. More often, however, buckwheat's circumnavigation of the globe has been marked by a recurrent contradiction between the plant's humble origins and its use in *haute cuisine*. Even as the groats evoke for some a distant (and often poor) homeland, their very foreignness to others makes the food exotic, worthy of celebration by epicures. But perhaps we should not be surprised. Although earthy and unrefined, buckwheat has tantalizing powers: The intensity of its flavor can transfigure the banal and bland. Surely the American settlers, in their dietary monotony, recognized this treasure once they tasted it. And so buckwheat prevailed against cultural odds to win a secure place at America's breakfast table.

Buckwheat Groats *(Grechnevaia Kasha)*

Buckwheat Groats with Bow Tie Noodles *(Kasha Varnishkes)*

Buckwheat Salad

Spicy Soba

Buckwheat Dumpling with Cheese *(Struklja)*

Preston County Buckwheat Cakes

Buckwheat Bread

Sweet Buckwheat Bread

Buckwheat Honey Cake

SEE ALSO:

Buckwheat Blini (page 80)

Sweet Buckwheat Crêpes *(Crêpes de blé noir)* (page 82)

Buckwheat Groats *(Grechnevaia Kasha)*

Anyone who has eaten buckwheat in Russia knows why it is so well loved there: the large groats cook up distinct and fluffy, with an inimitable nutty flavor. Russian *kasha,* as the cooked grains are called, hardly resembles the soft porridge many Americans may shy away from. The problem is that most packaged buckwheat is sold in a medium-fine cut, which doesn't give the buckwheat a chance to become anything but mush. Seek out the whole groats at a health food store and roast them yourself if necessary (see Note). Most important, bake the buckwheat instead of boiling it, as recipes usually direct. Prepared in an earthenware casserole, buckwheat makes a robust dish that marries well with winter vegetables.

1 cup coarse-cut buckwheat groats
½ teaspoon salt
2 cups boiling water or Mushroom Broth (page 51)
2 tablespoons unsalted butter, cut into bits (optional)

In a large skillet stir the groats over medium-high heat for about 5 minutes, until each grain begins to brown.

Preheat the oven to 350°F. Grease a 1½-quart earthenware casserole with a cover.

Place the groats in the casserole with the salt. Pour the boiling water or broth over all and dot with butter, if desired. Cover the casserole and bake for 20 minutes, until the liquid has been absorbed.

Serves 4 to 6.

VARIATIONS: Snipped dill, sautéed fresh mushrooms or onions, or reconstituted dried mushrooms may be added to the groats.

Leftover *kasha* may be pressed into a pan and chilled, then cut into pieces and fried lightly in butter or oil to make an interesting base for appetizers (top the *kasha* squares with cucumbers or radishes in sour cream). Cold *kasha* is also delicious with yogurt.

NOTE: To roast raw (green) buckwheat, spread 1 cup of groats in a jelly roll pan and bake at 300°F for 35 to 40 minutes, until browned. Stir the groats occasionally, especially toward the end.

Buckwheat Groats with Bow Tie Noodles
(Kasha Varnishkes)

Kasha varnishkes is a classic Jewish dish from Eastern Europe, its name reflecting its Slavic roots (varnishkes refers to the noodles, from the Slavic root for "boil"). Sautéed onions and egg add depth to the buckwheat's wild tang, creating a rich and satisfying dish.

2 medium onions, peeled and chopped (2 cups)
4 tablespoons unsalted butter (or less, if desired)
1 cup coarse-cut buckwheat groats
1 egg, lightly beaten
½ teaspoon salt
2½ cups boiling water
1 cup dried bow tie noodles (about 4 ounces)

In a small skillet sauté the onions in the butter until they begin to brown, 10 to 12 minutes.

Meanwhile, in a large saucepan cook the buckwheat groats with the beaten egg over medium heat, stirring, until the grains are well coated. Stir in the salt, the cooked onion, and the boiling water. Cover the pan and simmer until the water has been absorbed and the buckwheat is tender, 10 to 15 minutes.

While the buckwheat is cooking, bring a large kettle of salted water to a boil. Add the bow tie noodles and cook until tender but still firm, 8 to 10 minutes.

To serve, stir the noodles into the buckwheat and transfer the mixture to a serving dish.

Serves 6 to 8.

VARIATION: Sauté ½ cup sliced mushrooms in 1 tablespoon of butter and add to the cooked buckwheat along with the noodles.

Buckwheat Salad

Tibetans enjoy a salad of buckwheat greens, similar in taste to watercress and spinach. Here I've added cooked groats to greens in an unusual winter salad.

    1   cup coarse-cut buckwheat groats
    ½   teaspoon salt
    2   cups boiling water
    3   tablespoons vegetable oil
    3   tablespoons freshly squeezed lemon juice
    1   cucumber, peeled, seeded, and sliced ¼ inch thick
    3   scallions, thinly sliced, including the green parts
    1   bunch watercress (4 to 6 ounces), coarse stems removed
        Freshly ground black pepper
    2   tablespoons sour cream

Preheat the oven to 350°F.

Place the buckwheat and salt in a lightly greased casserole. Add the boiling water and bake for 20 minutes, until the water has been absorbed.

Turn the groats out into a large bowl and allow to cool slightly, then mix in the vegetable oil and lemon juice. Cool to room temperature.

Stir in the remaining ingredients, mixing well. Serve at room temperature.

Serves 6 to 8.

Spicy Soba

Japan is famous for its excellent buckwheat noodles, which are available in several forms: fresh, dried, and partially cooked. In this country the dried noodles are often sold as *zaru soba*. They are delicious served plain, or dipped in a light sauce made from broth, rice wine, and soy. When the weather turns cold, however, I like a spicier rendition. This one is sure to draw raves.

½ cup soy sauce
½ cup firmly packed light brown sugar
¼ cup tahini
2 garlic cloves, put through a garlic press
½ teaspoon dried red pepper flakes
¼ cup sesame oil
6 scallions, chopped, including the green part
1 pound dried soba

Bring a large kettle of salted water to a boil.

Meanwhile, prepare the sauce. In a small saucepan heat together the soy sauce, brown sugar, tahini, garlic, and red pepper, whisking until the sugar and tahini melt. Stir in the sesame oil and scallions and keep warm.

When the water boils add the soba to the kettle and cook until just tender, about 5 minutes. Drain.

Return the noodles to the kettle and toss with the sauce. Transfer to a bowl and serve immediately.

Serves 4.

Buckwheat Dumpling with Cheese *(Struklja)*

The dumplings of Eastern Europe are justly celebrated, and this recipe from Slovenia is especially savory. When the dumpling is sliced, its pale yellow filling is marbled against the rich brown of the buckwheat dough, making a striking dish. Although several steps are involved, the actual preparation of the dumpling is not difficult.

Dough

1¼	cups buckwheat flour
¾	cup unbleached white flour
½	teaspoon salt
1	egg
10	to 11 tablespoons warm water

Filling

2	tablespoons sour cream
½	pound farmer cheese
2	eggs
	Pinch of salt
2	teaspoons sugar

3½	quarts water
2	teaspoons salt
1	cup fresh bread crumbs
2	tablespoons unsalted butter
2	tablespoons grated Kasseri or Parmesan cheese

To make the dough, mix together the buckwheat flour, white flour, and salt. Make a well in the center and drop in the egg. Mix the egg into the flour, then add just enough water to make a soft, pliable dough. Knead the dough briefly. Place it on a floured surface and cover with an overturned bowl. Leave to rest for at least 15 minutes.

Meanwhile, make the filling by mixing the sour cream into the farmer cheese. Beat in the eggs, one at a time. Add the salt and sugar.

Heat the water and the 2 teaspoons salt in a large kettle.

On a floured surface, roll out the dough ⅛ inch thick into a 12 x 18-inch rectangle. Spread the filling over the dough, leaving 1 inch around the edges. Beginning with a long end, roll up the dough like a jelly roll, stopping at the last turn before the end. Fold the last section of dough up over the roll (this keeps the filling from oozing as the last bit is rolled).

Butter an 18-inch-long piece of aluminum foil. Place the filled roll on the foil, then bring the ends together to make a ring. Press them to seal. (Don't worry if the dough tears a little; it will not hurt the finished dumpling.) Wrap the roll tightly in the foil, sealing all the seams well to form a neat packet.

When the water comes to a rolling boil, place the foil packet in the kettle and cover. Boil for 30 to 35 minutes.

Meanwhile, in a small skillet toss the bread crumbs with the butter. Cook over medium heat for 5 minutes, until the crumbs are crisp and brown.

When the dumpling is done, remove the packet from the water. Open it carefully to avoid getting burned and slide the dumpling onto a cutting board. Slice the dumpling diagonally to reveal the filling. Place the slices in an overlapping pattern on a serving plate. Sprinkle with the grated cheese and top with the toasted bread crumbs. Serve at once.

Serves 6 to 8.

Preston County Buckwheat Cakes

This recipe comes from Bill Collins, who heads the honors program at West Virginia University. Bill's mother taught his sister to bake buckwheat cakes, and she in turn tutored Bill. Both Bill and his sister favor a recipe that was printed on the buckwheat flour packaged for Marrara's Market in Kingwood, West Virginia. These fabulous pancakes are similar to those sold by the thousands at the Preston County Buckwheat Festival, where electric drills are used to mix the vast quantities of batter. It's much easier to bake buckwheat cakes at home, though. Just be sure to use a heavy, well-seasoned griddle, preferably made of cast-iron. And, if cooking for a multitude, don't forget to dust your drill.

2½ teaspoons active dry yeast
4 cups lukewarm water
2 cups buckwheat flour
½ teaspoon baking soda
1 teaspoon salt
1 tablespoon sugar

The night before you plan to make the pancakes, dissolve the yeast in 2 cups of the warm water. Stir in the buckwheat flour, cover, and leave to rise overnight.

The next morning, remove ½ cup of the batter to use as a starter for the next batch of pancakes (see Note). Dissolve the baking soda in ½ cup of the remaining water. Stir this mixture into the batter along with the salt and sugar. Add the remaining 1½ cups water to the batter.

Heat a heavy griddle. Use a ¼-cup measure to drop the batter onto the griddle to make pancakes about ⅛ inch thick. Cook the pancakes for a few minutes until bubbles form on the surface, then turn and cook on the other side for just a minute until lightly browned. Serve immediately. Butter and maple syrup are the traditional accompaniments.

Serves 4.

NOTE: Store the reserved starter in a jar in the refrigerator (it will keep a long time). The night before you plan to bake pancakes, add 1 teaspoon of yeast to the starter before stirring in the water and buckwheat flour. Proceed as above. The pancakes will taste slightly more sour when made with a starter.

Buckwheat Bread

Dark buckwheat flour contains four times as much fiber as whole wheat flour. This hearty, nutritious loaf tastes especially good with cheese.

2½ teaspoons active dry yeast
2¾ cups unbleached white flour
1¼ cups warm water
2 tablespoons molasses
1½ teaspoons salt
2 cups buckwheat flour
Cornmeal for dusting

The day before you plan to bake the bread, make a sponge by mixing the yeast and ¾ cup of the white flour with ¾ cup of the water. Stir well, cover, and leave to sit at room temperature overnight.

The next day, stir in the remaining water, the molasses, salt, and buckwheat flour. Beat in the remaining 2 cups of white flour. Turn the dough out onto a floured surface and knead until smooth and elastic, about 10 minutes. Place the dough in a lightly greased bowl and turn to grease the top. Cover and leave to rise for 1½ hours, until the dough has doubled in bulk.

Dust a baking sheet with cornmeal. Punch down the dough and divide in half. Shape into two round loaves. Place the loaves on the baking sheet, cover them, and leave to rise for 40 to 45 minutes.

Preheat the oven to 375°F. Bake the bread for 30 minutes, until crusty and brown. Cool on racks.

Makes 2 loaves.

Sweet Buckwheat Bread

Moist and aromatic, this beautiful, caramel-brown loaf is more like a dense cake than a bread. It is also chock full of nutrients. I've adapted this recipe from one by food historian William Woys Weaver that appeared in *National Geographic Traveler*. The Pennsylvania Dutch serve this loaf either with a meal as a table bread, or at a coffee *klatsch*. I like it best with coffee, which complements its rather exotic flavor.

3   cups buckwheat flour
½   cup whole wheat flour
1   teaspoon baking soda
1   teaspoon ground anise
4   tablespoons unsalted butter
6   tablespoons dark brown sugar
1   teaspoon dried rosemary
3   tablespoons plus 1 teaspoon poppy seed
4   large eggs
2   cups plain yogurt

Preheat the oven to 375°F. Grease and lightly flour a 12-inch pie dish, preferably ceramic.

In a large bowl mix together the buckwheat flour, whole wheat flour, baking soda, and anise.

Place the butter and brown sugar in the bowl of a food processor and process to the consistency of fine crumbs. Add this to the flour mixture along with the rosemary and 3 tablespoons of the poppy seed.

In a separate bowl beat the eggs until light, then stir in the yogurt. Pour this mixture into the dry ingredients and stir until well blended. The batter will be stiff.

Turn the batter into the prepared pie dish and smooth the top. Sprinkle with the remaining 1 teaspoon of poppy seed. Bake for 40 minutes, then cool on a rack before slicing.

Makes 1 large loaf.

Buckwheat Honey Cake

I first tasted this cake over two decades ago in Kiev, but I still remember its mahogany color and richness, not to mention the bees swarming all around it. Since then I've baked many a honey cake, but none rivals this one in flavor or appeal. It should be prepared 2 days before serving. The recipe comes from my first cookbook, *A Taste of Russia*.

8	tablespoons (1 stick) unsalted butter
1	cup firmly packed dark brown sugar
1	cup buckwheat honey
4	eggs, separated
2½	cups all-purpose flour
2	teaspoons baking soda
1	teaspoon baking powder
	Pinch of salt
	Grated rind of 1 orange
1	cup sour cream
1	teaspoon ground cinnamon
½	teaspoon grated nutmeg
½	cup currants
1	cup chopped walnuts
½	cup chopped pitted dates

Preheat the oven to 300°F. Grease a 10-inch angel-food cake pan and line the bottom and sides with brown paper (the kind used for grocery bags). Grease the paper.

In a large mixing bowl cream the butter and sugar until light and fluffy, then beat in the honey. Beat in the egg yolks one at a time, mixing well after each addition. Stir in the flour, baking soda, baking powder, and salt. Add the orange rind and sour cream, beating until the batter is smooth. Stir in the cinnamon, nutmeg, currants, walnuts, and dates.

Whip the egg whites until stiff but not dry and fold them into the batter. Pour the batter into the prepared pan, spreading it evenly.

Bake the cake for 75 minutes, or until a cake tester comes out clean.

Remove the outer part of the pan and let the cake cool upright in the tube section. When completely cool, remove the cake from the pan.

Wrap the cake in aluminum foil and leave it to mellow at room temperature for 2 days before serving.

Makes 1 large cake.

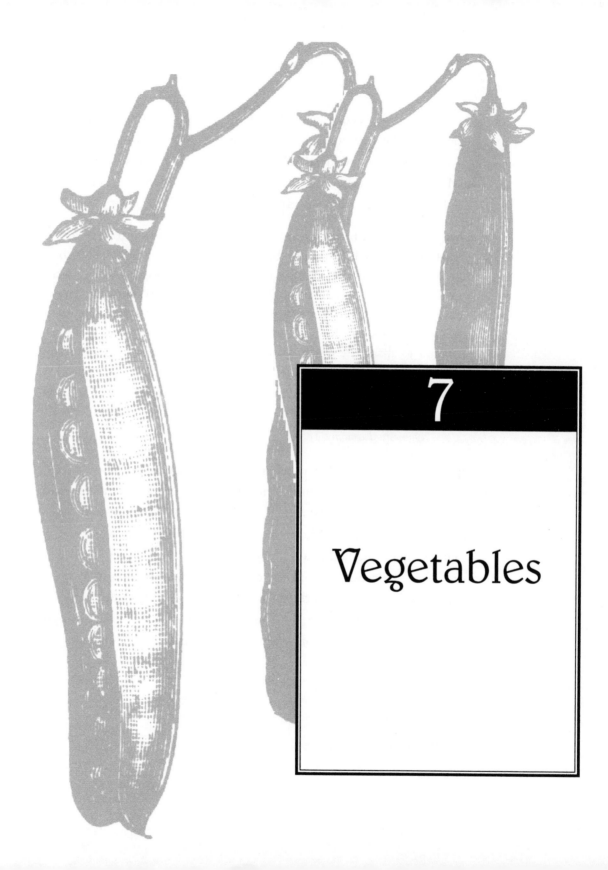

7

Vegetables

In a mid-nineteenth-century cookbook, the chef Alexis Soyer describes the devious culinary practices to which cooks of the past were sometimes reduced. He offers a recipe for a "Carthusian of Meat and Vegetables"—a chartreuse or old-fashioned mold of meat or poultry surrounded by vegetables:

> You will perhaps be surprised at the name I have given to this curious mixture of vegetable produce, but you will immediately perceive that I have taken it from those well-known monks who took vows to partake of no animal food, something like our strict vegetarians of the present day; but those jolly old dogs in former days were obliged, at times, to break their vow; as, however, it could not be done openly, they were obliged to mask the object cooked in [a] covering of vegetables, and thus cheated their oath and their own conscience.
>
> —ALEXIS SOYER, *A Shilling Cookery for the People*
> *Embracing an Entirely New System of Plain Cookery and*
> *Domestic Economy,* 1854

Happily, long gone are the days when vegetables had to be served duplicitously. Now we can proclaim their presence, stuffing vegetables with more vegetables, sautéing, baking, steaming, and roasting them with abandon. We need not masquerade in the style of the Chartreuse monks.

This chapter highlights a variety of cold-weather vegetables, all of which assert their essential earthy qualities. No longer must roots be boiled to death or hidden under layers of cream sauce. The recipes I offer here allow the vegetables to shine on their own; and not surprisingly, some even appear luminous on a dark winter's night.

Warm Beet Vinaigrette
Pureed Beets with Wine
Stuffed Cabbage Leaves

Savory Sauerkraut

Braised Fennel

Garlicky Winter Greens

Jerusalem Artichokes with Rice

Jerusalem Artichokes with Tomatoes

Stuffed Kohlrabi

Sautéed Mushrooms with Olives

Sautéed Mushrooms and Chestnuts

Brandied Onions

Hot Potato Snow

Potato Köfte *(Patates Köftesi)*

Mashed Potatoes and Celery Root

Curried Potato Casserole

Salsify Fritters

Salsify Vinaigrette

Baked Acorn Squash with Apples

Gratin of Turnips

Turnip and Onion Casserole

Roasted Winter Vegetables

Roasted Winter Vegetables with Mustard Sauce

Winter Vegetable Stew

SEE ALSO:

Potato Pancakes *(Latkes)* (page 289)

rutabaga recipes (pages 172–181)

Spinach and Watercress Puree (page 69)

Warm Beet Vinaigrette

These grated beets are wonderfully tangy and quite easy to prepare.

- 1 medium onion, peeled and finely chopped
- ¼ cup olive oil
- 4 garlic cloves, peeled and minced
- 1 pound beets, peeled and coarsely grated
- ¾ teaspoon salt
  Freshly ground black pepper
- 2 tablespoons red wine vinegar
- 1 teaspoon Dijon mustard

In a large skillet sauté the onion in the olive oil until golden, 10 to 12 minutes. Stir in the garlic, grated beets, salt, and pepper to taste. Cover the skillet and cook over low heat for 15 to 20 minutes, until the beets are tender. Stir in the vinegar and mustard and leave to rest for 10 minutes. Serve warm.

Serves 4 to 6.

Pureed Beets with Wine

Cornstarch gives this ruby puree a beautiful sheen, resulting in an elegant presentation.

1½ pounds beets
¼ cup dry red wine
2 tablespoons freshly squeezed lemon juice
⅛ teaspoon salt
    Freshly ground black pepper
1½ teaspoons cornstarch
1 teaspoon salted butter

Sprigs of dill or parsley

Preheat the oven to 400°F.

Place the unpeeled beets in a shallow dish and bake until soft, 1 to 1½ hours, depending on their size. Peel them and puree in a food processor with 2 tablespoons of the wine.

Transfer the puree to a medium saucepan and stir in the lemon juice, salt, and pepper to taste. Dissolve the cornstarch in the remaining 2 tablespoons of wine and add to the beets. Heat slowly for about 1 minute, stirring, until the beets turn shiny. Stir in the butter and serve, garnished with sprigs of dill or parsley.

Serves 4.

Stuffed Cabbage Leaves

These wonderfully sweet-and-sour bundles are presented in the Eastern European style, except that barley replaces the usual filling of meat. The cabbage must cook for a couple of hours to develop the best flavor, a boon if we are to believe the second-century Greek writer Athenaeus, who states that the smell of boiling cabbage drives away the headache caused by a hangover. Others may be less sanguine about cabbage and its smell. In *The Anatomy of Melancholy* Robert Burton warns readers away from the vegetable, stating that it "causeth troublesome dreams, and sends up black vapours to the brain." Rest assured that this cabbage mixed with onions and tomatoes is nonhallucinatory. In fact, it smells quite delicious as it cooks, so you need not hesitate to invite friends to dinner. And the stuffed leaves taste even better after reheating.

1 small head of white cabbage (about 2 pounds)
2 large onions, peeled and chopped
3 tablespoons olive oil

Filling

½ cup raw barley
1 cup water
1 teaspoon salt
Freshly ground black pepper
1 large carrot, peeled and grated
¼ cup minced parsley
1 garlic clove, peeled and minced
1 egg, lightly beaten

One 28-ounce can tomatoes, drained and chopped
⅓ cup freshly squeezed lemon juice
¼ cup firmly packed dark brown sugar
¼ teaspoon salt

Core the cabbage and blanch it in a pot of boiling water for 8 to 10 minutes. Remove from the pot and gently peel off the outer leaves. If the inner leaves are still too stiff to be removed, return the cabbage to the boiling water for another minute or so. Continue in this fashion until all of the leaves have been removed. Use the small inner leaves or any damaged ones to line the bottom and sides of a 3-quart saucepan. Reserve the blanching liquid.

Next, prepare the onions. Place the onions and olive oil in a heavy-bottomed frying pan and pour over just enough of the reserved water from the cabbage pot to cover them. Bring to a boil and simmer slowly, uncovered, for 45 minutes to 1 hour, until the water has evaporated and the onions are golden. Stir occasionally to make sure the onions don't stick to the pan.

While the onions are simmering, prepare the filling. In a small pan bring the barley and water to a boil and simmer, covered, for 15 minutes until the water has been absorbed. (The grains will still be firm.) Place the barley in a large mixing bowl and stir in the salt, pepper, grated carrot, parsley, garlic, and egg. Blend well.

Now, starting with the largest leaves, take a cabbage leaf and place a mound of the filling along the center. Tuck up the bottom edge of the leaf first, then roll and tuck until the filling is completely enclosed in the leaf. Continue until all the filling has been used. There will be about twelve rolls.

Place half of the rolls in the cabbage-lined pot in a single layer. Cover with half of the prepared onions, then top with the remaining cabbage rolls and the rest of the onions.

In a medium saucepan bring the tomatoes to a boil with the lemon juice, sugar, and salt. Pour over the cabbage rolls, cover the pan, and simmer for 1½ to 2 hours.

Makes about 12 rolls, serving 4 to 6.

VARIATION: For sweet-and-sour cabbage, shred the cabbage instead of separating the leaves. Prepare the onions and the tomato sauce as directed, but do not prepare the barley filling. Stir the shredded cabbage into the cooked onions, add the tomato sauce, cover the pan, and simmer for 1½ to 2 hours. This amount will serve 6 to 8 as a side dish.

Savory Sauerkraut

Here is an easy way to get your cabbage fix if you don't have either the time or the inclination to shred it laboriously. Simply heat prepared sauerkraut with wine and seasonings for half an hour before serving. The result is tangy, crisp, and delicious.

1 onion, peeled and finely chopped
1 tablespoon unsalted butter
1 pound best-quality sauerkraut (4 cups), rinsed and drained
1 cup dry white wine
½ teaspoon paprika
½ teaspoon caraway seed

In a large skillet sauté the onion in the butter until it begins to turn golden, about 8 minutes. Add the remaining ingredients. Cover the skillet and simmer for 30 minutes, until most of the liquid is absorbed. Serve hot.

Serves 4 to 6.

Braised Fennel

Slow cooking brings out the aromatic anise flavor of bulb fennel in this decorative dish.

2 fennel bulbs, trimmed of leaves and roots and
   halved lengthwise
2 tablespoons olive oil
1 medium onion, peeled and finely chopped
2 medium carrots, peeled and finely chopped
2 garlic cloves, peeled and minced
1 cup water
¼ cup dry white wine
4 sprigs of parsley
1 bay leaf
¼ teaspoon dried thyme
½ teaspoon salt
   Freshly ground black pepper

2 tablespoons minced parsley

In a large skillet gently cook the cut fennel in the olive oil for 5 minutes on each side. Remove to a plate with a slotted spatula. Add the onion, carrots, and garlic to the olive oil in the pan. Place the fennel, cut side down, on top of the vegetables. Add the water, wine, parsley sprigs, and seasonings.

Cover the skillet and simmer until the fennel is tender, about 45 minutes, turning once. Transfer the fennel to a serving platter. Remove the parsley sprigs and bay leaf from the skillet and discard. Boil the remaining liquid and vegetables for about 1 minute to thicken slightly, then pour over the fennel. Garnish with the minced parsley and serve.

Serves 4 to 8.

Garlicky Winter Greens

Here is an appealing way to prepare the bitter greens of winter. For robust flavor, I like to cook them with plenty of garlic. Toasted bread crumbs add a nice crunch.

2 pounds mixed bitter greens (such as mustard, turnip, and Swiss chard), trimmed
1 pound fresh spinach, trimmed
¼ cup olive oil
4 large garlic cloves, peeled and minced
    Salt
    Freshly ground black pepper
1 cup coarse fresh bread crumbs, toasted

Rinse the bitter greens thoroughly to rid them of any lingering dirt (I swish them around in a sink filled with cold water). Coarsely chop the greens, then rinse them again briefly. Remove them from the water but do not drain; transfer them, with the water still clinging, to a large kettle. Steam over medium heat for 10 minutes.

Meanwhile, wash the spinach, then chop it coarsely. Rinse it again briefly. After the bitter greens have cooked for 10 minutes add the spinach, with the water still clinging, to the pot. Steam all the greens together for 5 minutes more. Drain.

While the greens are cooking, heat the olive oil over low heat in a large skillet. Cook the garlic for 2 minutes. Add the drained, cooked greens, tossing to mix well. Cook over medium-high heat 3 minutes more. Season liberally with salt and pepper. At the last minute stir in the toasted bread crumbs and serve.

Serves 6.

Jerusalem Artichokes with Rice

Despite their name, Jerusalem artichokes are tubers, members of the sunflower family and native to North America. They are amazingly easy to grow and produce beautiful yellow flowers, yet the plant has fallen out of favor in the United States. Such disregard is a shame because the crunchy texture and sweet flavor of the tubers are so delightful. Jerusalem artichokes may be eaten right out of hand as a tasty snack, but when married with other ingredients they reach new heights. This lovely dish is prepared in the Turkish style, with olive oil and dill.

2   tablespoons olive oil
1   medium onion, peeled and finely chopped
1   medium carrot, peeled and cut in half lengthwise,
      then sliced ¼ inch thick
1   pound Jerusalem artichokes, well scrubbed and
      sliced ½ inch thick (see Note)
1   tablespoon freshly squeezed lemon juice
2   tablespoons raw rice
¾   cup water
¾   teaspoon salt
1   teaspoon sugar

1   tablespoon minced fresh dill

Heat the olive oil in a medium saucepan. Add the onion, carrot, and Jerusalem artichoke, in that order. Pour the lemon juice over the artichokes and sprinkle on the rice. Add the water, salt, and sugar. Cover the pan and simmer for 30 minutes. Spoon the mixture into a dish and serve hot or warm, garnished with the minced dill.

Serves 4 to 6.

NOTE: I like the added texture the peel gives the vegetable, so I usually just scrub the artichokes well without peeling. If you prefer a more delicate flavor, feel free to peel them.

Jerusalem Artichokes with Tomatoes

This recipe is tangier than the preceding one. Although the dish may be prepared just before serving, the flavors improve on standing, as the tomatoes mellow and blend with the artichokes.

½   pound Jerusalem artichokes, well scrubbed
1   tablespoon olive oil
1   tablespoon unsalted butter
One   16-ounce can tomatoes, drained and coarsely chopped
½   teaspoon salt
    Freshly ground black pepper
⅛   teaspoon dried thyme

Boil the Jerusalem artichokes in salted water to cover until just tender, 10 to 15 minutes depending on their size. Drain and slice ½ inch thick.

While the artichokes are cooking, simmer the remaining ingredients together in a medium saucepan. Stir the sliced artichokes into the tomato mixture and heat gently. Serve warm.

Serves 4.

NOTE: This dish may be made ahead of time and left at room temperature, or refrigerate it overnight and reheat.

Stuffed Kohlrabi

If you can find purple kohlrabies, mix them with the more common green ones for a colorful dish.

2 pounds small kohlrabies, including the leaves
  (about eight 2-inch roots)
1 tablespoon unsalted butter
1 small onion, peeled and finely chopped
1 garlic clove, peeled and minced
⅛ teaspoon dried thyme
1 egg, lightly beaten
¼ cup fine dry bread crumbs
2 tablespoons minced fresh dill
¼ teaspoon salt
  Freshly ground black pepper
1 cup vegetable broth

Remove the leaves from the kohlrabies. Finely chop enough leaves to make ¼ cup, and set aside. Parboil the roots in salted water to cover for 10 minutes, then drain and let sit until cool enough to handle. With a paring knife trim the bottoms of the roots so that they stand upright. Scoop out the insides, leaving a ½-inch shell.

Make the filling. In a small skillet heat the butter over low heat. Cook the onion and garlic over medium heat for 3 minutes, then stir in the thyme and the chopped kohlrabi leaves. Continue to cook 2 minutes longer. Transfer to a bowl and leave to cool. Stir in the egg, bread crumbs, dill, salt, and pepper to taste.

Preheat the oven to 350°F.

Stuff the hollowed-out kohlrabies with the onion and bread crumb mixture and place in a shallow baking dish. Pour the vegetable stock around them and cover. Bake for 1 hour, until the kohlrabies are tender. Serve hot.

Serves 8.

Sautéed Mushrooms with Olives

These piquant mushrooms come from Bulgaria, which, like its better-known neighbors along the Black Sea, produces excellent olives and wine.

¼ cup olive oil
1 pound mixed wild mushrooms, trimmed and sliced
1 shallot, peeled and minced
3 garlic cloves, peeled and minced
⅓ cup brine-cured black olives (such as Kalamata),
   pitted and coarsely chopped
2 tablespoons tomato paste
2 tablespoons water
¼ cup dry red wine
2 tablespoons minced parsley
¼ teaspoon salt (or more, to taste)
   Freshly ground black pepper

Heat the olive oil in a large skillet and add the mushrooms, shallot, and garlic. Cook over medium heat, stirring occasionally, for 5 minutes. Stir in the remaining ingredients and simmer 5 minutes more. Serve hot.

Serves 4 to 6.

NOTE: Leftover mushrooms make an excellent topping for pizza.

Sautéed Mushrooms and Chestnuts

This flavorsome sauté is a cold-weather tradition in our family, marking the appearance of the season's first chestnuts. I used to make it with an ample amount of cream, but the vegetables are really rich enough to stand on their own. Now I can enjoy as many servings as I like!

1   pound fresh chestnuts (see Note)
1   pound shiitake mushrooms
¾   cup water
1   large onion, peeled and chopped
1   small garlic clove, peeled and minced
2   tablespoons olive oil
¼   cup Madeira
¼   teaspoon dried thyme
½   teaspoon salt
    Freshly ground black pepper
1   tablespoon minced parsley

With a sharp knife cut a deep X on the flat side of each chestnut. Place the nuts in a large pot of boiling water and cook for 10 minutes. Remove the pan from the heat. With a slotted spoon take a few chestnuts at a time from the water and peel them, removing both the outer husk and the fine inner peel. Try to keep them whole.

Cut the stems from the mushrooms and place the stems in a small saucepan with the water. Bring to a boil and simmer for 15 minutes.

Coarsely chop the mushroom caps.

In a large skillet sauté the onion and garlic in the olive oil until soft, 5 to 8 minutes. Stir in the peeled chestnuts and cook over medium-low heat for about 5 minutes more.

Strain the mushroom broth and discard the stems.

Add the chopped mushroom caps to the chestnut mixture, along with the strained broth, Madeira, thyme, salt, and pepper. Mix well. Cook, covered, over low heat for 10 minutes.

Stir in the parsley and transfer to a serving dish.

Serves 4 to 6.

NOTE: Peeling fresh chestnuts is admittedly tedious. If you can find a good brand of *unsweetened* canned chestnuts, feel free to use them, calculating ¾ pound of prepared chestnuts for each pound of fresh. If you do use fresh chestnuts, always buy and prepare a few more than you think you will need—there are invariably a few spoiled ones in each batch.

Brandied Onions

Peppery and colorful, these onions may be served as a side dish or mounded on bread for a delicious appetizer.

    2 pounds yellow onions, peeled, sliced, and separated into rings
    2 tablespoons unsalted butter or olive oil
  One 28-ounce can tomatoes, drained and chopped
    ¼ cup water
    ¼ cup brandy
    1 scant teaspoon salt
    ¾ teaspoon freshly ground black pepper

In a large skillet sauté the onions in the butter or oil until golden, about 15 minutes. Stir in the remaining ingredients and simmer for 25 to 30 minutes, stirring occasionally. Serve warm or at room temperature.

Serves 6.

Hot Potato Snow

As I was flipping through *Leipoldt's Cape Cookery*, a marvelous book by C. Louis Leipoldt on South African food, this recipe immediately caught my attention. What could be more appropriate for a cold-weather cookbook than hot snow? This dish is indeed like an oxymoron, with its mound of flaked potatoes resembling snow that melts in the mouth. For the fluffiest texture, use the best baking potatoes you can find.

2 large russet potatoes, well scrubbed
½ teaspoon powdered ginger
½ teaspoon dried rosemary
   Grated rind of 1 lemon
   Salt
   Freshly ground white pepper
   Freshly grated nutmeg

Bring several inches of water to a boil in a large kettle. Rub each potato with ¼ teaspoon of ginger. Place the potatoes on a rack over the water and sprinkle with the rosemary and lemon peel. Steam until tender, 50 to 60 minutes.

Peel the potatoes and press them through a sieve onto a serving dish so that they flake into a mound. Season with salt, pepper, and nutmeg, and serve immediately.

Serves 4.

Potato Köfte *(Patates Köftesi)*

Most *köfte* are made with ground meat, but these spicy vegetarian ones use mashed potatoes to bind the bulgur. This recipe comes from my friend Nevin Halici, whose small kitchen in Konya, Turkey, regularly turns out fabulous food. This dish is typical of her culinary brilliance.

> 1 pound potatoes
> 1 cup raw bulgur
> 1½ cups boiling water
> 4 garlic cloves, peeled and minced
> 1 tablespoon tomato paste
> 1 teaspoon freshly ground black pepper
> 1 teaspoon cayenne
> 1 teaspoon salt
> ½ cup olive oil
> 5 scallions, trimmed and finely chopped, including the greens
> 1 tablespoon minced parsley
>
> Romaine leaves

Boil the whole, unpeeled potatoes in salted water to cover until tender, about 30 minutes. Peel and mash them.

While the potatoes are cooking, place the bulgur in a bowl and pour the boiling water over it. Cover the bowl and leave to rest until the potatoes are done. The bulgur should absorb all of the water; if it hasn't, turn the bulgur out into a sieve to drain any excess water.

In a large bowl mix the bulgur with the mashed potatoes, using your hands to knead thoroughly. Mix in the garlic, tomato paste, spices, and olive oil. Stir in the scallions and parsley.

Form the mixture into 3-inch-long, sausage-shaped *köfte*. When ready to serve, nestle each *köfte* in a small leaf of romaine.

Serve at room temperature.

Makes 2 dozen *köfte,* serving 6 to 8.

Mashed Potatoes and Celery Root

Celery root and potatoes are a match made in heaven; add garlic, and they become even more ethereal. This recipe was inspired by Lydie Marshall's method for garlic mashed potatoes. Because I like the vegetables home-style, with some chunks, I mash them by hand. If you prefer a more elegant presentation, use a food processor.

1 pound russet potatoes (2 medium-large)
4 garlic cloves, unpeeled
1 celery root (1 pound), peeled and cut into chunks
½ teaspoon salt
Freshly ground white pepper

Boil the unpeeled potatoes and garlic cloves in salted water to cover for 25 minutes. Add the celery root and continue to boil until the vegetables are tender, 10 to 15 minutes longer. Remove the potatoes, celery root, and garlic from the pan. Turn the heat to high and boil the water briskly while you prepare the vegetables.

Peel the potatoes and the garlic and mash them with the celery root. Add about ¼ cup of the reduced cooking water to make the potatoes creamy. Stir in the salt and add pepper to taste. Serve hot.

Serves 4 to 6.

VARIATION: Stir 1 cup grated Gruyère cheese into the mashed vegetables.

Curried Potato Casserole

These creamy potatoes with their piquant curry flavor are utterly satisfying.

3 large potatoes
2 tablespoons unsalted butter
1 medium onion, peeled and finely chopped
2 tablespoons tomato paste
2 teaspoons curry powder
5 tablespoons all-purpose flour
1½ cups evaporated skim milk (one 12-ounce can)
1 cup water
1 teaspoon salt
Freshly ground black pepper

Boil the whole, unpeeled potatoes in salted water to cover until just tender, 35 to 40 minutes. Drain and allow to cool slightly, then peel them and cut into 1-inch cubes. You should have about 5 cups of cubed potatoes.

While the potatoes are boiling, melt the butter in a large saucepan and sauté the onion for 10 minutes, until it begins to turn golden. Add the tomato paste, curry powder, and flour, mixing well. Gradually stir in the evaporated milk and the water. Add the salt and pepper to taste. Bring to a boil and simmer for 3 minutes.

Preheat the oven to 375°F. Lightly grease a 2-quart casserole.

Add the potato cubes to the sauce and stir to coat them well. Turn the mixture into the prepared dish and bake for 30 minutes, until bubbly. Serve hot.

Serves 6.

Salsify Fritters

Salsify is not always readily available, and you may need to do some sleuthing. After a summer of weeding pesky burdock from the yard, I was horrified to find salsify identified as burdock root. Salsify's black cousin, scorzonera, is sometimes labeled as salsify. But if you can find either the cream-colored salsify or black scorzonera, be sure to try these delicious fritters. Just remember to drop the peeled vegetable directly into acidulated water so that it doesn't discolor. And if you're peeling scorzonera, you may want to wear gloves to avoid stained hands.

2 pounds salsify
Juice of 1 lemon plus ¼ cup freshly squeezed lemon juice
1 teaspoon salt
Freshly ground white pepper
2 garlic cloves, put through a garlic press
2 tablespoons minced parsley
2 tablespoons minced fresh dill
2 eggs, lightly beaten
6 tablespoons fine dry bread crumbs

Vegetable oil for frying

Trim and peel the salsify but leave it whole. Place the whole roots in a kettle of boiling water containing the juice of 1 lemon. Boil gently until barely tender, 12 to 15 minutes.

Drain the salsify and grate it coarsely (this is most easily done in a food processor but may also be done by hand). Transfer to a bowl and stir in the ¼ cup lemon juice, the seasonings, herbs, eggs, and bread crumbs.

In a large skillet heat vegetable oil to a depth of ⅛ to ¼ inch. Take a large spoonful of salsify mixture and shape it into a patty. Drop in the hot oil and cook over medium-high heat for 4 to 5 minutes, until the underside is browned. Turn the fritters and cook for 3 minutes more. Drain on paper towels and serve hot.

Serves 4 generously.

Salsify Vinaigrette

This refreshing side dish pairs salsify with a lemony vinaigrette.

Juice of ½ lemon plus 2 teaspoons freshly squeezed
lemon juice
1 pound salsify
1½ teaspoons Dijon mustard
⅛ teaspoon salt
Freshly ground black pepper
2 tablespoons olive oil
2 teaspoons minced parsley

Fill a large saucepan with water and add the juice of ½ lemon. Bring the water to a boil.

Meanwhile, peel the salsify and slice it crosswise into 1-inch pieces. Drop the slices into the boiling water and cook gently for 10 minutes, until just tender.

To make the dressing, in a small bowl mix together the mustard, salt, pepper, and 2 teaspoons lemon juice. Whisk in the olive oil to form an emulsion, then stir in the parsley.

When the salsify is done, drain it and transfer to a serving dish. Add just enough dressing to coat the slices without drenching them. Serve warm or at room temperature.

Serves 4.

Baked Acorn Squash with Apples

Cut acorn squash makes a wonderful vehicle for sweet, citrus-scented apples.

2   small acorn squash, cut in half lengthwise and seeded
2   tart apples, peeled, cored, and diced
4   tablespoons unsalted butter, melted
½   cup firmly packed light brown sugar
2   tablespoons orange juice (prepared juice is fine)
1   teaspoon grated lemon rind

Preheat the oven to 400°F.

Place the prepared squash in a shallow baking dish cut side down and add about ½ inch of boiling water to the dish. Bake for 20 minutes.

Meanwhile, mix the apples with the remaining ingredients. Remove the squash from the oven and turn right side up. Place one quarter of the mixture in each hollow. Cover the dish with foil and bake for 20 minutes more, or until the squash is tender.

Serves 4 amply.

Gratin of Turnips

Because I love the intensity of root vegetables, I rarely doctor them with butter and cream as directed in most old-fashioned recipes. But turnips baked with cream are a weakness to which I readily succumb.

2 pounds small turnips, peeled and sliced ½ inch thick
1 tablespoon melted unsalted butter
    Salt
    Freshly ground black pepper
¼ teaspoon dried thyme
1 garlic clove, peeled and put through a garlic press
1 cup heavy cream
1 cup fresh bread crumbs

Preheat the oven to 350°F.

Place the turnip slices on a baking sheet, brush them with the melted butter, and sprinkle with salt, pepper, and thyme. Bake for 25 minutes, or until tender and slightly puffed.

Lightly grease a 1-quart gratin dish or shallow casserole. Layer the baked turnip slices in it. Mix the pressed garlic with the cream and pour over the turnips. Top with the bread crumbs. Bake for 20 to 25 minutes, until the cream has thickened. Serve hot.

Serves 4.

VARIATION: Sprinkle the gratin with ¼ cup grated Gruyère cheese and set it under the broiler to brown before serving.

Turnip and Onion Casserole

Baked turnips and onions are more mundane than a gratin, but this homey casserole is surprisingly satisfying. The onions remain crisp and add nice texture to the dish.

1 pound small turnips, peeled and sliced ¼ inch thick
Salt
Freshly ground black pepper
3 small onions, peeled and thinly sliced
½ cup vegetable broth
1 tablespoon melted unsalted butter (optional)
½ cup grated Cheddar cheese

Preheat the oven to 400°F. Lightly grease a 1-quart casserole.

Place one third of the turnip slices in the bottom of the prepared casserole and season with salt and pepper. Top them with half of the onions and season well. Repeat with the remaining turnips and onions, ending with a layer of turnips. Pour the broth over the vegetables and drizzle with melted butter, if desired.

Bake, uncovered, for 75 minutes, basting occasionally. Sprinkle on the grated cheese and bake for 5 minutes more, until the cheese has melted. Serve hot.

Serves 4 to 6.

Roasted Winter Vegetables

This lush vegetable medley appears frequently on our table because sweet winter roots make such a satisfying one-dish meal. No strict rules govern the recipe: just keep color variety in mind and use whatever combination appeals, allowing about 1 pound of mixed vegetables per person if they are to be served as a main course. Choose from among the following:

Beets, peeled and sliced
Carrots, peeled and thickly sliced
Celery root, peeled and sliced
Fennel, trimmed and sliced
Garlic cloves, peeled and left whole
Yellow onions, peeled and cut into wedges
Parsnips, peeled and thickly sliced
Potatoes, peeled and cut into wedges
Rutabagas, peeled and sliced
Shallots, peeled and separated into sections
Sweet potatoes, peeled and cut into wedges
Turnips, peeled and sliced
Winter squash, peeled, seeded, and sliced
Olive oil
Balsamic vinegar
**Salt, freshly ground pepper, dried summer savory,
  and dried thyme**

Preheat the oven to 425°F. Lightly grease a baking dish large enough to hold the prepared vegetables without crowding.

Toss the vegetables with a little olive oil and balsamic vinegar and season to taste (use about 2 teaspoons of oil and 1 teaspoon of vinegar for each pound of vegetables). Place the dish in the oven and roast for about 45 minutes, turning the vegetables occasionally, until they are tender and browned.

Roasted Winter Vegetables with Mustard Sauce

For a richer dish, serve the vegetables with this simple sauce:

  1 tablespoon salted butter
  1 tablespoon all-purpose flour
1½ teaspoons dry mustard
  1 cup Roasted Vegetable Broth (page 44) or other
     vegetable stock
  2 tablespoons Dijon mustard
     Dash each of salt, freshly ground black pepper, and paprika

Melt the butter in a medium saucepan and whisk in the flour. Cook over medium heat for a minute, stirring constantly, then mix in the dry mustard. Gradually whisk in the vegetable broth. Bring to a boil and simmer until the sauce thickens slightly, about 5 minutes. Stir in the mustard and season to taste.

Makes about 1 cup of sauce, serving 4.

Winter Vegetable Stew

The rich flavor of this stew suggests that it has cooked for hours, but 20 minutes of simmering is all that is needed. Serve piping hot in shallow soup bowls.

1 small onion, peeled and finely chopped
3 garlic cloves, peeled and minced
1 tablespoon olive oil
¼ pound brussels sprouts, trimmed and blanched for
   1 minute in boiling water
½ pound cauliflower florets, blanched for 1 minute in
   boiling water
1 sweet potato, peeled and sliced ½ inch thick, then cut
   into ¼ inch sticks
1 large red potato, scrubbed and cut into 1-inch cubes
2 large carrots, peeled and sliced ½ inch thick
½ pound celery root, peeled and cut into 1-inch cubes
½ acorn squash, peeled, seeded, and sliced ¼ inch thick,
   then each slice halved
1 teaspoon minced gingerroot
1 teaspoon salt
   Freshly ground black pepper
½ teaspoon dried thyme
   Generous pinch of dried savory
1 quart Roasted Vegetable Broth (page 44) or other
   vegetable stock
3 tablespoons unsalted butter, softened
3 tablespoons all-purpose flour

In a large stockpot sauté the onion and garlic in the olive oil until soft, 10 to 12 minutes. Add the remaining vegetables, the seasonings, and the vegetable broth, mixing well. Bring the stew to a boil and simmer until the vegetables are tender, about 20 minutes.

Make *beurre manié* by mixing the butter and flour together with your fingers. Stir bits of this mixture into the stew and cook for about 3 minutes more, until the broth has thickened slightly.

Serve hot.

Serves 4 to 6.

Rutabaga Stories

ONE OF THE WORLD'S least understood vegetables, rutabaga may also be the most maligned. Noses turn up at the very word. Yet under the rough skin of this unprepossessing tuber a treasure lies hidden: flesh rich and flavorful, the color of gold.

The origins of rutabaga are as poorly understood as the vegetable itself. Unlike its close cousins, the cabbage and turnip, rutabaga is not an ancient food, having made its first appearance only in the seventeenth century. Some consider Bohemia its birthplace, while others insist that it originated in Scandinavia. We do know that a Swiss botanist, Caspar Bauhin (whose name is inexplicably anglicized as Cooper Bartin in some sources), first described rutabaga in 1620. The plant was given the Latin name of *Brassica napobrassica*, but beyond that, little is certain. Scientists are unsure whether Bauhin himself developed the plant through experimentation, or whether it arose spontaneously in nature. As its French name of *chou-navet* suggests, the rutabaga is a cross between cabbage and white turnip. Its thirty-eight chromosomes represent a hybridization of the turnip's twenty chromosomes and the cabbage's eighteen. As such, the rutabaga is not strictly a root vegetable, even though usually treated as one. Rather, the tuber that we eat is a swelling of the plant's stem underground.

The rutabaga's strange pattern of growth and mysterious provenance have led to much confusion. For a vegetable that so few claim to like, the number of claims for its genesis is surprising. Rutabaga's colloquial names reflect its common association with various countries. Russians know it as German *(nemka)*, Swede *(shvedka)*, and even Dutch *(gollandka)*. As for the English "rutabaga," the word apparently derives from the Swedish *rotabagge*, which most sources translate as either "red bags" or "baggy roots." My own sojourn in Sweden inclines me to render the word as "ram's foot," whether for its resemblance to same or for the ram's propensity to dig up the sweet bulb (never having observed a ram in a field of rutabagas, I cannot be sure). *Rotabagge* must be a dialect form, for in standard Swedish the vegetable is quite sensibly called *kålrot,* or "cabbage root." Whatever its etymology, the rutabaga's association with Sweden has yielded its most common moniker in English: swede or Swedish turnip. Regional names dominate, though. In certain parts of the United States, rutabaga is also called yellow turnip, Russian turnip, Bulgarian turnip, or Canadian turnip, the latter reflecting recent marketing trends rather than the predominance of any particular ethnic group. I myself am fond of the dialect form "rootybaker," since the vegetable bakes so beautifully. Nowhere, perhaps, is the confusion of names greater than in Britain, where rutabaga and turnip are used so interchangeably that it is sometimes hard to know which vegetable is meant. Minnesotans, however, face special difficulties: a popular joke tells of a local requesting "swedes" in a grocery store outside of her state, only to be told that the store is hardly in the business of selling people.

Misunderstanding is bad enough, but the poor rutabaga has also had to endure its share of aspersions. For many, the vegetable is closely associated with poverty, the food of hardship. In *Soyer's Cookery Book* the nineteenth-century chef Alexis Soyer notes that "swedes" were not generally eaten until the year of the Irish famine. The French evince a particular dislike for rutabaga, even though bourgeois cuisine works wonders with turnips, which possess a stronger flavor. *Love and Rutabagas,* Claire Hsu Accomando's memoir of World War II France, proclaims the positive and negative markers of her childhood experience. As for Russians, they complain that "I'm as sick of you as of rutabagas." And none other than Percy Bysshe Shelley, although generally sympathetic to vegetarianism, maligns rutabaga in his implicit equation of the vegetable to fodder in *Oedipus Tyrannus:* "Hog-wash or grains, or ruta-baga, none/has yet been ours since your reign begun." Setting his satire in ancient Rome, Shelley evidently was unaware of the rutabaga's relatively recent entry into the world.

But let us refrain from further aspersions here, since food aversions can be catching. In England and Ireland, rutabagas were put to practical use as jack-o'-lanterns well before the New World crop of pumpkins usurped their place. The hollowed-out vegetables carried glowing coals (not candles) that lit the way on dark nights. Rutabagas had their culinary devotees, as well: the earthy, soulful Mr. Morel, in D. H. Lawrence's *Sons and Lovers,* was especially partial to "swede-turnip"— not surprising for someone named after a mushroom. The aesthetic appeal of rutabaga has best been captured by the English poet Edward Thomas. His poem "Swedes," written not long before the poet's death in World War I, stands as a great encomium to this lowly vegetable. Thomas revels in the rutabaga's hidden brilliance, a gem waiting to be unearthed:

SWEDES
They have taken the gable from the roof of clay
On the long swede pile. They have let in the sun
To the white and gold and purple of curled fronds
Unsunned. It is a sight more tender-gorgeous
At the wood-corner where Winter moans and drips
Than when, in the Valley of the Tombs of Kings,
A boy crawls down into a Pharaoh's tomb
And, first of Christian men, beholds the mummy,
God and monkey, chariot and throne and vase,
Blue pottery, alabaster, and gold.

But dreamless long-dead Amen-hotep lies.
This is a dream of Winter, sweet as Spring.

How can we best enjoy this "dream of Winter, sweet as Spring," with its purple top and golden bottom? There are many ways. We can learn from northern cultures, where cool soil yields the sweetest vegetables. Rutabagas reach a pinnacle at the Finnish Christmas table, baked into *lanttulaatiko,* a creamy pudding enriched with butter and seasoned with the comforting triad of nutmeg, cinnamon, and allspice. When I studied in Finland many years ago, this hearty dish carried me through many a dark day. The Russians use rutabaga inventively. Elena Molokhovets, Russia's nineteenth-century doyenne of cooking, suggests adding Malaga wine to rutabagas, a combination that admittedly appeals to me more than her recipe for sweet stuffed rutabagas with vanilla sauce. The Scots like to puree rutabaga, considering "bashed neeps," like their more standard cousin, the turnip, a traditional accompaniment to the national dish of haggis. Being no fan of haggis, I prefer rutabaga "bashed" with Scotch, which, like Malaga, adds a fruity depth of flavor. The Irish mash rutabaga with butter and pepper or enjoy it plain. In the United States, mashed rutabaga frequently graces the Thanksgiving table, its inherent sweetness enhanced with apples or perked up with lemon peel. Though many feel the need to moderate rutabaga's distinctive flavor by mixing it with potatoes or carrots, true aficionados relish its earthiness. Rutabaga is an extremely adaptable vegetable, taking equally well to boiling, steaming, sautéing, or baking. It can be caramelized in cubes like small new potatoes or simply roasted until brown in the oven. Or try wrapping pieces of rutabaga in foil and roasting the vegetable in the hot ashes of a fireplace, as the early American settlers did. The colonists also made pies out of rutabaga (instead of pumpkin), since they could store it longer and found its flavor actually improved after a hard frost. Rutabaga can be cooked in chunks or mashed, turned into a savory casserole or sweet pie, or used as a base for an excellent soufflé. When rutabaga is young and tender, it can be enjoyed raw and is far more interesting than the ubiquitous carrot and celery sticks. Rutabaga is also delicious grated raw and seasoned with a simple vinaigrette. Even the greens of the young plant can be eaten, much like the turnip, collard, and mustard greens of the same family.

Despite its versatility, rutabaga remains largely underappreciated in the United States today—although those who grow the vegetable recognize its many virtues. And no wonder. Rutabaga is rich in vitamins, especially vitamin C, and was a common scurvy preventative on long sea voyages. In this way rutabaga likely made its way to America, where it was recorded by the beginning of the nineteenth century. (It was already established in the British Isles by the end of the eighteenth century; the 1791 edition of the *Encyclopedia Britannica* describes "the Swedish turnip [as] a plant from which great expectations have been formed.") Thomas Jefferson is said to have enjoyed the vegetable, although he makes no mention of it in his *Farm Book;* and even if he had planted rutabaga, he probably would have had poor luck with it, as he did with buckwheat, another cold-climate crop. By the middle of the nineteenth century, pioneers migrating West, especially those from Scandinavia, carried rutabaga in their wagon trains, planting it as one of the first crops in the Great Plains. There the vegetable thrived, and thanks to its excellent keeping qualities helped the settlers to survive their first difficult winters. (Today, commercially grown rutabagas are coated with an edible wax, or paraffin, to prolong their shelf life, but even without this protective coating they last for months.) The most frugal housewives, fearing hard times, often saved the peeled skins of rutabagas to dry and use for flavoring soups when supplies of the fresh vegetable were depleted. No doubt this sort of rutabaga soup is the stuff of painful wartime memories.

Over the years, scientists have worked to develop new varieties of the vegetable, so that it can be grown in warmer climates. As recently as June 1995, a lively debate took place in the North Carolina General Assembly when some legislators proposed that rutabaga be named the official state vegetable. To their disappointment, the sweet potato prevailed instead, thanks to passionate lobbying by a group of fourth graders. These well-meaning youngsters obviously had not been exposed to the delights of the tuberous rutabaga. Moreover, the legislators missed an opportunity to place their state in the vanguard, for if any vegetable represents the food of the future, it is the rutabaga. Really. Rutabaga is extraordinarily good to eat, in terms of both flavor and health. Low in calories, it has no choles-terol and virtually no fat, and contains nearly twice as many carbohydrates as the turnip. Rutabaga also boasts goodly amounts of vitamins A and C in addition to all of the necessary minerals, including more calcium than other root vegetables. For a maligned vegetable, that's not too bad. Perhaps more of us should journey back to the simple pleasures afforded by this lowly vegetable. We can follow Carl Sandburg's advice: "And so if you are going to the Rootabaga country you will know when you get there because the tracks change from straight to zigzag . . ." Easier still, we can go to the nearest greengrocer and buy a beautiful yellow bulb crowned with a purple top, and cook it lovingly, as befits the riches of the earth.

Rutabaga Salad
Oven-Roasted Rutabaga and Potatoes
Pureed Rutabaga with Scotch
Braised Rutabaga with Onions and Mushrooms
Finnish Rutabaga Pudding *(Lanttulaatiko)*
Rutabaga and Cheese Soufflé
Oven-Glazed Rutabagas
Fireplace-Roasted Rutabagas
Sweet Rutabaga Pie

SEE ALSO:
Turnips in Wine Sauce (page 228)

Rutabaga Salad

This crunchy New England salad is a surprising and delicious way to eat rutabaga, and it adds a bright spot of color to the winter table. You can vary the proportions of vegetables, but don't be timid with the rutabaga, which should take center stage.

2 cups grated raw rutabaga (about half a 1-pound rutabaga)
3 scallions, trimmed and chopped, including the greens
5 radishes, thinly sliced
2 cups torn pieces of romaine

Dressing

1 teaspoon Dijon mustard
½ teaspoon dry mustard
½ teaspoon salt

½ teaspoon freshly ground white pepper
¼ teaspoon sugar
1 small garlic clove, peeled and minced
2 tablespoons white wine vinegar
¼ cup olive oil
2 tablespoons snipped fresh dill

In a salad bowl mix together the rutabaga, scallions, and radishes. Chill in the refrigerator. Just before serving, toss with the romaine pieces.

To make the dressing, mix together the mustards, salt, pepper, sugar, garlic, and vinegar in a small bowl. Gradually whisk in the oil to form an emulsion, then stir in the dill.

When ready to serve, toss the vegetables with just enough of the dressing to coat them lightly.

Serves 4.

Oven-Roasted Rutabaga and Potatoes

Rutabaga and potatoes have a natural affinity, and roasting the two together with a hint of brown sugar brings out the best in both.

1 rutabaga (1 pound), peeled and sliced lengthwise,
   then sliced again crosswise into ½-inch sticks
2 large potatoes (1 pound), peeled and sliced lengthwise,
   then sliced again crosswise
2 tablespoons olive oil
2 tablespoons light brown sugar
½ teaspoon salt
   Freshly ground black pepper

Preheat the oven to 450°F.

Place the prepared vegetables in a baking dish large enough to hold them in a single layer. Toss with the olive oil, sugar, salt, and pepper. Roast for 50 to 60 minutes, until tender and browned.

Serves 4 generously.

Pureed Rutabaga with Scotch

A golden puree with a hint of Scotch, this dish is elegant enough to serve at a special dinner party.

1 rutabaga (1¾ to 2 pounds)
3 tablespoons unsalted butter
3 tablespoons Scotch
¼ teaspoon salt (or more, to taste)

Peel and cube the rutabaga. Cook it in boiling salted water to cover until tender, about 25 minutes, then drain.

Transfer the rutabaga to the bowl of a food processor fitted with the metal blade and puree it. Add the butter, Scotch, and salt to taste. Process until smooth.

Turn the puree out into a bowl and serve immediately.

Serves 4.

Braised Rutabaga with Onions and Mushrooms

This earthy medley is the way I enjoy rutabaga most. A good broth made from roasted root vegetables lends an appealing sweetness to this dish. The vegetables can be mixed together for serving, but the presentation will be more elegant if you place the rutabaga on a platter and arrange the mushrooms decoratively on top.

1 rutabaga (1 pound), peeled and cut into matchsticks
2 medium onions, peeled and chopped (2 cups)
1 garlic clove, peeled and minced
3 tablespoons olive oil
¼ teaspoon salt
  Freshly ground black pepper
1 tablespoon all-purpose flour
1 cup Roasted Vegetable Broth (page 44)
½ pound shiitake mushrooms, trimmed and coarsely chopped
¼ cup port
2 tablespoons minced parsley

In a large skillet cook the rutabaga, onion, and garlic over medium-high heat in 2 tablespoons of the oil until they begin to brown, about 5 minutes. Season with the salt and pepper to taste. Sprinkle on the flour and toss to combine with the vegetables. Stir in the broth. Cover the skillet and simmer for 20 minutes, or until the vegetables are just tender.

Meanwhile, in another skillet quickly cook the mushrooms in the remaining 1 tablespoon of oil for 3 minutes. Add the port and parsley and cook for 2 to 3 minutes more.

Combine the mushrooms with the rutabaga mixture and serve hot.
Serves 6.

Finnish Rutabaga Pudding *(Lanttulaatiko)*

L anttulaatiko was my first introduction to rutabaga. I have to admit that initially I was more attracted to this pudding's mellifluous name than to its contents, but the rutabaga proved as mellow on the tongue as its name. Recipes for *lanttulaatiko* are fairly standard, although some American ones (predictably) add sugar. Other versions call for adding mashed potatoes, or separating the eggs to make a lighter pudding. The recipe that follows is for the real thing; the only change I've made is to use milk instead of the more traditional heavy cream. *Lanttulaatiko* is an important part of the Finnish Christmas table.

     2 rutabagas (2 to 2½ pounds), peeled and cubed
     2 eggs
     ½ cup milk
     ½ teaspoon salt
     ½ teaspoon freshly grated nutmeg
        Dash of allspice
     3 tablespoons all-purpose flour
     1 tablespoon unsalted butter, softened
     2 tablespoons fine dry bread crumbs

Preheat the oven to 350°F. Butter a 1½-quart soufflé dish.

Boil the rutabagas in salted water to cover until soft, 25 to 30 minutes. Drain and mash, either by hand or in a food processor (the pudding will be creamier if you use a food processor, but do not process the rutabagas into an absolutely smooth puree—there should still be some texture).

Beat in the eggs one at a time, then add the milk, salt, spices, and flour. Turn the mixture into the prepared dish.

With a fork mash together the butter and bread crumbs and sprinkle them over the top of the rutabaga mixture.

Bake, uncovered, for 1 hour, until lightly browned. Serve hot.

Serves 6 to 8.

Rutabaga and Cheese Soufflé

This savory soufflé emerges from the oven golden and light.

- 2 pounds rutabagas, peeled and cubed
- 2 tablespoons unsalted butter
- ¼ cup finely chopped onion
- 2 tablespoons minced parsley
- ½ teaspoon salt
  Freshly ground black pepper
- ¼ cup grated sharp Cheddar cheese
- 3 eggs, separated
- ½ cup fresh bread crumbs (preferably from whole wheat bread)

Boil the rutabagas in salted water until tender, 25 to 30 minutes. Drain and mash (for this recipe it is best to puree the rutabagas in a food processor fitted with the metal blade). You should have about 3 cups of puree.

While the rutabagas are cooking, melt the butter in a small skillet. Sauté the onion in the butter until soft, about 5 minutes. Stir in the parsley and set aside.

Preheat the oven to 350°F. Grease a 1½-quart soufflé dish.

Transfer the rutabaga puree to a bowl. Stir in the onion mixture, the salt, pepper, and cheese. Beat in the egg yolks one at a time.

Whip the egg whites until they form soft peaks, then fold them carefully into the rutabaga puree. Turn the mixture into the prepared dish and sprinkle the bread crumbs on top.

Bake for 50 to 60 minutes, until puffed and brown.

Serves 6.

Oven-Glazed Rutabagas

Rutabaga receives a sweet treatment here, more familiar to American tastes. Because of its assertiveness, bottled orange juice works better than fresh for this recipe, which takes very little effort to prepare.

  2 rutabagas (2 pounds), peeled and halved, each half cut into ¼-inch-thick slices
  ¾ cup firmly packed light brown sugar
  ½ cup prepared orange juice
  1 teaspoon grated lemon rind
  2 tablespoons salted butter

Parboil the rutabaga slices in salted water to cover for 10 minutes.

Preheat the oven to 350°F. Lightly grease a 10-inch pie plate.

Mix the brown sugar, orange juice, lemon rind, and butter in a small saucepan. Bring to a boil and cook gently for 10 minutes, until the mixture is slightly syrupy.

Drain the rutabaga and place the slices in overlapping layers in the pie plate. Pour the hot syrup over them.

Bake for 50 to 60 minutes, basting once or twice, until lightly browned. Cut in wedges to serve.

Serves 6 to 8.

Fireplace-Roasted Rutabagas

Roasted in the coals of a hot fire, rutabaga turns mellow and creamy inside, with a smoky, charred crust that adds some bite. Try experimenting with different herbs to flavor the vegetable—you may even want to blacken it in the Cajun style. This method of preparing rutabaga is very simple, and it's unbelievably good.

    2 rutabagas (about 1 pound each)
       Olive oil
       Dried marjoram
       Salt
       Freshly ground black pepper

Peel the rutabagas and place each one on a double thickness of aluminum foil. Drizzle with olive oil and season to taste with crushed dried marjoram, salt, and pepper. Wrap the rutabagas tightly in the foil and place in the hot coals of a fire. Roast for about 1½ hours, or until charred on the outside and tender within. Slice to serve.

    Serves 4.

Sweet Rutabaga Pie

Only the most discerning palates will detect rutabaga in this custardy pie, which easily masquerades as pumpkin.

Crust

- 1½ cups all-purpose flour
- ½ teaspoon salt
- ½ cup vegetable shortening
- 4 to 5 tablespoons ice water

Filling

- 1 rutabaga (1 pound), peeled and cubed
- ½ cup firmly packed light brown sugar
- 2 tablespoons molasses
- 2 eggs
- 1¼ cups half-and-half or light cream
- 1½ teaspoons ground cinnamon
- ½ teaspoon grated nutmeg
- ½ teaspoon ground ginger
- ½ teaspoon salt
- ½ teaspoon pure vanilla extract

Crystallized ginger (optional)

In a medium bowl mix together the flour and salt. Cut in the shortening until the mixture resembles coarse meal. Add just enough water for the dough to hold together—do not overmix. Roll the dough out on a floured surface to a round about 11 inches in diameter. Carefully lift the dough into a 9-inch pie plate. Trim and crimp the edges.

Boil the rutabaga in salted water to cover until tender, 25 to 30 minutes. Drain and puree until smooth in a food processor fitted with the metal blade. You will have about 1½ cups of puree.

Preheat the oven to 450°F.

Transfer the puree to a bowl and add the sugar and molasses. Beat in the eggs one at a time. Stir in the remaining filling ingredients, mixing well. Pour the filling into the prepared pie shell and bake at 450°F for 15 minutes. Reduce the heat to 350°F and bake for 40 to 45 minutes longer, until the filling is set.

Cool to room temperature before serving, decorated with crystallized ginger, if desired.

Makes one 9-inch pie.

8

Salads

If you love salads as much as I do, winter presents a challenge. Every autumn, after the last of the tender lettuces and ripe tomatoes had disappeared from the market, I used to buy a head of hydroponically grown lettuce and hothouse tomatoes, trying to convince myself that they couldn't possibly be as tasteless as I remembered from the previous season. But they inevitably were. So now I no longer attempt to approximate the glories of summer salads. Instead, I seek out seasonal produce, which can be combined into refreshing, colorful salads that bring cheer to the winter table and a surprising variety of tastes into our lives.

New Year's Black-Eyed Peas

Mediterranean Orange Salad

Spanish Escarole Salad

Watercress and Endive Salad

Celery Root and Carrot Salad with Mustard Vinaigrette

Central Asian Cabbage Salad *(Karam salati)*

Warm Mushroom Salad

New Year's Black-Eyed Peas

Eating beans for good luck in the new year is a Southern American tradition. Although I live in New England, I prepare these delicious black-eyed peas every January 1, thanks to my sister, Ardath Weaver, who gave me the recipe. I like to offer the beans plain, but they are also attractive when served on romaine leaves. The ingredients can easily be doubled for a crowd.

½ pound dried black-eyed peas
1 medium onion, peeled and finely chopped
One 14½-ounce can stewed tomatoes, including the juice
¼ cup dark molasses
1¼ cups water
1 teaspoon salt
Freshly ground black pepper
Pinch of dried oregano

Soak the beans in water to cover overnight. The next day, drain and rinse them, then place in a large saucepan with the onion, stewed tomatoes, molasses, and water. Bring to a boil and simmer until the beans are tender, about 1 hour. Do not allow them to become mushy.

Stir in the salt, black pepper, and oregano. Serve at room temperature.

Serves 6.

Mediterranean Orange Salad

My favorite winter salad, colorful and refreshing.

- 1 red bell pepper, cored, seeded, and cut into thin strips
- ¼ cup olive oil
- 4 large navel oranges
- ½ small red onion, peeled and sliced paper-thin
- ½ cup Niçoise olives
- 2 garlic cloves, peeled and coarsely chopped
- ½ teaspoon salt
- 2 tablespoons sherry vinegar

In a small skillet sauté the red bell pepper strips in the olive oil for 10 minutes, until softened.

Meanwhile, peel the oranges and remove the white pith. Cut them into thin rounds, discarding any seeds, and arrange in overlapping circles on a serving plate. Scatter the onion slices over the oranges.

Remove the peppers from the oil with a slotted spoon, reserving the oil. Strew the peppers over the oranges and onions. Scatter the olives on top.

In a mortar with a pestle pound the garlic with the salt to make a paste. Mix this paste into the oil remaining in the pan and add the vinegar, stirring to mix well.

Pour the dressing over the oranges and leave the salad to sit for 1 hour at room temperature before serving.

Serves 4 to 6.

Spanish Escarole Salad

This beautifully composed salad is a specialty of Seville. I've adapted the recipe from Elisabeth Luard's charming *Flavours of Andalucia*.

- 1 small head of escarole
- 1 red bell pepper, cored, seeded, and sliced into thin rings
- ½ cucumber, peeled and sliced
- 3 slices of sweet onion, separated into rings
- 6 artichoke hearts, halved (see Notes)
  - Sea salt
- ⅓ cup green olives (see Notes)
- 1 tablespoon capers

Dressing

- 1 hard-boiled egg
- 1 garlic clove, peeled and put through a garlic press
- 2 tablespoons sherry vinegar
- ½ cup extra-virgin olive oil

Choose a large, shallow bowl for serving the salad.

Thoroughly wash and dry the escarole and tear it into medium-sized pieces. You should have about 8 cups of loosely packed leaves.

Place the escarole in the bowl and top it with a layer of red bell pepper rings. Place a layer of cucumber slices over the peppers, then a layer of onion rings, then the artichoke hearts. Sprinkle lightly with sea salt. Top the artichokes with the green olives. Sprinkle the capers over all.

To make the dressing, remove the white from the egg, chop it finely, and set it aside. In a small bowl mash the yolk. Stir in the pressed garlic and the vinegar. Gradually whisk in the olive oil until an emulsion is formed.

Pour the dressing over the salad. Sprinkle a little more salt over the salad and garnish it with the chopped egg white.

Serves 6.

NOTES: Canned artichokes (not marinated) are fine for this salad. You will need one 14-ounce can. Drain before using. I like the look of whole olives, but be sure to warn your guests if the olives are not pitted.

Watercress and Endive Salad

Winter's dearth of garden-fresh lettuce is admittedly trying, but this elegant salad has all the refreshing crispness of summertime greens. Its lovely hues will brighten your table.

2 large heads of Belgian endive
1 bunch watercress (about 6 ounces)
½ pink grapefruit

Dressing

1 tablespoon raspberry vinegar
1 small garlic clove, peeled and minced
¼ cup walnut oil
Salt
Freshly ground black pepper

Cut the endive into julienne strips. Rinse the watercress and remove the tough stalks. Mix the greens together in a salad bowl, preferably glass.

With a sharp knife, remove the peel and all of the white pith from the grapefruit half. Cut the grapefruit into small chunks.

To make the dressing, place the vinegar and garlic in a small bowl, then slowly whisk in the oil until an emulsion is formed. Season with salt and plenty of black pepper.

Toss the salad with about 4 tablespoons of the dressing. Garnish with the grapefruit pieces and serve.

Serves 4.

NOTE: This recipe makes about twice as much dressing as you will need for the salad. The rest may be stored in the refrigerator for about a week.

Celery Root and Carrot Salad with Mustard Vinaigrette

This vitamin-rich salad keeps well in the refrigerator and offers a light counterpoint to a heavy winter meal.

¾ pound celery root, peeled and shredded
¾ pound carrots, peeled and shredded
2 to 3 scallions, trimmed and chopped, including the greens

Dressing

2 tablespoons plus 2 teaspoons white wine vinegar
2 tablespoons Dijon mustard
½ teaspoon salt
   Freshly ground black pepper
½ cup olive oil
2 tablespoons minced parsley
2 tablespoons minced fresh dill

In a salad bowl mix together the shredded celery root, carrots, and scallions. In a small bowl mix the wine vinegar with the mustard, salt, and black pepper. Slowly whisk in the olive oil to form an emulsion. Stir in the parsley and dill.

Pour enough of the dressing over the vegetables to moisten them generously, but do not drench the salad. Toss well. The salad tastes best after it has been left to stand for at least an hour.

Serves 6 to 8.

Central Asian Cabbage Salad (*Karam salati*)

Root vegetables flourish in Central Asia's harsh climate. From Tashkent to Almaty markets display kaleidoscopic rows of radishes in shades of red, green, black, and white, and carrots ranging from deep orange to bright yellow in hue. Central Asians use winter vegetables inventively, steaming them to fill dumplings, grating them into pilafs, salting them for pickles, even cooking them into sweet jams. Here, hearty vegetables are combined in a piquant salad that makes a nice change from coleslaw.

- 1 medium onion, peeled and chopped
- 2 garlic cloves, peeled and minced
- 3 tablespoons vegetable oil
- ¼ pound white cabbage, shredded
- 5 large red radishes, trimmed and coarsely grated
- 1 large carrot, peeled and coarsely grated
- ⅛ teaspoon salt (or more, to taste)
  Freshly ground black pepper
- 4 teaspoons tomato paste
- 2 tablespoons minced parsley
- 1 tablespoon minced fresh dill

In a skillet sauté the onion and garlic in 1 tablespoon of the oil until soft, about 10 minutes. Set aside to cool.

Combine the shredded cabbage, grated radishes, and grated carrot in a large bowl. Stir in the onion mixture, then add the salt and pepper to taste.

In a small bowl whisk together the remaining 2 tablespoons of oil and the tomato paste. Stir into the vegetable salad, mixing well. Chill.

Just before serving, stir in the minced parsley and dill.

Serves 4.

Warm Mushroom Salad

Scandinavia's late-summer mushroom salads inspired me to create this winter version, in which a bed of cool lettuce receives a lush blanket of warm mushrooms.

2 cups water
2 tablespoons freshly squeezed lemon juice
½ teaspoon salt (or more, to taste)
¾ pound white mushrooms, trimmed and thinly sliced
1 generous tablespoon freshly grated onion
¼ teaspoon sugar
4 tablespoons heavy cream
Freshly ground white pepper
Boston lettuce

In a medium saucepan bring the water, lemon juice, and salt to a boil. Add the mushrooms, return to a boil, and simmer, covered, for 3 minutes. Drain well.

In a medium bowl combine the grated onion, sugar, and cream. Toss with the mushrooms. Season to taste with salt and pepper.

Place several leaves of lettuce on each of four salad plates. Spoon some mushrooms and cream over the lettuce and serve warm.

Serves 4.

NOTE: The mushrooms may also be served at room temperature. Spoon them over the lettuce just before serving.

9

Breakfast
Favorites

Today, in our frantic, late-twentieth-century lives, we have all but forgotten the appeal of an unhurried breakfast; we are too rushed, always on the run. In *The House of the Seven Gables,* Nathaniel Hawthorne depicted the pleasures of the nineteenth-century breakfast:

> Life, within doors, has few pleasanter prospects than a neatly arranged and well-provisioned breakfast table. We come to it freshly, in the dewy youth of the day, and when our spiritual and sensual elements are in better accord than at a later period; so that the material delights of the morning meal are capable of being fully enjoyed. . . .

At least on weekends, it would do us good to recapture the delights of a languorous morning spent lingering over coffee at a well-provisioned table. The recipes that follow should help to provide a luxurious start to your day.

Bran Muffins

Old-Fashioned Oatmeal

Porridge

Danish Tapioca and Pear Porridge *(Paerevaelling)*

Dutch Baby Pancake

Sweet Cheese Pancakes *(Syrniki)*

Snow Pancakes

Snow Griddle Cakes

SEE ALSO:

Basque-Style Scrambled Eggs *(Pipérade)* (page 64)

Finnish Cardamom Braid *(Pulla)* (page 236)

Puffed Cheese Ring *(Gougère)* (page 68)

Rusks (page 241)

Bran Muffins

Unlike many bran muffins, these are pale and delicate. They come from the Swedish grandmother of a friend who gave me the recipe nearly twenty years ago. I've been making them ever since.

1½ cups bran
½ cup boiling water
¼ cup (heaping) vegetable shortening
¾ cup sugar
1 egg, beaten
1¼ cups all-purpose flour
1¼ teaspoons baking soda
¼ teaspoon salt
1 cup buttermilk

Preheat the oven to 400°F. Grease a 12-cup muffin pan or line with paper muffin cups.

Place ½ cup of the bran in a small bowl and pour the boiling water over it. Let stand for 5 minutes, until soft.

Meanwhile, cream together the shortening and sugar. Beat in the egg. Mix together the flour, baking soda, and salt. Add the dry ingredients to the creamed mixture alternately with the buttermilk, mixing only enough to blend. Stir in the softened bran and the remaining 1 cup of bran.

Spoon the batter into the muffin cups and bake for 18 to 20 minutes, until lightly browned.

Makes 1 dozen muffins.

Old-Fashioned Oatmeal

With each passing decade, oats seem to become more processed. From oat flakes the breakfast industry moved to quick-cooking oats, but even those weren't fast enough for time-pressed Americans. Next came instant oatmeal; now it's sometimes hard to find whole oats in the grocery store. I suspect that many people have never even tried the whole grain, yet a bowl of real oatmeal is an extraordinary experience: slightly chewy, extremely flavorful, and absolutely satisfying. Nothing is more sustaining on a cold morning. Once you've tried this hot cereal, you'll find it hard ever to microwave a convenience packet again.

> 4 cups milk
> 1 cup Irish oatmeal (whole grain, not quick-cooking or instant oats)
> ¼ teaspoon salt
> ¼ teaspoon ground cinnamon
> A few gratings of nutmeg
> 3 to 4 tablespoons light brown sugar
> 1 small apple, peeled, cored, and finely chopped
> ½ cup raisins

Preheat the oven to 350°F.

Bring the milk to a boil in a large saucepan. When it boils, stir in the remaining ingredients and return to a boil, then transfer the mixture to a 2-quart casserole. Bake, uncovered, for 30 to 35 minutes, until the milk has been absorbed but the oatmeal is still creamy. Stir before serving.

Serves 4.

Porridge

When I was growing up, my mother prepared great batches of this hot and filling cereal. She always had to dish out my portion first, because I refused to eat raisins.

4½ cups milk
½ cup regular (not instant) farina (such as Cream of Wheat)
6 tablespoons hot wheat cereal
¼ teaspoon salt
¼ cup raisins (optional)
   Brown sugar (optional)

Heat the milk in a large saucepan over medium heat. When bubbles begin to appear on the surface, gradually stir in the cereals and salt, mixing well to avoid lumps. Cook over low heat until thickened, 4 to 5 minutes. Stir in the raisins, if desired, and serve hot, sprinkled with brown sugar.

Serves 4.

Danish Tapioca and Pear Porridge *(Paerevaelling)*

There is, admittedly, something Dickensian about gruel, and so the recipe I offer here may not be to everyone's taste. I've chosen to adapt a very old form of porridge from Bodil Jensen's *Take a Silver Dish . . .* , a fascinating compendium of Danish food. Based not only on tapioca but also on barley or rice, this porridge was traditionally eaten as a first course at dinner rather than breakfast. Because I love tapioca and soured milk products, this homey-homely gruel makes me happy on cold mornings. Whole pearls of tapioca are cooked in buttermilk, which lends the porridge both tang and texture, while poached pears contribute a welcome sweetness. If visions of *David Copperfield* don't haunt you, you'll find this an interesting addition to your breakfast repertoire.

- 3 cups buttermilk
- 2 cups milk
- ½ cup small pearl tapioca
- ⅓ cup sugar
- 2 Bosc pears (¾ to 1 pound), peeled, cored, and sliced

In a large pan bring the buttermilk, milk, and tapioca to a boil. (Commercial buttermilk will separate and curdle, but once the pudding thickens the curds will add interesting texture, even if they make a less than lovely dish.) Simmer, uncovered, for 45 minutes, stirring occasionally to prevent the tapioca from sticking. Stir in the sugar and sliced pears and cook for 25 to 30 minutes longer, until the pears are tender and the porridge has thickened.

Serve warm.

Serves 4 to 6.

NOTE: The porridge reheats well, so it may be made in advance.

Dutch Baby Pancake

Baked in a hot oven, this dramatic pancake rises several inches above the sides of the pan. It can be served directly from the skillet. Lemon juice and powdered sugar make the pancake luxurious.

2 tablespoons unsalted butter
3 eggs
½ cup plus 2 tablespoons milk
½ cup plus 2 tablespoons all-purpose flour
   Pinch of salt

Lemon wedges
Powdered sugar

Preheat the oven to 425°F. Place the butter in a heavy 10-inch skillet, preferably cast-iron. Set the skillet in the oven until the butter melts. Be careful not to let it burn.

Crack the eggs into a blender and whir until just mixed. Add the milk and whir until blended, then add the flour and pinch of salt and blend for 30 seconds, no longer.

Remove the hot skillet from the oven and tip it so that the butter coats the bottom. Immediately pour the batter into the skillet and return to the oven. Bake for 20 minutes until the pancake is puffed and brown on the edges.

Serve immediately, with lemon wedges and powdered sugar.

Serves 4.

Sweet Cheese Pancakes *(Syrniki)*

When I lived in Russia these pancakes, topped with jam, were my favorite breakfast food. They taste like the filling in cheese blintzes, only somewhat more tart.

1 pound farmer cheese
1 egg
6 tablespoons all-purpose flour
⅛ teaspoon salt
3 tablespoons sugar
½ teaspoon pure vanilla extract

1 tablespoon unsalted butter
1 tablespoon vegetable oil

In a medium bowl mix together the farmer cheese, egg, flour, salt, sugar, and vanilla. Turn the mass out onto a sheet of wax paper and shape it into a 10-inch log. Roll up in the wax paper and refrigerate for at least 30 minutes, or overnight.

In a large skillet heat the butter and oil. Cut the cheese log into 1-inch slices, shaping them gently into rounds. Fry the pancakes for about 10 minutes over medium heat, turning once, until they are plump and golden.

Serves 4.

VARIATION: For brunch or supper, make savory pancakes by substituting 1 tablespoon sugar and omitting the vanilla. Serve with sour cream.

Snow Pancakes

Ever resourceful, New Englanders used snow in surprising ways. Many early American cookbooks call for fresh snow as an ingredient in pancake batter. Added at the last minute, the snow quickly chills the batter and keeps it from spreading on the griddle. This recipe is from *Miss Parloa's New Cook Book and Marketing Guide,* published in Boston in 1880. Maria Parloa was a well-known cooking school teacher, whose great popularity enabled her to command extraordinarily, even exorbitantly, high fees. These lightly fried pancakes are more like fritters than traditional griddle cakes and benefit from a sweet topping.

Vegetable oil for frying

1½ **cups unbleached white flour**
¼ **teaspoon salt**
1 **cup milk**
1 **egg, well beaten**
1 **large apple, peeled, cored, and finely chopped**
½ **cup packed fresh snow**

Powdered sugar, maple syrup, honey, or jam for topping

Pour vegetable oil into a large skillet to a depth of ⅛ to ¼ inch and heat.

Place the flour and salt in a medium bowl. Add the milk and beaten egg, stirring only until just mixed. Stir in the chopped apple.

When the oil is hot but not smoking, stir the snow into the pancake batter, and immediately drop the batter by heaping tablespoonfuls into the pan. Cook over medium-high heat, turning once, until the pancakes are a rich brown.

Serve hot with a sweet topping.

Serves 4.

Snow Griddle Cakes

The nineteenth-century cookbook author Lucia Gray Swett was not to be outdone by Maria Parloa: her *New England Breakfast Breads,* published in Boston in 1891, also includes a pancake recipe calling for the addition of fresh, powdery snow. Jan Longone of Ann Arbor's Wine and Food Library kindly provided me with a copy of Swett's instructions for "Snow Griddle Cakes," which are rich with sour cream. My adaptation yields lighter pancakes that are more suited to contemporary taste. Try them with Hot Orange Sauce (page 263).

   1½ cups all-purpose flour
   ½ teaspoon baking soda
   ¾ teaspoon baking powder
   ½ teaspoon salt
   2 tablespoons sugar
   1¼ cups buttermilk
   ¼ cup sour cream
   1 egg, lightly beaten
   1 cup fresh, powdery snow

In a medium bowl mix together the flour, baking soda, baking powder, salt, and sugar. Stir in the buttermilk, sour cream, and egg, mixing only enough to blend. Last of all mix in the snow. Drop the batter by heaping tablespoonfuls onto a lightly greased, heated griddle. Cook the pancakes over medium heat until bubbles appear on the surface, then turn and cook for another minute or so on the other side until lightly browned. Serve hot.

    Serves 4 to 6.

Tolstoy's Table

VEGETARIANISM IN RUSSIA inevitably conjures up Count Leo Tolstoy, a guru for vegetarians of all stripes in his day. Although best known for his epic novels, Tolstoy also authored "The First Step," an impassioned preface to the 1891 Russian translation of Howard Williams's *The Ethics of Diet: A Catena of Authorities Deprecatory of the Practice of Flesh-Eating*. By linking his name with the vegetarian crusader's and publicly associating himself with the vegetarian cause, Tolstoy directly influenced the development of vegetarianism in Russia. Vegetarian promoters repeatedly invoked his name; and so forcefully did Peter Verigin, the leader of the Dukhobor religious sect, preach Tolstoy's method to his followers that they willingly gave up not only meat, but also alcohol and tobacco. Meanwhile, Tolstoy's own disciples practiced vegetarianism in the communities they founded based on their understanding of his teachings.

Although mythologized as a vegetarian pacifist, Tolstoy's abstinence did not initially arise from ethical considerations. Tolstoy struggled against carnal and gustatory temptation alike; the renunciation of sex and meat were equally important for attaining moral purity. Thus his treatise on the first step toward ethical living shows far greater concern with the rigors of asceticism than with compassion for animals. For Tolstoy, the disavowal of meat was simply another step in his quest for moral self-perfection, a search that soon drove his wife, Sophia, to exasperation.

The long-suffering Sophia oversaw a household of thirteen children in addition to her difficult husband, and each day she endeavored to compose nourishing menus for their daily meals. The Tolstoys' cook, Nikolai Rumiantsev, had formerly been a flutist in Prince Nikolai Volkonsky's serf orchestra. But when he lost his teeth to decay, he was unable to continue playing, and the Tolstoys took him into their employ as a cook. At first, Nikolai was a disaster in the kitchen. From Sophia's diary entries we know that Nikolai's initial cooking efforts were less than successful (his beignets were as tough as the soles of shoes). But eventually Nikolai proved as talented in the kitchen as in the orchestra, making beignets so light that the family dubbed them "Nikolai's Sighs." As the batter cakes swelled on the griddle, Nikolai would blow air into the corners to puff them up further, then quickly fill them with jam.

The Tolstoys kept to a strict routine, with lunch served at one o'clock for everyone except the master himself, who arrived just before the table was cleared at two or two-thirty. At lunchtime the children were spared their father's rigid meal, which each day consisted only of oatmeal and a small pot of *prostokvasha,* a soured-milk product like yogurt. Dinner was served promptly at six, with two servants presiding. Their presence troubled Tolstoy no end, but he apparently yielded to his wife on this point. At dinner the entire family enjoyed four courses of vegetarian foods, followed by coffee. Evening tea was much more informal. The family gathered in the parlor to enjoy cookies, jam, honey, and tea from a steaming samovar.

In 1874 Sophia and her brother Stepan compiled a cookery book of the family's favorite recipes, complete with a humorous title page stating that the manuscript had been passed by the official censor. The nearly two hundred recipes give a good idea of the kinds of dishes the Tolstoys enjoyed. Sophia's worldliness shows in her instructions for "Sabayon," "Bavaroise," and "Stufato." At the same time she includes a large number of recipes making use of black bread crumbs and semolina, very much in the Russian style. We also find useful household hints, such as "How to Cook Spinach So That It Remains Green," "A Face Mask," and "Aunt Pelageya's Elixir for Teeth." The manuscript is unsystematic, running not from soup to nuts but from a Viennese Cake to a remedy for cockroaches. In between we are treated to such delicacies as the flaming "Plump-Pudding" that the Tolstoys' English governess, Hannah, prepared, and "Anke's Cake," a lemon-filled layer cake baked for special occasions. We also find a recipe for koumiss, the fermented mare's milk drunk by Central Asian nomads. In Sophia's rendition, the beverage is made from cow's milk and is intended to ease Tolstoy's frequent stomach upsets, as prescribed by the family doctor.

The Russian public, of course, knew little of Tolstoy's upsets, and many yearned for a ready way to emulate the master. A convenient avenue was found through the publications of the Posrednik Publishing House, which Tolstoy and his disciple Vladimir Chertkov founded in 1885. Posrednik's editorial staff made clear to its readers that good eating habits could generate the same sort of "pure bright life" that Tolstoy experienced. In the 1890s, the publishing house began to issue numerous books on vegetarianism. The vegetarian diet was meant to appeal to cultured readers—the overfed, gouty, leisured class who needed to eat less. No one expected to make converts of the Russian peasantry, who practiced vegetarianism perforce. Posrednik also aimed to develop a social conscience against the slaughter of helpless animals, as well as a sense of justice in the face of widespread hunger.

The Russians already enjoyed a wide variety of meatless dishes, without actually calling them vegetarian. These dishes were prepared on a regular basis according to the strictures of the Russian Orthodox Church. Nearly two hundred days of the year were considered fast days by the Church, each requiring varying degrees of abstention. During the four major fast periods, lasting up to forty days at a time, all meat and dairy products were proscribed. Thus, as an established feature of Russian cuisine, the meatless meal was hardly a radical innovation to a Russian, particularly a religious one. All of the cookbooks of the time reflect the division of the Russian table into feast- and fast-day meals. Fast-day recipes substituted nut oils and almond milk for dairy products in cooking and baking. Main courses revolved around a wide array of vegetables, notably mushrooms, and grains.

Posrednik's publications represented vegetarianism not only as ethically based but also as grounded in religious thought. Practical and dietary considerations were similarly important. Therefore anyone suffering from malaise, whether physical or spiritual, could turn to vegetarianism for revival. Even Esperantists found vegetarianism entirely in keeping with their internationalist goals. A separate League of Vegetarian Esperantists vowed "to make esperantists vegetarians, to esperantize vegetarians, and to be of practical benefit to one another." Esperanto was often used as the official language for speeches and debates at international vegetarian congresses.

Two of Posrednik's greatest proselytizers were the husband and wife team of Aleksandr and Olga Zelenkov. A practicing biologist and physician, Aleksandr Zelenkov published books on homeopathy and the biological sciences and also edited a translation of Plato's writings on vegetarianism. He is best known as a founder and chairman of Russia's first vegetarian society. An ideological pioneer, Zelenkov simultaneously crusaded against alcohol, and as may well be imagined, his temperate stance did little to enhance the popularity of vegetarianism in Russia. Although his wife held the same sober beliefs, she wisely chose instead to approach vegetarianism as any conscientious housewife would, by emphasizing its benefits. Writing in a chatty manner quite dissimilar to her husband's tendentious theorizing, she published four pamphlets and a lively (if idiosyncratic) cookbook, *I Don't Eat Anyone.*

In Olga Zelenkova's first pamphlet we find brief articles about Tolstoy's vegetarianism and the ease of realizing a vegetarian diet. She knowingly appeals to the housewife by pointing out that not only are vegetarian food products always fresh, but also economical because they can be purchased in bulk. Vegetarian ideology is important to Zelenkova, but so are the way food tastes and the ease with which it can be prepared. Using Tolstoy's admonitions against intoxicants as a model, Zelenkova is adamant in her imprecations against alcohol. As elsewhere in Europe, the Russian temperance and vegetarian movements were generally allied, but Zelenkova carries her exhortations to extremes. In addition to alcohol, she condemns all sorts of spices and singles out coffee, tea, kola nuts, and guarana seeds as especially dangerous. She seems to have a particular prejudice against America and its uncivilized inhabitants, citing the addiction of American women to coffee, which she compares to American men's drunken need for whiskey. America even gets blamed for the lowly potato—neither a spice nor an intoxicant—which she anathematizes for its relatively high content of potassium and sodium. In *I Don't Eat Anyone* Zelenkova concludes: "One can only regret the initial export of the potato from America and its introduction onto European soil."

Such diatribes notwithstanding, the founding of the St. Petersburg Vegetarian Society early in 1902 ushered in an era of intense activity and interest in vegetarianism in Russia. Two serious journals, *The Vegetarian Herald* and *The Vegetarian Review,* reported on the activities of the various Russian societies as well as international trends in vegetarianism. Special cafeterias were set up throughout Russia, serving food of such generally high quality that even nonvegetarians frequented them. From these journals we learn that by 1915 the publishing of vegetarian cookbooks had become an established industry, and a profitable one at that. Russia's involvement in World War I forced the vegetarian journals to close down for a time, although the cafeterias continued to function. Several years of political turmoil ensued. When *The Vegetarian Herald* began publishing again in April 1917, it had adopted a noticeably political tone. One article from this issue, entitled "Toward the Second Step" (following Tolstoy's first), hails the government's abolition of capital punishment and calls for abolishing capital punishment for animals as the next step. The July issue is disheartening in its report that capital punishment has been reintroduced into Russia.

Vegetarians worldwide still mention Tolstoy's name with reverence, but the most fascinating Russian vegetarian remains obscure even in Russia today. Natalia Nordman-Severova crusaded for the liberation of domestic servants from excessive labor, for the liberation of the housewife from the kitchen, and for the abolition of world hunger. Significantly, all of these grand social schemes were contingent upon vegetarianism, which became Nordman's main platform. Yet her brand of vegetarianism was unlike any other. Progressing from a standard meatless diet, she gradually excluded all dairy products from her meals, and eventually came to eat almost all of her food raw. In her most extreme period of vegetarianism, she touted the diet for which she became famous: a regimen based almost entirely on grass and hay. Despite the obvious asceticism of her program,

Nordman expressed great *joie de vivre* both in person and in her writings, always emphasizing the pleasure and well-being to be gained from her diet.

In 1891 Nordman met the celebrated Realist painter Ilya Repin, and though infatuation was not immediate, their attraction gradually grew. By 1899 Repin had purchased a small house in Nordman's name in the Finnish village of Kuokkala, not far from St. Petersburg. There they set up house together in the beautiful, newly renovated *dacha* that Nordman named "Penaty" after the Roman gods of the household. Repin appreciated the comfortable domesticity of his new life. Many of his friends, however, could barely tolerate Nordman and considered her influence over Repin deleterious. But Repin publicly applauded Nordman's efforts, declaring that thanks to the enforced vegetarian diet at Penaty, he had never felt better. Repin's enthusiastic acceptance of vegetarianism indicates the degree to which Nordman did in fact hold sway over him, for she succeeded in converting him where the great Tolstoy had failed. Repin had visited Tolstoy more than once to paint his portraits, and like others before him was deeply moved by the writer's beliefs. For a time he had tried "to live by some of Tolstoy's moral precepts," if only out of infatuation with Tolstoy's daughter, Tatiana. In his memoirs Repin claims that he could do nothing but "submit to Tolstoy's will," yet despite several attempts at vegetarianism, he was unable fully to embrace it. He succumbed, however, to Nordman's earnest suasion.

Nordman worked to convert not only Repin, but all visitors to Penaty, holding an open house each Wednesday afternoon that provided the perfect opportunity to proselytize. Her guests included some of the most gifted writers and artists of the time. The rules Nordman established at Penaty were highly original, and even those visitors who did not care for the hostess could hardly help being amused, even charmed, by her regulations. It all began in the front hall, where guests were immediately confronted with a bold sign proclaiming "Take off your own coats and beat on the tom-tom!"—the first indication that egalitarianism reigned. The ethos of self-service extended into the dining room, where it reached a brilliant intensity. A prominently placed sign reminded everyone that

"Equality and Self-help" were the order of the day. To put her rules into effect, Nordman had set up a separate table at which guests were expected to cut their own bread with a special machine of her own devising. But her greatest innovation—truly the talk of the town—was the dining table itself, a large round table with a sort of lazy Susan in the center that enabled guests to help themselves without being waited on by servants. As part of her larger, social agenda, Nordman had revolutionized the household. Intrepid guests could enjoy the surprises with which they were met and allow themselves to be drawn into the household's prevailing spirit of play.

While such a system might seem unduly rigorous for diners accustomed to the finest in mealtime service, Nordman's dining room was in fact always beautifully appointed. The table was covered with red lacquer and bordered in green, so that no tablecloth was necessary. Fine china, crystal, and flatware sparkled, and fresh flowers or leaves of the season were always strewn decoratively across the table. For place cards Nordman used postcards with photographs of a painting by Repin or another artist. But the real ingenuity of the table lay in its two-tiered construction. The central, upper tier turned by means of nickel-plated hooks that were positioned all along the edges so that each person could take hold of a hook and turn any portion of the table toward himself to reach whatever he needed. On the lower tier, in front of each place setting, stood two small, interior shelves holding clean plates, so that the diner could exchange his dirty plate for a clean one without the aid of a servant. Guests were expected to adhere rigidly to the motto about self-help; they were not even supposed to serve one another. If a newcomer made the mistake of offering a dining partner food, he or she was forced to make a speech, which could be short or quite long, depending on the seriousness of the infraction. The more infractions, the livelier the dinners at Penaty, so newcomers were always welcome.

The food—all vegetarian—was artistically arranged in the middle of the lazy Susan, with the symbol of the Repins—a large turnip—rising as a centerpiece above all. (The Russian word for turnip is *repa,* from which the name Repin derives.) Nordman seems to have had a special fondness for *trompe l'oeil* presentations: To their surprise, diners found mashed bananas in the butter dishes. On the table also stood various *zakuski* or hors d'oeuvres, *pirozhki* or pies, and miniature barrels holding sauerkraut and pickles. All of these delights alternated with bottles of port, Madeira, and other fine wines carrying the name "Sun's Energy." Unlike most of her fellow vegetarians, Nordman eschewed neither spices nor wine; in fact, she considered wine "the energy of the sun" and a necessary accompaniment to any meal. As "the blood of the sun," wine caused all of the human juices to flow.

Before sitting down to a Penaty dinner, other rituals had first to be observed. Nordman would put on music to heighten the mood and stimulate the appetite, and all of the guests were expected to begin "plastic dancing" with exaggerated gestures and steps. In probable imitation of Isadora Duncan, Nordman would wave a white scarf and flirtatiously float like a swan past Repin, who kept his arms taut at his sides while stamping his feet like a Cossack dancer. These "plastic dances" were an integral part of Nordman's program for health, as were cross-country skiing and *Schneetreten*, the practice of walking barefoot on snow, which she reputedly accomplished with a beatific look on her face. These outdoor rituals likely exacerbated the tuberculosis that eventually caused Nordman's death in 1914. As for the dancing, Tolstoy's son recalls one visit Repin and Nordman made to Yasnaya Polyana, the Tolstoy estate. Although pleased by Repin's conversion to vegetarianism, Tolstoy was greatly distressed by the "dancing orgies to a gramophone" that took place in the room above his and could hardly wait for the eccentric couple to leave.

Even after Nordman's death, Repin preserved the order she had established at Penaty. The meals served at the Wednesday salons were vegetarian, and the lazy Susan still revolved. The Futurist poet David Burliuk recalls the difficulties of self-service at the dining table. As he frantically tried to move in his direction a crock of tasty-looking sauerkraut studded with cranberries and lingonberries, another guest suddenly decided he wanted a helping of salted mushrooms and grabbed the table's hooks, jerking it back.

More than an advocate for healthy living, Nordman truly believed she could save the world. In a tireless crusade she presented public lectures, published articles and brochures, and organized courses for women workers in Kuokkala, at which Repin himself sometimes lectured. As Nordman contemplated the problem of eradicating widespread hunger, her views crystallized into the solution that made her at once famous and notorious: her diet of grass and hay. This discovery came in a moment of epiphany as she watched her favorite workhorse, Liuba, hungrily munching hay. She suddenly realized that man, too, could benefit from this produce, becoming as healthy and strong as a horse. And Russia would never again have to suffer from hunger, since hay was not only abundant, it was also free.

In 1911, Nordman published a cookbook in which she explicitly presents the merits of her hay diet, *A Cookbook for the Hungry*. She purposely had the book printed on cheap gray paper to make it accessible to the poor. She dedicated it, however, to the "overfed," explaining that "vegetarianism is necessary for the very rich and the very poor. The poor need it because it is cheap and nourishing. The rich, in order to cleanse all the poisons from the corpses that have accumulated in their overfed organism." The book methodically details a comprehensive method for changing the human diet, including an important project for feeding the hungry, in which every large apartment house or yardman's lodge would daily provide a huge kettle of free soup for the poor. The soup would be free in all respects. The indigent would not have to pay for it, and neither would the providers, since the ingredients would consist of the discards from wealthy kitchens. Kindergartens and factories could establish similar soup kitchens, and thus, without spending a cent, the rich could feed the needy.

Nourished by grass in the summer, and hay in the winter, everyone would be healthy. Other greens would supplement the diet. City dwellers could easily get scraps from cooks and shopkeepers who regularly discarded cabbage stalks, beet tops, and turnip greens as unfit provender. They could also take delight in the rejected greens from carrots, cauliflower, celery, parsley root, rutabaga, Jerusalem artichokes, potatoes, radishes, beans, and peas.

A search for greens could turn into a summer holiday with an excursion to the countryside to pick the freshest and tastiest grasses—a special treat for the children. Like the fruit of the vine, grasses kissed by the sun and wind give humans vitality. They also provide important vitamins, and Nordman cites chemical analyses of different grasses to show just how nourishing each variety is. A further advantage of cooked grass or hay is that the broth rapidly quells hunger, so that a hearty bowl at noon satisfies the body for virtually twenty-four hours. One need only partake of a cold, light snack in the evening if the stomach begins to complain.

In keeping with her expansive theory, Nordman adduces further benefits to the simple consumption of broth made from hay: by not having to toil endlessly in the kitchen, the cook can be liberated from the most menial tasks and return home to her family at four o'clock. Close reading reveals that this liberation entails an eight-hour day, a significant "first step" beyond the usual seventeen.

Here I should note that the idea of using hay in the kitchen is not in itself so farfetched. Good Russian cooks took advantage of the aromatic properties of hay in many ways. For instance, in her famous cookbook, *A Gift to Young Housewives,* Elena Molokhovets (the Russian Mrs. Beeton) advocates tossing hay into the water in which fresh ham is boiled to add extra flavor. She also uses it to impart a special taste to fish as it smokes and often spreads it on the floor of the wood-fired Russian oven when baking cabbage or bread. But Nordman appears to have been the first to brew hay systematically into an edible broth. And this she did with a vengeance, forcing distinguished visitors to swallow what must have seemed a bitter brew. The human capacity to digest hay may not rival the cow's four-part stomach, but Nordman's cookbook offers a number of intriguing recipes, and she explains how a standard hay broth can be used in combination with other ingredients to make a variety of delicious soups. Here is her recipe for the basic "Hay Soup in a Teapot":

> Take a teapot, depending on the number of people either a small porcelain one or a huge tin one for a whole worker's cooperative,

toss in two *zolotniks* [about 8.5 grams] of hay per person, chop an onion, add some bay leaves (one leaf for every 3 people) and 2 peppercorns per person, pour on rapidly boiling water, simmer for ten minutes, and the soup is ready.

Nordman admits that hay can smell a bit medicinal, but cheerfully adds "that's not so bad." If you really can't stand it plain, she suggests simply adding it to other soups for the nutritional value and you won't even notice its presence.

Ever concerned with expenses, Nordman offers in her book an economical weekly menu for which she provides the cost per person. For instance, the Tuesday menu calls for "Simple oatmeal, served as a puree. This soup is made at absolutely no cost, since the oats are strained for the puree and given to the horse. Baked turnip with bread crumbs and onions. Fried celery." Assuming the ongoing expense of oats for the animals, this meal costs only five kopecks per person. Nordman has a special fondness for celery because it is "cheap, filling, aromatic and tasty." Surprised that it is not better known in Russia, she offers an entire section on the sorts of dishes that can be prepared from celery. The twenty recipes include *zakuski*, soups, and stews; Nordman also suggests an interesting meal of fried celery cutlets with tomatoes and chestnuts.

At some Penaty dinners, at least in the earlier stages of her vegetarianism, Nordman would serve a soup of freshly mown hay from the Penaty meadows, flavored with carrots, potatoes, and other vegetables, offering on the side such tasty dishes as vegetable ragouts, *pirozhki* with rice or cabbage, fruit puddings *(kisel'),* and compotes. In her later, more extreme period, however, everything at Penaty was served raw and cold on the beautiful round table. One guest recalls a Wednesday meal of turnip pastry with barley filling, olives, raw grated celery, and the like.

Nordman insisted that a Russian meadow, with its many grasses, could provide a more varied and nutritious diet than any in Italy, where produce is available only in season. In Russia, for a quick and tasty meal, one need simply go out into the summertime fields and pick fresh grasses like lady's mantle, goutweed, angelica, mountain sorrel, yarrow, timothy grass, and canary grass, then sauté them with celery, parsley, dill, and onion in a little olive oil. As the gentle season draws to a close, dry the grasses and tie them in cheesecloth to make an instant boullion to have on hand for a variety of soups throughout the year. After the soup has boiled, the grasses can be strained from the bag and mixed with an equal proportion of flour to make an excellent dough. She offers other tips, many of them quite appetizing as well as innovative. Pies made from strained, cooked turnip mixed into a dough with flour and filled with cabbage are particularly delicious, claims Nordman. To make lovely black currant, raspberry, and rhubarb fruit puddings, dry the young leaves of these plants in summer. As a substitute for black tea, use dried wild strawberry blossoms and leaves. Replace coffee with dried beets and chicory. Nordman emphasizes that nothing need ever be thrown away. Leftover broth can be boiled up several times with various new additions, and even used tea leaves can be dried and brewed again, and again. Nordman also includes many recipes from Zelenkova's *I Don't Eat Anyone,* which seem delicious by any standards. Chestnut puree with Jerusalem artichokes, stewed green peppers with tomatoes, onions, and olive oil, and "vegetarian herring" of olives and potatoes dressed with a mustard vinaigrette.

Strident and eccentric, Nordman herself was too unappealing to garner a following, and her views never really caught on in her native land. Rich and poor alike found the thought of eating discards too distasteful. And although vegetarian cafeterias continued to flourish in the 1920s, for most of the Soviet period meat represented a status symbol, its procurement an obsession. Thus Nordman's grand vision fell into obscurity. Few remember the special footwear she invented, or the winter jackets stuffed peasant-style with wood shavings so that she could avoid wearing fur; her innovative comforters stuffed with (what else?) hay in place of goose down have been similarly forgotten. It is particularly unfortunate that no one paid closer attention to the "magic chest" she insulated with pillows. An early version of a crockpot or slow-cooker, this chest was designed to ease the busy housewife's burden. Half-cooked food placed in the chest would finish cooking unattended. "Just think," said Nordman, "any working woman can start fixing soup or kasha, put it in my magic chest, and calmly go off to work, to her job. Returning home, she'll find everything ready! Just think how this will liberate women!" The possibility of an instant meal was extremely important to Nordman: "At last the time has come for women's liberation from the yoke of endless domestic cares that humiliate her." In her commentary to recipes for dried soup powders, Nordman expressed the hope that this sort of instant soup would become widespread in Russia. But it never did. Soviet housewives labored for decades without the benefit of Nordman's labor-saving devices. And even if they had been exposed to her vegetarian ideas, they would have had no patience with her unconventional diet, preferring instead to dream of extravagant dining in the grand nineteenth-century style.

Vegetarian Borshch

Mixed Vegetable Salad *(Vinegret)*

Garlic Buns

Carrot Pie *(Pirog s morkov'iu)*

Baked Mushroom Dumplings

Stewed Mushrooms

Turnips in Wine Sauce

Countess Tolstoy's Hot Apple Compote

Orange Rice Pudding

Vegetarian Borshch

In Russia and Ukraine, where beet soup originated, over one hundred different varieties of *borshch* exist. I'm especially fond of this rustic version, which is thick and chunky, Slavic soul food at its best. This recipe makes enough for a crowd, but the sheer abundance of vegetables celebrates the neglected roots of winter. Don't be put off by the long list of ingredients. Once the chopping is done, the soup cooks itself.

2	large onions, peeled and finely chopped
4	garlic cloves, peeled and minced
1	large carrot, peeled and thinly sliced
1	small parsnip, peeled and thinly sliced
1	small turnip, peeled and finely chopped
2	tablespoons olive oil
6	medium beets (1½ pounds), peeled and finely chopped
3	medium potatoes, peeled and finely chopped
1	small celery root (¼ pound), peeled and finely chopped
1	pound white cabbage, shredded
1	cup pitted brine-cured black olives
1	tart apple, peeled, cored, and finely chopped
8	cups water
One	28-ounce can tomatoes in thick puree, finely chopped (reserve the puree)
2	tablespoons tomato paste
10	black peppercorns
3	allspice berries
1	bay leaf
1¼	teaspoons salt
1	tablespoon freshly squeezed lemon juice
	Freshly ground black pepper
	Minced fresh dill
	Sour cream (optional)

In a large stockpot sauté the onions, garlic, carrot, parsnip, and turnip in the olive oil until soft, 12 to 15 minutes. Stir in the beets, potatoes, celery root, cabbage, olives, apple, and water. Add the tomatoes along with the reserved puree, then stir in the tomato paste, spices, and salt. Bring to a boil. Reduce the heat and simmer the soup, covered, for 1½ to 2 hours. (At this point the soup may be cooled, then held for several days in the refrigerator.)

Just before serving, stir in the lemon juice and pepper to taste. Serve hot, garnishing each bowl with minced dill and a dollop of sour cream, if you like.

Serves 10 to 12.

NOTE: The bright color of *borshch* tends to fade on standing. If you plan to reheat the soup, you can perk it up by grating a small roasted beet and stirring it into the soup 10 minutes before serving.

Mixed Vegetable Salad (*Vinegret*)

This vegetable mixture is arguably Russia's most famous salad, having crossed international boundaries to become the "Russian Salad" of supermarkets and restaurants throughout the world. Interestingly, though, Russians know it as either Olivier Salad—after the superstar French chef who took Moscow by storm in the 1880s—or, more prosaically, Capital Salad, the standard first course of Soviet-era restaurants. But no matter what it's called, a well-made *vinegret* is sensational. Feel free to tinker with the ingredients and proportions I give here, which are simply guidelines for making a salad that must above all be piquant. You might try adding sauerkraut or pickled mushrooms, or a few canned white beans. Or you could substitute prepared mustard for the dry, or omit the hard-boiled eggs as Orthodox Russians would on fast days. This salad mixes into a brilliant shade of red, thanks to the beets, but you can also make a White Russian version by leaving them out.

2 pounds waxy potatoes
1 large beet (about 8 ounces)
1 cucumber, peeled, seeded, and diced (1½ cups)
3 large scallions, including the green part, finely
    chopped (1 cup)
2 hard-boiled eggs, diced
⅔ cup diced dill pickle
⅓ cup finely chopped brined black olives
1 tablespoon capers
1 tablespoon minced fresh dill

Dressing

3 tablespoons plus 2 teaspoons white wine vinegar
1 teaspoon dry mustard
2 teaspoons sugar
1½ teaspoons salt
    Freshly ground white pepper
6 tablespoons olive oil

    Sprigs of fresh dill

Boil the potatoes in salted water to cover until just tender, about 30 minutes, depending on their size. Drain and allow to cool slightly.

In a separate pan, boil the beet in water to cover until just tender, about 45 minutes. Drain and allow to cool slightly.

While the potatoes and beet are boiling, prepare the rest of the salad. Place the diced cucumber, scallions, eggs, pickle, olives, and capers in a large bowl. When the potatoes and beets are cool enough to handle, peel and dice them. Add to the vegetables in the bowl, stirring to mix well. Stir in the minced dill.

To make the dressing, stir together the vinegar, mustard, sugar, salt, and pepper. Gradually whisk in the olive oil until an emulsion has been formed. Pour over the vegetables, mixing well.

Chill the salad for at least 1 hour to allow the flavors to blend (the salad improves on standing). Test for seasoning, adding more salt, pepper, or vinegar, if necessary. Serve garnished with sprigs of fresh dill.

Serves 8.

Garlic Buns

If you love garlic, you'll find these plump buns divine.

2½ teaspoons active dry yeast
1½ cups plus 3 tablespoons lukewarm water
1 teaspoon salt
4 to 4½ cups bread flour or unbleached white flour
3 large garlic cloves
4 teaspoons light olive oil
1 teaspoon coarse sea salt

Proof the yeast in ¼ cup of the water for 10 minutes, until bubbly. Stir in 1¼ cups more water, 1 teaspoon salt, and 4 cups of flour, beating to mix well. Turn the dough out onto a floured surface and knead until smooth and elastic, about 10 minutes, adding up to ½ cup more flour if necessary.

Place the dough in a large, lightly greased bowl and turn it to grease the top. Cover and leave to rise until doubled in bulk, about 1½ hours. Punch down the dough and divide into twelve pieces.

Roll each piece of dough into a ball and place on a lightly greased baking sheet.

Preheat the oven to 425°F. Leave the buns to rise for 20 minutes.

Bake the buns for 10 minutes at 425°F, then reduce the heat to 350°F and bake for 10 minutes longer, until they are lightly browned.

While the buns are baking, put the garlic cloves through a garlic press into a small bowl. Stir in the remaining 3 tablespoons of water and the olive oil. Set aside.

Let the buns cool for 10 minutes, then brush them with the garlic mixture, making sure that each bun gets some bits of garlic. Sprinkle the tops of the buns with the sea salt. Either serve immediately or transfer to a rack to finish cooling.

Makes 1 dozen buns.

Carrot Pie *(Pirog s morkov'iu)*

Russians believe that a house is judged by its pies, not its walls. And what pies there are! They can be savory or sweet, simple or lavish. Puff pastry, short pastry, or yeast-raised dough encloses the filling or embraces it lightly around the edges. Round, oval, rectangular, or square, multilayered or flat, Russian pies are enjoyed for breakfast, lunch, snack, and dinner, as well as evening tea.

Russian cuisine is hard to imagine without its myriad pies. The most popular pies are filled with meat, fish, cabbage, mushrooms, or rice and hard-boiled eggs. The one I offer here is a bit more unusual, with a tender yeast dough surrounding a tasty filling of carrots and scallions. This type of *pirog* is often small and traditionally served as an accompaniment to soup. Here, the entire batch of dough is shaped into one large, golden envelope. To a Russian eye, however, such dramatic size is not excessive: in the nineteenth-century novel *Oblomov*, Ivan Goncharov describes a huge holiday pie that a family of gentry works to consume for two days, only then passing on the still considerable remains to their servants, who enjoy the pie for two days more and still can't finish it all. Try this *pirog* with a light vegetable or mushroom soup, and if you do have any left over, simply refrigerate it and reheat gently.

Dough

2½ teaspoons active dry yeast
¼ cup lukewarm water
1 cup milk
½ cup (1 stick) unsalted butter, cut into pieces, at room temperature
1 teaspoon salt
2 teaspoons sugar
1 whole egg, at room temperature
2 egg yolks, at room temperature
4½ to 5 cups unbleached white flour

1 tablespoon fine dry bread crumbs

Filling

1¼ pounds carrots, trimmed, peeled, and cut into chunks
5 tablespoons unsalted butter
4 large scallions, including the green part, finely chopped (1¼ cups)
1¼ cups fresh bread crumbs
1½ teaspoons salt
Freshly ground black pepper
3 tablespoons sour cream
½ cup minced parsley
1 to 2 tablespoons minced fresh dill

1 egg yolk
1 teaspoon cold water

Dissolve the yeast in the warm water. Heat the milk to lukewarm and add the butter, then stir the mixture into the yeast. Add the salt, sugar, whole egg, and

2 egg yolks, mixing well. Gradually stir in enough flour to make a soft dough. Turn out onto a floured board and knead until the dough is smooth and elastic, about 10 minutes. Place the dough in a large greased bowl, turning to grease the top. Cover and leave to rise until doubled in bulk, about 1½ hours.

While the dough is rising, make the filling. Boil the carrots in salted water to cover until just tender, 12 to 15 minutes. Drain and chop them finely.

Melt the butter in a medium saucepan. Cook the carrots, scallions, and fresh bread crumbs over medium heat for 10 minutes. Remove from the heat and stir in the salt, pepper, sour cream, parsley, and dill. Allow the filling to cool slightly before using.

When the dough has risen, punch it down and divide into two pieces, one slightly larger than the other. On a floured surface roll out the larger piece into a 10 x 12-inch rectangle and place it on a lightly greased baking sheet. Sprinkle with the fine dry bread crumbs to within 1 inch of the edges, then spread the carrot filling over the crumbs.

Roll out the second piece of dough into a slightly smaller rectangle than the first, then carefully lay it over the filling to cover it entirely. Turn the edges of the bottom piece of dough up over the top piece to form a rolled border. Seal by pinching with your fingers or crimping with a fork.

Preheat the oven to 350°F. Cover the pie and leave it to rise for 20 minutes. Brush all over with the egg yolk that has been lightly beaten with the cold water. Bake for 25 to 30 minutes, until nicely browned. Serve slightly warm or at room temperature.

Makes 1 large pie, serving 8 to 10.

VARIATION: To make small pies or *pirozhki,* divide the dough into four dozen pieces. Roll out each piece into a circle about 3½ inches in diameter, and place a heaping tablespoon of filling on each round. Press the edges together to seal, gently shaping the pies into ovals. Place seam side down on lightly greased baking sheets. Leave to rise for 20 minutes, brush with the egg wash, and bake for 15 to 20 minutes.

Baked Mushroom Dumplings

These tender packets of dough filled with fresh and dried mushrooms may be as close to paradise as mushroom lovers can get in this world. Soft, silky, and redolent of the forest, these dumplings satisfy the soul as well as the senses. In his book on Russian cuisine, food historian Vil'iam Pokhlebkin describes a similar dish, dating its origin to the Middle Ages. I've streamlined the sixteenth-century method to make it possible to enjoy these succulent dumplings without the benefit of serfs laboring in the kitchen for hours.

⅓ cup raw rice

⅔ cup water

½ teaspoon salt

1 medium onion, peeled and very finely chopped

4 tablespoons olive oil

2 garlic cloves, peeled and minced

10 ounces fresh exotic mushrooms (such as portobello, shiitake, and cremini), trimmed and finely chopped

½ cup minced reconstituted dried mushrooms (see Notes)

1 hard-boiled egg, finely chopped

2 tablespoons minced fresh dill

Freshly ground black pepper

One 12-ounce package Gyoza (pot sticker) wraps (see Notes)

12 cups hot Mushroom Broth (page 51) or vegetable broth (see Notes)

Freshly minced dill (optional)

Sour cream (optional)

Cook the rice in the water over very low heat with ¼ teaspoon of the salt for 10 minutes, until the liquid has been absorbed.

In a medium skillet, sauté the onion in the olive oil for 5 minutes, then stir in the garlic and the fresh mushrooms. Cook over medium heat for about 5 minutes longer, stirring occasionally. Remove the pan from the heat and stir in the cooked rice, dried mushrooms, egg, and dill. Season with the remaining ¼ teaspoon of salt and the black pepper.

Preheat the oven to 350°F. Lightly grease several baking sheets.

Place a heaping teaspoon of mushroom filling on each noodle wrapper. Moisten the edges with water to seal, forming half-moon-shaped dumplings. Place the dumplings on the sheets and bake for about 12 minutes, until crisp and browned at the edges.

Pour the hot broth into a 6-quart ovenproof casserole, preferably earthenware. Drop the dumplings into the broth. Cover the pot and place in the oven. Bake at 350°F for 30 minutes. Carefully ladle into shallow bowls and serve hot, garnished with minced dill and sour cream, if desired.

Makes about 60 dumplings, serving 8 to 10.

NOTES: If you can't find prepared pot sticker or wonton wraps, you can still make these dumplings with your favorite noodle dough. Roll out the dough very thin and cut out 3½-inch rounds. Proceed as directed above.

If you are using the Mushroom Broth on page 51, you will need 1½ times the recipe. Mince enough of the dried mushrooms after they have cooked to make ½ cup. If you are using vegetable broth, pour 2 cups of boiling water over about 1 ounce of dried mushrooms and leave them to soak for 30 minutes. Strain the liquid through a coffee filter to remove any grit and use it for part of the broth. Mince the mushrooms and add to the filling.

If you want to use a mushroom broth but don't have the time to prepare the one on page 51, a quick broth may be made as follows:

3 to 4 ounces dried mushrooms
4 quarts water
8 garlic cloves, peeled
8 bay leaves
8 sprigs of parsley
1 teaspoon whole black peppercorns
1 teaspoon salt

Place all of the ingredients except the salt in a large stockpot. Bring to a boil, then simmer, covered, for 30 minutes. Strain the broth through a coffee filter to remove any grit. Stir in the salt. These proportions yield approximately 12 cups.

Stewed Mushrooms

Recipe number 102 in Sophia Tolstaya's cookery book describes a simple dish of stewed mushrooms: "Clean the mushrooms well, cut them up, remove their stems, and place them in an earthenware pot with salt, butter, a spoonful of flour, some dill, pepper, and bay leaf or tarragon. Place them in a slow oven to stew, covered. One hour before serving add some sour cream." Slow cooking brings out the intense flavor of the mushrooms, which is best if you use a mixture of exotics such as portobello, shiitake, and crimini. Here is my interpretation of Mrs. Tolstoy's recipe, a real taste of Russia.

1   pound mixed exotic mushrooms (such as portobello, shiitake, and cremini), stems removed, coarsely chopped
½   teaspoon salt
    Freshly ground black pepper
1   tablespoon all-purpose flour
2   tablespoons snipped fresh dill
1   bay leaf
2   tablespoons unsalted butter, cut into bits
2   tablespoons sour cream

Preheat the oven to 300°F. Lightly grease a 3-quart casserole with a cover, preferably earthenware.

Toss the mushrooms with the salt, pepper, flour, and dill and place them in the casserole. Bury the bay leaf among the mushrooms and dot with the butter. Cover and bake for 1 hour.

Remove the cover and stir in the sour cream. Cover again, return to the oven, and bake for 1 hour more. Serve hot.

Serves 4 to 6.

Turnips in Wine Sauce

This recipe is based on one in Elena Molokhovets's famous nineteenth-century cookbook, *A Gift to Young Housewives*. Although her instructions call for Malaga wine, sweet sherry is easier to find in twentieth-century America, and considerably easier on the pocketbook. Whether you use Malaga or sherry, the fortified wine produces a rich, sweet sauce that adds a touch of sophistication to the common turnip.

1 pound small turnips, peeled, halved, and sliced ½ inch thick
1 tablespoon unsalted butter
1 tablespoon all-purpose flour
1 cup vegetable broth or Roasted Vegetable Broth (page 44)
½ cup sweet (cream-style) sherry
  Freshly ground white pepper

1 tablespoon minced parsley

Bring a large pot of water to a boil. Blanch the turnip slices for 2 minutes. Drain.

In a medium saucepan melt the butter. Whisk in the flour and cook, stirring, for a minute, then gradually whisk in the vegetable broth. Stir in the sherry, then add the turnips. Cover and bring to a boil. Cook over medium-low heat until the turnips are tender, 10 to 15 minutes. Grind on a dusting of white pepper and transfer the turnips with their sauce to a serving dish. Garnish with the minced parsley and serve immediately.

Serves 4.

VARIATION: Rutabaga may be substituted for the turnips. Peel and dice a one-pound rutabaga, than parboil for 15 minutes. Drain and proceed as directed above.

Countess Tolstoy's Hot Apple Compote

A dessert recipe in Sophia Tolstaya's book reads: "Take 10 sour apples, cut them into pieces, mix them with sugar in a frying pan, add a cup of jam or candied peel or apple rind; turn this hot mass out onto a plate, then whip 6 egg whites with sugar, make a border, sprinkle it with almonds, and place it in the Russian stove an hour before serving." My rendition produces a marvelous, showy dessert, with billows of golden meringue drifting over a base of tart apples.

2   tablespoons unsalted butter
3   pounds tart apples, peeled, cored, and finely chopped
1   tablespoon freshly squeezed lemon juice
1¼   cups sugar
6   tablespoons apricot jam
¼   cup diced candied orange or lemon peel
6   egg whites, at room temperature
¼   cup slivered almonds

Melt the butter in a large skillet. Add the finely chopped apples. Sprinkle them with the lemon juice and ¼ cup of the sugar, stirring to coat them well. Cook, covered, over medium-low heat for about 8 minutes, until the apples are soft but still hold their shape. Remove the pan from the heat and stir in the jam and candied peel.

Lightly grease a shallow 3-quart baking dish. With a slotted spoon transfer the apples to the dish and spread them evenly.

Preheat the oven to 300°F.

Beat the egg whites until they form soft peaks, then gradually beat in the remaining 1 cup of sugar, 1 tablespoon at a time, until a stiff meringue is formed. Using a spatula, lavishly spread the meringue around the edges of the baking dish, leaving an opening in the center for the apples to peek through. Sprinkle the meringue with the slivered almonds.

Bake for 1 hour, until the meringue is puffed and golden. Serve immediately.

Serves 8 amply.

Orange Rice Pudding

Oranges have long been considered a luxury in Russia, so this nine-teenth-century pudding represented the height of elegance. It is a lovely dessert, with fresh oranges offering nice balance to the sweet, creamy rice.

½ cup raw rice
1 cup water
1 cup milk
¼ teaspoon salt
½ vanilla bean
¼ cup sugar

Syrup

⅔ cup water
⅓ cup sugar
3 whole cloves
   Grated rind of 2 navel oranges
2 tablespoons freshly squeezed orange juice
1 teaspoon orange liqueur, such as Grand Marnier

2 navel oranges, peeled, white pith removed, and separated into
   sections

Place the rice, water, milk, and salt in the top portion of a double boiler that has been set over gently boiling water. Split the vanilla bean and scrape the seeds into the rice mixture, then add the bean. Cover the pot and cook the rice, stirring occasionally, until all the liquid has been absorbed, about 75 minutes.

To make the syrup, in a small saucepan stir together the water, sugar, cloves, and orange rind. Bring to a boil and cook gently until syrupy, about 10 minutes. Remove the cloves, then stir in the orange juice and liqueur. Keep warm.

When the rice is done, remove the vanilla bean and stir in the sugar. Mound the rice in the center of a serving dish and place the orange sections decoratively around it. Pour about two thirds of the syrup over the orange sections, then pour the remaining syrup over the rice, making sure that some of the orange rind garnishes it on top. Serve immediately.

Serves 4.

10

Sweet and Savory Breads

There is no denying our emotional attachment to bread. It's not just that the aroma of bread baking is so comforting, or a fresh loaf so satisfying. Bread making also replicates the cycle of life, and if only subliminally, we feel kinship with the live yeast that billows and swells the dough until ultimately meeting its end in a fiery oven. Russian folklore goes so far as to equate the life of grain with that of a saint: "They beat me, flail me, rend me, yet I remain silent."

What better time to bake bread than when the weather turns cold and the oven can provide some welcome heat? The rhythms of bread making fit well with the seasonal slowdown of winter. Bread should not be rushed. It urges us to temper our pace, to nurture and marvel as small changes occur: the momentary transformation of stolid, stiff dough into a silken mass; the first, minute bubbles that break on its surface. Plan your bread making for a leisurely afternoon, or stretch it over an evening and morning by refrigerating the dough in between. Any way you do it, the processes of bread making are most gratifying when the weather is cold.

Finnish Cardamom Braid *(Pulla)*

Cinnamon Walnut Wreath

Plum Buns *(Zwetschgennudeln)*

Date and Nut Loaf

Rusks

Boston Brown Bread

Popovers

Squash Crescents

Sour Rye Bread

Georgian Cheese Bread *(Khachapuri)*

Finnish Cardamom Braid (*Pulla*)

*P*ulla ranks as one of my great comfort foods, although I was twenty-one before I tasted it. While studying at the University of Helsinki, I lived in a dormitory quite far from the classrooms, and as autumn progressed, the daily trek became increasingly difficult. Soon it was not only cold but dark when I set off for class. What saved me—and my studies—was the discovery of a modest bakery about a fifteen-minute walk from the university. This bakery soon became my morning ritual, as I stopped in for a cup of rich hot chocolate and a loaf of *pulla,* Finland's wonderful cardamom-scented bread. I'd sip my chocolate and tear off chunks of the warm bread, taking whatever was left with me. More often than not I arrived at the university empty-handed. These days, a loaf lasts longer, and I even manage to freeze some bread when I make up a batch. But *pulla* still spells comfort to me.

2½ teaspoons active dry yeast
¼ cup lukewarm water
1 teaspoon plus ¾ cup sugar
2 cups lukewarm milk
1 teaspoon salt
2 teaspoons ground cardamom (from about 32 pods)
12 tablespoons (1½ sticks) salted butter, melted
4 eggs, at room temperature, lightly beaten
7 to 8 cups unbleached white flour

1 egg white, lightly beaten until frothy
3 tablespoons sliced almonds
3 tablespoons pearl sugar or coarsely crushed sugar cubes

Dissolve the yeast in the water with 1 teaspoon of sugar until bubbly. Stir in the milk, remaining ¾ cup sugar, salt, cardamom, melted butter, eggs, and 4 cups of the flour. Beat well. Gradually add just enough flour to form a soft dough. Turn out onto a floured board and knead until the dough is smooth and elastic, about 10 minutes.

Place the dough in a large greased bowl, turning to grease the top. Cover and leave to rise until doubled, 1½ to 2 hours. Punch down the dough and let rise again until nearly doubled, about 1 hour.

Divide the dough into three pieces. Divide each piece into three balls of equal size. Roll each ball out between your hands into a rope about 12 inches long. Braid three ropes together, turning the ends under. Place the loaf on a lightly greased baking sheet (you will need two sheets). Repeat with the remaining dough. Cover the loaves and leave them to rise until slightly puffy, 20 to 30 minutes.

Preheat the oven to 375°F. Brush the loaves with the beaten egg white, then sprinkle each with 1 tablespoon of almonds and 1 tablespoon of pearl sugar. Bake for 25 to 30 minutes, until nicely browned.

Makes 3 loaves.

Cinnamon Walnut Wreath

True to form, this divine loaf is shaped like a wreath, but unlike most Scandinavian coffee cakes it contains walnuts instead of the more usual almonds.

5   teaspoons active dry yeast
½   cup lukewarm water
1½ cups lukewarm milk
½   cup sugar
2   teaspoons salt
2   eggs, at room temperature, lightly beaten
8   tablespoons (1 stick) unsalted butter, softened
7   to 8 cups all-purpose flour

Filling
4   tablespoons unsalted butter, softened
1   cup sugar
4   teaspoons ground cinnamon
1   cup finely chopped walnuts
½   cup currants

Glaze

    2 cups confectioners' sugar
    3 tablespoons hot milk
    1 teaspoon pure vanilla extract

In a large bowl, dissolve the yeast in the water until bubbly. Stir in the milk, sugar, salt, eggs, butter, and half of the flour. Beat well. Gradually add enough flour to form a soft, slightly sticky dough. Turn out onto a floured board and knead until the dough is smooth and elastic, about 10 minutes.

Place the dough in a large greased bowl, turning to grease the top. Cover and leave to rise until doubled, 1½ to 2 hours. Punch down the dough and let rise again until nearly doubled, 30 to 40 minutes.

Divide the dough into two pieces. Roll out each piece into a 9 x 18-inch rectangle. Spread each rectangle with 2 tablespoons butter and sprinkle with ½ cup sugar, 2 teaspoons cinnamon, ½ cup nuts, and ¼ cup currants. Starting with a long end, roll each rectangle tightly as for a jelly roll. Pinch the seam to seal. Transfer the rolls seam side down to lightly greased baking sheets. Bring the ends of the rolls together to form a ring and seal tightly.

With kitchen shears make cuts every 1 inch or so around the rings, cutting two thirds of the way through the dough. Gently turn the slices to one side, then the next, as you move around the rings, revealing the filling. Leave the loaves to rise until slightly puffy, 35 to 40 minutes.

Preheat the oven to 375°F. Bake for 25 to 30 minutes, until browned. Meanwhile, prepare the glaze by mixing together the confectioners' sugar, milk, and vanilla. When the loaves are done, transfer them to racks set over wax paper. Spoon the glaze over them while they are still warm.

Makes 2 loaves.

Plum Buns *(Zwetschgennudeln)*

*Z*wetschgennudeln are fruit-filled buns. Their fanciful German name, "plum noodles," refers to the plum dumplings that are popular throughout Germany and Central Europe. This wintertime rendition substitutes yeast dough for the noodle dough and jam for the fresh fruit, transforming the dumplings into tender buns, which I like best when still warm from the oven. Uschi Fischer kindly shared her recipe with me.

2½ teaspoons active dry yeast

¼ cup lukewarm water

¾ cup lukewarm milk

½ cup sugar

6 tablespoons unsalted butter, melted

3 to 3¼ cups unbleached white flour

⅓ cup plum jam or preserves

2 tablespoons finely chopped canned plums
(about 2 whole plums)

Confectioners' sugar

Proof the yeast in the lukewarm water for 10 minutes, until bubbly. Stir in the milk, sugar, 2 tablespoons of the butter, and enough flour to make a soft dough. Knead the dough on a floured surface until smooth and elastic, about 10 minutes. Place it in a lightly greased bowl and turn to grease the top. Cover with plastic wrap and leave to rise until doubled in bulk, about 2 hours.

Mix together the plum jam and chopped plums. Have ready a 9-inch cake pan. Melt the remaining 4 tablespoons butter and pour into a shallow bowl.

Divide the dough into sixteen pieces and shape each piece into a ball. With your thumb make an indentation in each ball and fill it with about ½ tablespoon of the plum filling. Pinch the edges of the dough around the filling to seal it. Dip each bun into the melted butter, turning to coat on all sides. Place the buns in the pan, cover, and leave to rise until puffy, 20 to 25 minutes.

Preheat the oven to 350°F. Bake the buns until nicely browned, about 30 minutes. Dust with confectioners' sugar before serving.

Makes 16 buns.

Date and Nut Loaf

My sister, Ardath Weaver, gave me this recipe nearly thirty years ago. She and her college roommates were famous for this date lovers' loaf, which uses twice as many dates as most. I still remember my midwinter visit to the Northeast from Texas and how we trudged through the snow to the funky house that my sister, an art major, had decorated. The front door was painted over with giraffes, bears, dogs, and cats. Inside, an old cast-iron stove stood in the corner of the kitchen, painted a deep brick-red to match the refrigerator. From my perspective as younger sister, this house seemed the height of sophistication, as did the bread my sister served. Though I don't know the fate of that house on Charlesfield Street, I still find this bread delicious.

1 pound dates, chopped
1 teaspoon baking soda
1 cup boiling water
1 tablespoon unsalted butter
1 cup sugar
1 egg, lightly beaten
1 teaspoon pure vanilla extract
   A dash each of ground cinnamon, grated nutmeg, and salt
1½ cups all-purpose flour
½ cup chopped walnuts

Place the dates in a medium bowl and sprinkle with the baking soda, then pour the boiling water over them. Set aside.

Preheat the oven to 350°F. Generously grease a 2-pound coffee can to use as a pan.

In a large bowl cream the butter. Stir in the sugar, egg, vanilla, and spices. Add half of the flour, then stir in the dates. Add the remaining flour and the nuts. Scrape the batter into the prepared can and bake for 90 minutes, or until a cake tester inserted in the center comes out clean.

Makes 1 loaf.

Rusks

Rusks are Northern Europe's answer to biscotti. Twice baked to crispness, they are perfect for dunking in coffee or hot chocolate, or simply eating out of hand. They are also excellent for breakfast in a bowl of hot milk. In this recipe I use baker's ammonia, a common ingredient in Scandinavia for adding extra lightness and crispness to baked goods.

> 1¼ cups milk
> 8 tablespoons (1 stick) unsalted butter, cut into pieces
> 2½ teaspoons active dry yeast
> 1 small egg
> ¾ cup sugar
> ½ teaspoon salt
> ½ teaspoon baker's ammonia (see Note)
> 4½ to 5 cups all-purpose flour
> ¼ cup cinnamon sugar (optional)

Heat the milk to lukewarm, then add the butter and stir until it melts. Pour the milk mixture over the yeast in a large bowl. Beat in the egg, sugar, and salt. Mix the baker's ammonia with 1 cup of the flour and stir into the batter, then add enough remaining flour to make a soft dough. Beat vigorously with a wooden spoon, then turn out onto a floured surface and knead until smooth and elastic, about 10 minutes. Place the dough in a greased bowl and turn to grease the top. Cover and leave to rise for 2 hours, until doubled in bulk.

Preheat the oven to 400°F. Lightly grease two baking sheets. Punch down the dough and divide into thirty pieces. Shape each piece into a bun and place on the baking sheets. Bake for 10 minutes, then remove the buns from the oven. Reduce the heat to 350°F.

With a serrated knife carefully split each bun in half horizontally. (It's all right to let the buns sit for a few minutes until they are not too hot to handle.) Place each bun half cut side up on the baking sheets and sprinkle with cinnamon sugar, if desired. Return the rusks to the oven and bake for 10 minutes, until they begin to turn golden. Reduce the heat to 225°F and continue to bake until the rusks are crisp and dry, 35 to 45 minutes longer.

Makes 5 dozen rusks.

NOTE: Baker's ammonia (ammonium carbonate) is available from the King Arthur Baker's Catalogue, 1-800-827-6836. One-half teaspoon baking powder may be substituted for the ammonia.

Boston Brown Bread

American steamed bread has fallen out of favor, but it is a tradition that should be revived. Steaming is especially appealing on a cold afternoon, rewarding with moisture in the air as well as a healthy, delicious loaf that makes a nice change from yeast and quick breads. Virtually all recipes for brown bread are standard, calling for equal parts of whole wheat flour, rye flour, and cornmeal, with molasses added for a touch of sweetness. I can't improve on these time-honored proportions, which yield a moist, nut-brown loaf. Steamed bread connoisseurs insist that the bread should be cut with a string while still warm, but you can use a serrated knife in a pinch. Serve brown bread with its traditional partner of baked beans, or as a wholesome snack, either plain or spread with a little sweet butter.

½ cup whole wheat flour
½ cup rye flour
½ cup yellow cornmeal
½ teaspoon salt
½ teaspoon baking soda
6 tablespoons molasses
1 cup buttermilk
½ cup raisins

Generously grease a 1-quart pudding mold or coffee can and set aside.

In a bowl mix together the dry ingredients, then stir in the molasses and buttermilk. Add the raisins. Scrape the batter into the prepared pudding mold. Cover the mold with a lightly greased piece of aluminum foil and stretch a rubber band around the top to hold the foil in place.

Set the mold in a pan deep enough to hold it and pour water halfway up the sides of the mold. Cover the pan and bring the water to a boil, then turn the heat to low and allow the water to simmer. Steam the pudding for 2 to 2½ hours, until a cake tester inserted in the center comes out clean. (Check the water level halfway through the cooking to make sure that it remains high enough.)

Remove the mold from the water and allow the bread to cool for 15 minutes. Slide the loaf out of the pan and serve warm or at room temperature.

Makes 1 loaf.

Popovers

Steaming hot from the oven, with their dramatic crowns, popovers are a delightful bread. Here, a small amount of cheese gives the standard recipe a flavorful boost.

2 tablespoons unsalted butter
1 cup all-purpose flour
½ teaspoon salt
½ cup milk
½ cup water
3 eggs
⅓ to ½ cup grated Gruyère or Cheddar cheese

Preheat the oven to 450°F. Place eight 6-ounce custard cups on a baking sheet and put ¾ teaspoon of butter in each one.

In a medium bowl mix together the flour and salt. Stir in the milk and water, then beat in the eggs one at a time. Mix in the cheese. Do not overbeat.

Place the custard cups in the hot oven for a minute to melt the butter, then remove. Immediately pour in the popover batter, filling each cup about half full. Bake for 10 minutes at 450°F, then reduce the heat to 350°F and bake for 25 to 30 minutes longer, until the popovers are puffed and golden. Serve immediately.

Makes 8 popovers, serving 4.

Squash Crescents

Dinner rolls as golden as the sun.

2½ teaspoons active dry yeast
1 cup lukewarm water
¾ cup lukewarm milk
4 tablespoons unsalted butter, softened
1 egg, at room temperature, lightly beaten
1 cup mashed cooked winter squash (from 1¼ pounds squash; see Notes)
¼ cup firmly packed light brown sugar
1 teaspoon salt
5 to 5½ cups unbleached white flour

Proof the yeast in ¼ cup of the lukewarm water for 10 minutes, until bubbly. Stir in the remaining water, the milk, butter, egg, squash, sugar, salt, and enough flour to make a soft, somewhat sticky dough. Turn the dough out onto a floured surface and knead until smooth and elastic, about 10 minutes. Place it in a lightly greased bowl and turn to grease the top. Cover with plastic wrap and leave to rise until doubled in bulk, 1½ to 2 hours.

Punch down the dough and shape it into two balls. Roll out each ball into a 12-inch circle. With a sharp knife cut each circle into twelve triangles. Starting with the wide end, roll each triangle up toward the point. Place the rolls, point side down, on two lightly greased baking sheets. Cover and leave to rise for 30 minutes.

Preheat the oven to 375°F. Bake the rolls for 20 minutes, until golden. Transfer to racks to cool.

Makes 2 dozen crescents.

NOTES: To prepare the squash, cut it in half lengthwise and scoop out the seeds. Place cut side down in a baking dish. Pour ½ inch of boiling water around the squash and bake at 375°F for 30 minutes. Scoop out the cooked flesh and allow it to cool before using.

If you don't have time to shape crescents, simply divide the dough into twenty-four balls and place them in greased muffin tins. Bake as directed above.

Sour Rye Bread

Hearty wintertime meals require a hearty bread, and this sour rye adds a flavorful counterpoint to vegetable soups and stews, as well as making an excellent sandwich bread. The first time you bake these loaves, you'll have to make a starter, but it keeps well in the refrigerator, ready for each subsequent baking.

Starter

- ½ pound russet potatoes
- 3 to 3¼ cups water
- 1 tablespoon sugar
- ½ cup bread flour or unbleached white flour
- ½ cup rye flour

Bread Dough

- 1½ teaspoons active dry yeast
- 2¼ cups lukewarm water
- 1 teaspoon sugar
- ½ cup starter (see Note)
- 2 teaspoons salt
- 2 tablespoons molasses
- 2 tablespoons unsalted melted butter
- 2 cups rye meal
- 3 cups rye flour
- 3 cups (approximately) bread flour or unbleached white flour

- 1 teaspoon whole coriander seed
- Cold water
- Cornmeal for dusting

A week before you plan to bake the bread, boil the potatoes, covered, in 3 cups of water until tender, 25 to 35 minutes. Reserve the potato water. Peel and mash the potatoes, then stir in the reserved potato water, the sugar, and the flours, beating well. You should have a somewhat loose batter; add up to ¼ cup more water, if necessary. Cover the bowl and leave at room temperature for a week, stirring once a day. The starter will begin to ferment and give off a sour smell.

When you are ready to make the bread, proof the yeast in ¼ cup of the lukewarm water with the sugar until bubbly, about 10 minutes. Stir in the starter. Add the remaining 2 cups water, the salt, molasses, butter, and rye meal. Beat in the rye flour, then gradually beat in enough bread flour to make a stiff dough.

Knead the dough on a floured surface for 10 to 15 minutes, until it is smooth and elastic. (This stiff dough takes some work at first, but it will eventually yield.) Place the dough in a large greased bowl and turn to grease the top. Cover and leave to rise until doubled in bulk, about 2 hours. Punch down the dough and leave to rise for 1 hour more.

Divide the dough in half. Shape each half into a round and place on a baking sheet that has been sprinkled with cornmeal. Cover the loaves and leave to rise for 35 to 40 minutes.

Preheat the oven to 400°F. Crush the coriander seed with a mallet or the side of a heavy knife blade. Brush the loaves with cold water and sprinkle with the crushed seeds. Bake at 400°F for 15 minutes, then reduce the heat to 375°F and bake for 20 to 25 minutes longer, until the loaves sound hollow when tapped. Cool on racks.

Makes 2 loaves.

NOTE: Transfer the remaining starter to a covered jar and store it in the refrigerator, once a week adding a little flour and water. When you are ready to bake bread again, bring ½ cup of the starter to room temperature and proceed as directed above. This starter can also be used in other breads.

Georgian Cheese Bread *(Khachapuri)*

Asignature dish of the Republic of Georgia, *khachapuri* is eaten in many different ways—as a yeast bread or flaky pastry, as a turnover or an open boat with a near-liquid filling. In this version, a tender yeast dough is pleated around a savory filling of cheese subtly flavored with garlic. The ends of the dough are twisted into a topknot to make a golden loaf that looks gorgeous on a buffet table.

- ¾ cup milk
- 2½ teaspoons active dry yeast
- ½ teaspoon honey
- 6 tablespoons unsalted butter, at room temperature, plus
    - 1 tablespoon melted unsalted butter
- 1¾ teaspoons salt
- 2 cups unbleached white flour
- ½ pound farmer cheese
- 1 pound Muenster cheese, grated
- 3 eggs, lightly beaten
- 1 garlic clove, put through a garlic press

Heat the milk to lukewarm. Dissolve the yeast and honey in ¼ cup of the milk. Set aside to proof for 10 minutes, then stir in the remaining milk. Add the 6 tablespoons butter, 1½ teaspoons of the salt, and the flour, mixing well.

Turn the dough out onto a floured surface and knead until smooth and elastic, about 10 minutes. Place in a greased bowl, turning the dough to grease the top. Cover and leave to rise in a warm place until doubled in bulk, 1½ to 2 hours.

To prepare the filling, cream the farmer cheese in a medium bowl. Stir in the grated Muenster until well blended, then add the eggs and the remaining ¼ teaspoon salt. Push the garlic clove through a garlic press into the mixture and beat until smooth and light. Set aside.

When the dough has doubled in bulk, punch it down and then let it rise again until doubled, about 45 minutes. Punch down and divide into three equal pieces.

Grease three 8-inch cake or pie pans. On a floured surface, roll out each piece of dough into a circle about 12 inches in diameter. Center a round of dough in each pan.

Divide the cheese mixture into three equal parts. Place one third of the filling on each circle of dough, mounding it in the center. Then begin folding the edges of the dough in toward the center, moving in a clockwise direction, allowing each fold of dough to overlap the previous one, until the cheese mixture is completely enclosed in the pleated dough. Grasp the excess dough in the center of the bread and twist it into a topknot to seal.

Preheat the oven to 375°F.

Let the breads stand for 10 minutes, then brush with the melted butter. Bake for about 45 minutes, or until browned. Slip the *khachapuri* out of the pans and serve hot or at room temperature.

Makes 3 loaves, serving 8 to 12.

NOTE: For hors d'oeuvres, the dough may be shaped into several dozen miniature loaves, using 1 tablespoon of filling each. Place the loaves on lightly greased cookie sheets. These miniature *khachapuri* will take only 12 to 15 minutes to bake.

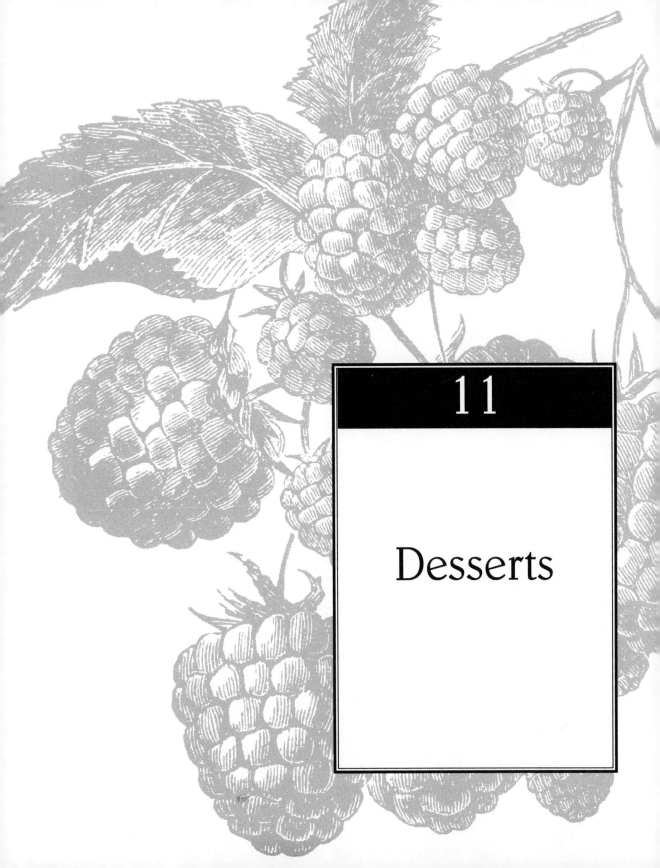

11

Desserts

If summer desserts are light and airy, then winter sweets are more complex. Fruits still define the season, only now they no longer stand alone, but in intricate combination with other ingredients: pears simmered in wine, apples baked with cider. Winter also means spices, as cinnamon, ginger, and cloves fill the air with wonderful fragrance. Happily, we work hard in cold weather, burning extra calories to stay warm, so an occasional rich dessert is not amiss.

Baked Apples with Cider

Poached Pears with Sabayon Sauce

Glazed Chestnuts with Oranges

Cranberry Apple Pie

Upside-Down Apple Tart *(La Tarte des Demoiselles Tatin)*

Gingerbread with Hot Orange Sauce

Lemon Marmalade Cake

Bread Pudding with Custard Sauce

Apricot Diamonds

Old-Fashioned Molasses Cookies

Russian Lace

Sugar-on-Snow

Snow Ice Cream

SEE ALSO:

Countess Tolstoy's Hot Apple Compote (page 229)

Orange Rice Pudding (page 230)

Sugarplums (page 295)

Swedish Gingersnaps *(Pepparkakor)* (page 292)

Baked Apples with Cider

Here is my favorite way to bake apples—adding cider at the last minute intensifies their luscious flavor. In *Visions of Sugarplums* Mimi Sheraton describes a similar dessert that originated in Tuscany, where the apples were baked with red wine. To my mind, this is the ultimate dessert for a cold evening.

Dough

1   cup all-purpose flour
2   tablespoons sugar
    Pinch of salt
4   tablespoons cold unsalted butter, in pieces
1   egg yolk
3   to 4 tablespoons ice water

Filling

4   large baking apples
4   tablespoons unsalted butter
4   tablespoons light brown sugar
1   teaspoon ground cinnamon
1   teaspoon grated lemon rind
¼   cup lemon marmalade (not rough-cut)
2   tablespoons golden raisins
2   cups Mulled Cider (page 20)

    Heavy cream (optional)

To make the dough, place the flour, sugar, and salt in the bowl of a food processor fitted with the metal blade. Add the butter and pulse until the mixture resembles fine meal. Add the egg yolk and water, pulsing only until the dough begins to pull away from the side of the bowl. Wrap in wax paper and chill for 1 hour.

Preheat the oven to 425°F. Lightly grease a 2-quart soufflé dish.

Core, but do not peel, the apples, making a generous hollow in each one.

In a small bowl cream the butter and sugar. Stir in the cinnamon, lemon rind, marmalade, and raisins. Fill the apples with this mixture, mounding any extra on top. Place the apples in the prepared dish.

On a floured surface roll out the dough into an 8-inch round. Carefully drape it over the apples so that it conforms to their shapes. Place the dish in the oven and bake for 10 minutes, then reduce the heat to 350°F and continue baking for 20 to 30 minutes, until the crust is golden.

Meanwhile, heat the cider and keep it warm.

When the apples are done, cut the crust around each one to separate them. Carefully lift out the apples and place each with a piece of crust in a shallow soup bowl. Pour ½ cup hot cider around each apple. Serve plain or drizzled with heavy cream.

Serves 4.

Poached Pears with Sabayon Sauce

This fabulous dessert may serve four—or one, if that one happens to be my husband left alone in the house on a snowy afternoon.

Syrup

    3 cups water
    1 cup dry red wine
    1 cup sugar
    2 tablespoons freshly squeezed lemon juice
  Two 3-inch cinnamon sticks
    2 whole cloves

    4 Bosc pears
      Juice of ½ lemon
      Sabayon Sauce (recipe follows)

First, make the syrup. Place all of the ingredients for the syrup in a large saucepan. Bring to a boil and simmer, covered, for 15 minutes.

While the syrup is simmering, prepare the pears. Fill a bowl large enough to hold the pears with cold water to cover and add the juice of ½ lemon. Peel the pears, leaving them whole and with stems intact. Core them from the bottom. Drop the pears as they are peeled into the lemon water to prevent darkening.

When the syrup is ready, remove the pears from the lemon water and carefully lower them into it. Simmer them, covered, until tender, 30 to 45 minutes, depending on their size.

Place the cooked pears upright on individual plates and serve warm, surrounded by the sabayon sauce.

Serves 4.

Sabayon Sauce

3 egg yolks
6 tablespoons sugar
    Pinch of salt
¼ cup brandy
½ cup heavy cream

Beat the egg yolks with the sugar until thick and lemon-colored. Transfer to a double boiler and heat over simmering water for 6 minutes, until thickened. Beat in the salt and brandy and allow the mixture to cool. Whip the cream until it forms soft peaks and fold into the brandy sauce.

Glazed Chestnuts with Oranges

Oranges provide beautifully contrasting flavor and texture to the rich sweetness of the chestnuts. This festive dessert may be assembled several hours in advance.

1 pound fresh chestnuts
2 cups water
2¼ cups granulated sugar
½ vanilla bean
1 tablespoon grated orange rind
6 navel oranges
3 tablespoons confectioners' sugar

Prepare the chestnuts by cutting a deep X on the flat side of each nut with a sharp knife. Place the nuts in a large pot of boiling water and cook for 10 minutes. Remove the pan from the heat. With a slotted spoon take a few chestnuts at a time from the water and peel them, removing both the outer husk and the fine inner peel. Try to keep them whole.

In a medium saucepan heat the water and granulated sugar over medium heat, stirring until the sugar dissolves. Add the vanilla bean and bring to a boil, then simmer for 5 minutes. Add the peeled chestnuts and boil gently until they are tender, about 15 minutes. Turn off the heat and leave the chestnuts to cool in the syrup while preparing the oranges.

Grate 1 tablespoon of orange peel and set aside.

With a sharp knife remove the peel and all of the white pith from the oranges. Cut the peeled oranges into ½-inch slices.

Arrange a layer of orange slices in a circle around the edge of a 10-inch round plate. Sprinkle with 1 tablespoon of the confectioners' sugar. Repeat with the remaining oranges and sugar, making three tiers.

With a slotted spoon remove the chestnuts from the syrup and mound them in the center of the ring of oranges. Return the syrup to a boil and cook until thickened, then pour over the chestnuts.

Before serving, sprinkle the oranges with the reserved orange peel.

Serves 6 to 8.

Cranberry Apple Pie

Cranberry pie, often chockablock with raisins, is a New England standard. Sometimes it is prepared like a crisp, with a butter-rich topping and no bottom crust. I like to pair the cranberries with apples in a more traditional pie that is not too sweet. A lattice crust shows off the cranberries' brilliance and makes the pie especially beautiful.

Crust

    3 cups all-purpose flour
    1 teaspoon salt
    1 cup vegetable shortening
    8 to 9 tablespoons ice water

Filling

    2 cups fresh cranberries
    ½ cup sugar
    ¾ cup firmly packed light brown sugar
    3 tablespoons all-purpose flour

Dash of salt
½ teaspoon ground cinnamon
½ teaspoon grated lemon rind
¼ cup pure maple syrup
2 tablespoons water
4 cups thinly sliced peeled apples
1 tablespoon unsalted butter (optional)

To make the crust, in a medium bowl mix together the flour and salt. Cut in the shortening until the mixture resembles coarse meal. Add just enough water for the dough to hold together, being careful not to overmix. Divide the dough in half. Roll out one piece of dough on a floured surface to a round about 11 inches in diameter. Carefully lift the dough into a 9-inch pie plate.

Preheat the oven to 400°F.

Mix together the cranberries, sugars, flour, salt, cinnamon, lemon rind, maple syrup, and water in a large saucepan. Stir the mixture over medium heat until the berries burst, 5 to 8 minutes. Stir in the apples, then turn the mixture into the unbaked piecrust. Dot with butter, if desired.

Roll out the remaining piece of dough into a round about 11 inches in diameter. With a pastry wheel cut strips to make a lattice crust, or place the whole round over the filling to make a full crust. Seal and crimp the edges.

Bake the pie for 45 minutes, until nicely browned.

Makes one 9-inch pie.

Upside-Down Apple Tart
(La Tarte des Demoiselles Tatin)

There is something magical about flipping baked desserts upside down to reveal the hidden patterns of their ingredients. *La Tarte des Demoiselles Tatin* looks spectacular turned out onto a plate, and it tastes every bit as good as it looks. This dessert is a cold-weather favorite at our house.

Crust
    1 cup all-purpose flour
    2 tablespoons sugar
       Pinch of salt
    4 tablespoons cold unsalted butter, in bits
    1 egg yolk
    3 to 4 tablespoons ice water

Filling
    5 to 6 Granny Smith apples (about 2 pounds)
    6 tablespoons unsalted butter
    ½ cup sugar
    3 tablespoons light brown sugar

To make the crust, in a medium bowl mix together the flour, sugar, and salt. Cut in the butter until the mixture resembles coarse meal. Add the egg yolk and just enough water for the dough to hold together. Do not over-mix. Form the dough into a ball, wrap in wax paper, and refrigerate for at least 1 hour.

Peel, core, and thinly slice the apples.

Place 4 tablespoons of the butter and the granulated sugar in a 10-inch Pyrex pie plate. Place a flame-tamer on a stove burner and carefully heat the mixture, stirring periodically, until the sugar caramelizes and turns golden brown. This could take as long as twenty minutes. The sugar has to be stirred frequently toward the end and watched closely to make sure that it doesn't burn. Remove the plate from the heat.

Arrange the apple slices in concentric rings over the caramelized sugar, mounding them slightly toward the center. As you layer the apples, dot them with the remaining 2 tablespoons butter and sprinkle with the brown sugar.

Preheat the oven to 450°F.

Remove the dough from the refrigerator and roll out on a floured surface to a circle 11 inches in diameter. Place the crust over the apples; do not seal the edges.

Bake the tart for 10 minutes at 450°F, then reduce the heat to 375°F and bake for 35 to 40 minutes more, until the crust is golden. Cool the tart on a rack for 10 minutes. Place a serving plate over the tart and invert it onto the plate to reveal the caramelized apples.

Serve warm or at room temperature.

Serves 8.

Gingerbread with Hot Orange Sauce

I love gingerbread in all of its forms—crisp snaps, chewy bars, and traditional English cake. This recipe makes a cakelike gingerbread that is extremely moist and tender. When served with hot orange sauce, it is pure bliss.

1	egg
6	tablespoons light brown sugar
½	cup dark molasses
6	tablespoons unsalted butter, melted
1	teaspoon ground ginger
¾	teaspoon ground cinnamon
¼	teaspoon ground cloves
¼	teaspoon grated nutmeg
	Pinch of salt
1	teaspoon baking soda
¼	teaspoon baking powder
1	cup all-purpose flour
½	cup boiling water
	Hot Orange Sauce (optional; recipe follows)

Preheat the oven to 350°F. Grease an 8-inch-square pan.

Beat the egg into the brown sugar in a medium bowl. Stir in the molasses, melted butter, and spices, mixing well, then add the salt, baking soda, baking powder, and flour. Beat in the boiling water. The batter will be loose. Pour the batter into the prepared pan and bake for 30 minutes, or until a cake tester inserted in the center comes out dry. Allow to cool before cutting into squares. Serve plain or with hot orange sauce.

Serves 6 to 8.

Hot Orange Sauce

½ cup sugar
¼ cup firmly packed light brown sugar
4 teaspoons cornstarch
½ cup freshly squeezed orange juice
2 tablespoons freshly squeezed lemon juice
1 teaspoon grated orange rind
  Pinch of salt
2 tablespoons unsalted butter
1 tablespoon light corn syrup
¾ cup water

Mix the sugars with the cornstarch in a medium saucepan. Gradually add the orange and lemon juices, stirring vigorously to avoid lumps. Stir in the orange rind, salt, butter, corn syrup, and water. Bring to a boil over medium heat and cook until the sauce thickens, 5 to 8 minutes. Serve hot.

Lemon Marmalade Cake

Beautifully glazed with a marmalade topping, this home-style cake is served warm from the oven. It makes a good dessert for unexpected guests, since it can be put together in minutes from ingredients that are generally on hand.

¾ cup lemon marmalade (not rough-cut)
4 tablespoons unsalted butter, softened
⅔ cup sugar
2 eggs
1 teaspoon grated lemon peel
¼ teaspoon pure lemon extract
1 cup all-purpose flour
1½ teaspoons baking powder
¼ teaspoon salt
½ teaspoon ground cinnamon
½ cup milk

Preheat the oven to 350°F. Lightly grease the sides of a 1-quart soufflé dish. Spread the marmalade over the bottom of the dish.

In a medium bowl cream the butter and sugar until light and fluffy, then beat in the eggs, one at a time. Stir in the lemon peel and extract.

Mix the dry ingredients together, then add them to the batter alternately with the milk. Pour the batter into the prepared dish (it will be loose).

Bake the cake for 40 to 45 minutes, until a cake tester inserted in the center comes out clean. Leave the cake to cool in the dish for 10 minutes, then invert it onto a plate and serve warm.

Serves 8.

VARIATION: Orange marmalade may be substituted for the lemon peel, in which case use almond extract instead of lemon extract.

Bread Pudding with Custard Sauce

lthough bread pudding originated as a frugal measure—a way to use up leftover bread—in our era it has become an indulgence. Bread puddings appear in all sorts of flavors and textures. This one is light and cinnamony, and so easy to make that it's already part of my five-year-old's repertoire. The pudding is delicious plain, but if you feel like pampering yourself, it's even better with custard sauce.

> 2 cups cut-up day-old French bread cubes (in 1-inch pieces)
> 2 tablespoons unsalted butter, melted
> 2¼ cups milk
> 3 eggs, lightly beaten
> ½ cup firmly packed light brown sugar
> ½ teaspoon ground cinnamon
> 1 teaspoon pure vanilla extract
> ¼ teaspoon salt
> ⅓ to ½ cup raisins
> Custard Sauce (optional; recipe follows)

Preheat the oven to 350°F. Heat a kettle of water. Lightly grease a 1½-quart soufflé dish.

Place the bread cubes in the prepared dish and drizzle them with the butter. Mix together the remaining ingredients except the sauce, and pour over the bread.

Place the dish in a pan and pour in boiling water to come 1 inch up the sides of the dish. Bake the pudding for 50 to 60 minutes, until firm. Serve warm, with custard sauce, if desired.

Serves 4.

Custard Sauce

1½ cups milk
½ vanilla bean, split lengthwise
4 egg yolks
½ cup sugar

Pour the milk into a medium saucepan. With a sharp knife scrape the seeds from the vanilla bean into the milk. Drop the bean into the milk and heat to boiling.

Meanwhile, beat the yolks with the sugar until light and fluffy. When the milk comes to a boil, remove the vanilla bean. Slowly pour the hot milk into the egg yolks, whisking constantly. Return the mixture to the pan and cook over low heat for 3 to 5 minutes, until the custard coats the back of a spoon. Pour through a strainer into a pitcher or serving bowl. Serve warm or chilled.

Apricot Diamonds

These rich butter cookies are similar to German *Spitzbuben,* but much less time-consuming to make. Instead of being rolled out, the dough is simply pressed into a baking dish, then topped with jam and a second layer of dough. The cookies are perfect for late-afternoon coffee or tea.

- 1 cup (2 sticks) unsalted butter
- 1 cup sugar
- 1 teaspoon pure vanilla extract
- 2 egg yolks
- 2 cups all-purpose flour
- 1 cup thick apricot jam

Preheat the oven to 375°F. Grease a 9 x 13-inch pan.

Cream the butter and sugar, then beat in the vanilla and egg yolks. Stir in the flour to make a soft, slightly sticky dough.

With floured hands pat about two thirds of the dough onto the bottom of the baking pan. Spread the jam evenly over the dough. Break off small bits of the remaining dough, flatten them between your palms, and arrange them over the jam so that it is almost entirely covered (don't worry if a little peeks through—the dough will spread as it bakes).

Bake for 30 minutes, or until golden. Cool in the pan, then cut into diamonds with a sharp knife.

Makes about 3 dozen cookies.

Old-Fashioned Molasses Cookies

These all-American cookie-jar treats are nice and chewy. Unlike most molasses cookies, this dough can be quickly mixed and dropped onto a baking sheet, a boon when you're craving something sweet.

½ cup (1 stick) unsalted butter
½ cup firmly packed light brown sugar
1 egg
¾ cup molasses
3 cups all-purpose flour
1 teaspoon baking soda
½ teaspoon salt
1½ teaspoons ground ginger
1 teaspoon ground cinnamon
½ cup buttermilk
3 tablespoons sugar

Preheat the oven to 375°F.

In a medium bowl cream the butter and brown sugar. Beat in the egg, then the molasses.

In a separate bowl, mix together the flour, soda, salt, ginger, and cinnamon.

Add one third of the dry ingredients to the molasses mixture, then beat in half of the buttermilk. Alternate with the remaining dry ingredients and buttermilk, mixing well after each addition.

Drop heaping tablespoonfuls of the batter about 2 inches apart onto three lightly greased baking sheets.

Place the 3 tablespoons of sugar in a small bowl. Dip a flat-bottomed glass in cold water, then into the sugar. Flatten the cookies with the glass, dipping it into sugar before pressing down on each cookie. Sprinkle any extra sugar over the cookies.

Bake for 10 to 12 minutes, until golden. Cool on a rack.

Makes about 3 dozen cookies.

Russian Lace

The Russians love snow; they also adore chocolate. Put the two together and you get Russian lace, a charming yet elegant candy that is great fun to make. In some recipes, chocolate enrobes a filling of crisp, caramelized sugar. My version is simpler and safer, and allows the chocolate to stand unabashedly on its own.

8 ounces bittersweet or semisweet chocolate

Melt the chocolate in the top part of a double boiler over hot water. Working quickly, scrape the chocolate into a pastry tube that has been fitted with a small piping tip. Take the pastry tube outside and pipe the chocolate directly onto clean snow in a decorative pattern, making a lacy design with overlapping squiggles and swirls. The chocolate will harden in just a few minutes. Carefully lift the lace from the snow with a spatula and place it on a platter. Break off pieces of chocolate to serve.

Serves 6 to 8.

Sugar-on-Snow

Sugar-on-snow is a seasonal New England treat. Traditionally served outdoors at sugaring-off parties, this simple confection can also be enjoyed in the warmth of the kitchen. It is a favorite with children and makes a good cooking project for a snowy afternoon. New Englanders often serve sugar-on-snow with sour pickles and plain raised doughnuts to balance the sweetness of the candy and provide contrasting textures.

1   **cup pure maple syrup**
    Fresh snow

Bring the syrup to a boil in a small pan and cook it over medium heat until a candy thermometer registers 232°F. Meanwhile, fill a large, wide-brimmed bowl with fresh snow, packing it down. When the syrup is ready, pour it by tablespoonfuls onto the packed snow. The syrup will harden into a soft, chewy candy like taffy. Lift the candy from the snow with a fork and enjoy it immediately.

Serves 8.

NOTE: If no fresh snow is on the ground, the hot syrup may also be poured onto a bowl of firmly packed crushed ice.

VARIATION: If fresh snow is available, you need not boil the maple syrup to enjoy it. Simply pour bottled syrup over a bowl of snow and eat it like syrup over ice cream.

Snow Ice Cream

This lush dessert takes only minutes to prepare and it provides good entertainment during a snowfall.

   1 cup heavy cream
One 10-ounce package frozen raspberries or strawberries
       in heavy syrup, thawed
   1 quart fresh snow

In a large bowl whip the cream until stiff, then fold in the thawed berries and syrup. Working quickly, fold in the snow. Serve immediately for a soft confection, or chill briefly in the freezer for an ice-cream-like dessert.

    Serves 4.

Celebrations of Light

OUR ANCESTORS STUDIED THE SKIES, seeing portents and omens in the changing celestial patterns. Twice a year, in winter and summer, the sun seemed to stand still in the sky, and they called this period of apparent inertia *solstice*. The winter solstice, especially, was a time of superstition, prompted by long, dark nights and days of weak sunlight that made our forebears uneasy; so they devised all sorts of magic rituals to encourage the sun to return to full strength. As a symbol of the sun, fire could keep the evil spirits of darkness at bay. Thus the ancient Celts lit great fires to banish the dark, while Greeks and Romans practiced ritual libations at their domestic hearths.

At the center of the home, the hearth and its fire represented the promise of sunshine and agricultural prosperity. The task of keeping the home fires burning was not taken lightly, and the cult of Vesta, the goddess of the hearth, was one of the most important and mysterious in ancient Rome. Elsewhere, throughout the world and through the centuries, the magic of fire and the light it provides have continued to offer symbolic hope in the season of darkness. Even in modern times, when we pride ourselves on having shed the superstitions of the past, we still brighten the winter with images of fire and light (candles and Christmas trees), subconsciously responding as our ancestors did to the weakness of the sun in the sky.

Perhaps in our need for brightness and light, in our search for winter cheer, we are still pagan at heart. Though our holidays are steeped in religious tradition, they nevertheless reflect a more visceral response to nature as we invoke the powers of light. Such kinship with the past should not surprise us, as seasonal rituals existed long before calendars regulated time. Besides, coincidences with the past can help us feel connected to a larger, more permanent world. Christmas offers a good example.

According to the Julian calendar, on which our present calendar is based, the winter solstice falls on December 25. The solstice was also the time for worshiping Mithras, the ancient Indo-Iranian god of light and truth. Around A.D. 270, under the Roman emperor Aurelian, this day was named the official birthday of the Imperial divinity *sol invictus,* the Invincible Sun that never lost its strength. Within the next century, as Christianity took hold, the Church fathers wisely fitted the ancient patterns of worship into an ecclesiastic framework instead of suppressing them entirely. Thus it made sense to fix the date of Christ's birth on December 25, already a sacred day. When the Christ Child was presented at the Temple forty days after his birth, St. Simeon declared him the "light of the world," and in this way a new bearer of light and truth came to replace the old. The festivities heralding Christ's birth also corresponded nicely with what had been the traditional Roman season of merriment between the rowdy Saturnalia of mid-December and the Kalends, or first days, of January.

Winter celebrations throughout the world reveal a luminescent focus. The Jewish holiday of Hanukkah is also known as the Festival of Lights. Although scholars dispute the origins of this name, the basic story of Hanukkah is well established. Nearly two hundred years before the birth of Christ, the Syrian king Antiochus ruled in Jerusalem. For three years he forbade the Jews to worship in their Temple, until Judah Maccabee and his ragtag army came down from the mountains and defeated the Syrians. The Maccabees set out to rededicate the Temple, but were able to find only one flask of oil—enough to keep the lamp lit for a single day. Miraculously, though, the oil burned for eight days. Today Jews celebrate Hanukkah by lighting an eight-branched candelabrum as a reminder of the wondrous burning oil. But many scholars believe that the real origins of the Hanukkah lights lie in older, pagan ceremonies, the details of which have been lost. Just as Christmas became fixed at the winter solstice, so the Jewish holiday commemorating the rededication of the Temple appropriated older winter solstice celebrations in praise of fire and light.

With time, what began as a nature festival took on religious meaning, and new customs accrued. For Jews of Eastern European ancestry, *latkes,* or potato pancakes, are traditional Hanukkah fare, since the oil they are fried in recalls the miracle in the Temple. A lavish hand with oil is also seen in other Hanukkah foods, such as fried noodles and *sufganiyot,* jelly doughnuts. Older traditions, however, called for pancakes made with cheese. Cheese dishes were once the food of choice for the holiday, in honor of Judith, a Maccabee daughter, who is said to have served salty cheese to the Syrian commander Holofernes. Having plied Holofernes with wine to assuage his great thirst, Judith promptly beheaded him, thereby helping to save the Temple. Although potato pancakes lack such a colorful history, the absence of gore likely makes them more palatable to contemporary diners.

Jews celebrate the new year at harvest time, in September, but the early Romans observed it on March 1, when nature began to stir after a winter's rest. By the second century B.C., however, civic considerations usurped natural cycles, and January 1—the day when Roman consuls took office—became the fixed date of the new year in Western culture. Nevertheless, peasants throughout the world persisted for many centuries in adhering to seasonal rhythms, basing their celebrations on the sun and its position in the sky.

The Celts celebrated their new year in early November by lighting huge bonfires, then rolling flaming wheels down hillsides. For the Vikings, the feast of *Joulu* or *Jol* proclaimed the return of the sun, even as it reflected a primitive fear of the dark. Light made the world less forbidding, and fire could banish the spirits of the dead believed to haunt the living during Yule. Vestiges of these fires can be seen in Scandinavia today, as thousands of lights in windows and storefronts magically transform the otherwise bleak surroundings into a fairyland—helped, too, by the comforting smells of gingerbread and mulled wine in the air.

December 13 was another significant day in various civil and ecclesiastic calendars. According to some calculations, the winter solstice fell on this day, which the Christian Church reckoned as St. Lucy's Day. Lucy's name derives from the Latin *lux* or *lucis,* for "light," and with the homage paid the saint, ancient solstice practices involving light took on new religious meaning. Sicilians used to light bonfires and stream through the countryside in torchlight processions. In her book on Italian holidays and foodways, Carol Field describes Santa Lucia (St. Lucy) celebrations in Realmonte, where logs were piled high in front of every house and then kindled to make the town appear engulfed in flames. These fires were intended to encourage the sun to return to full power at its moment of greatest weakness.

Although Lucy hailed from Sicily, her day is most avidly celebrated in Sweden, where it is customary to crown a bride for *Lusse* on December 13. Since the second decade of this century public competitions, not unlike beauty pageants, have been held to choose the loveliest brides. Legend has it that Lucy was martyred for renouncing carnal love. Rather than succumb to a suitor's advances after he had admired her eyes, she resolutely plucked them out and sent them to him on a platter. The Swedes tell a gentler story of Lucy, or Lucia as she is known in that country: as a young girl, she refused to bring her new husband a dowry, preferring instead to distribute her wealth to the poor. The husband proclaimed her a witch and had her burned at the stake, at which time a brilliant blaze illuminated the countryside for miles around. In the centuries since her death, Lucy has appeared to needy people throughout Europe, always providing succor. She is said to have showed up quite miraculously during a famine in Sweden to offer food to the hungry, her head encircled in light. Religious images of Lucy in Italy depict her carrying her eyes on a plate, much as Salome is typically shown bearing the head of John the Baptist, but in Sweden Lucy's image is literally all sweetness and light. Modern Lucys (Lucias), dressed in long white gowns with crowns of candles in their hair, carry trays of *lussekatter*, sweet breads baked in the shape of cats, or sometimes hearts and wreaths. The girls are often accompanied by *Stjärngossar*, Star Boys who wear peaked silver hats festooned with moons and stars. The Lucia bride is traditionally the oldest daughter in the family. To ensure a propitious year, before dawn on the morning of the thirteenth she brings her parents a breakfast tray of coffee, *pepparkakor* (crisp gingerbread), and *lussekatter*, golden as the sun from the butter and saffron kneaded into the dough. In some communities, a whole retinue of Lucias, candles ablaze, walks in procession, singing songs.

St. Lucy's Day falls midway in the holiday season, which in most

Western countries begins on the fourth Sunday before Christmas when the first Advent candles are lit. This ritual assures continual light as the days decline; it also marks the customary start of the holiday baking. In England, "Stir-up Sunday" is the day for making the Christmas pudding. The whole family participates in the task, each making a wish as he or she stirs. The pudding makers must take care to stir the batter clockwise, following the presumed course of the sun, for trouble will undoubtedly befall anyone who stirs "widdershins," in the wrong direction. Several of the most well-loved Christmas specialties imitate nature in winter. Russian *khvorost* ("twigs"), Swedish *klenäter,* and Italian *pan di Spagna* all resemble piles of dry twigs or logs covered with a fresh dusting of snow. Many holiday dishes share honey as a common ingredient, to ensure the sweetness of the coming year. In Alicante, Spain, a special Christmas nougat, *turrón,* is made from honey, toasted almonds, sugar, and egg whites, while in nearby Jijona, the confection is flavored with pine nuts and ground coriander. Germans prepare *Lebkuchen,* a medieval honey cake dense with spices. Slavs serve numerous versions of a wheat berry porridge that is sweetened with honey and dried fruits. A spoonful of the porridge is sometimes thrown up to the ceiling during the Christmas Eve feast; if it is sufficiently saturated with honey, the porridge will stick, boding well for the year ahead.

Because so many superstitions revolved around the turning of the new year, fortune-telling and divination reached a peak during the Christmas season. On Christmas Eve Swedes, Danes, and Norwegians still serve a sweetened, cinnamon-flavored rice pudding, in which an almond or other charm has been hidden. Whoever gets the serving with the almond is assured good luck for the year to come. This practice of baking a charm into pudding, bread, or cake is part of holiday-making throughout Europe and the Americas, where it most often occurs on Epiphany or Twelfth Night. Today, numerous charms are usually baked into a King's Cake to guarantee good luck for all; but in this process of equalization, the age-old sense of portent and trepidation has been lost. Other forms of augury relied on sources of fire or light. Signs of the future could be read in the ashes of the great yule log, as well as in the contorted shapes formed by molten lead or hot wax poured into a bucket of cold water. The shadow thrown on a wall by a burning piece of paper could reveal a young girl's fate, as could mirrors set up to reflect one another, with a lighted candle set before them.

Until recent times, most Christian cultures continued to believe in the prevalence of otherworldly spirits at Christmas. Although Scandinavia now welcomes its Christmas gnomes, and American children adore Santa's friendly elves, spirits were once seen as less benevolent. Because evil spirits roamed the world freely on Christmas Eve, Yuletide was considered the best time to banish troublesome demons from the hearth and safeguard the family. Every peasant culture developed special rituals. Norwegian families used to sleep on hay together for three nights at Christmas to ward off malicious trolls, while Spanish peasants would gather at midnight on New Year's Eve to swallow twelve grapes, one at each stroke of the clock, to guard against future trouble. Some rituals protected crops at Christmastime. In Greece, crumbs from the first slice of *Christopsomo,* or Christ's bread, a sweet loaf glazed with sugar and decorated with nuts, were sprinkled under trees in the belief that the bread's powerful symbolism would increase their yield. In Italy, the ground was fertilized with ashes from a yule log that had burned for twelve nights. The universally sure way to keep demons at bay was by lighting candles or a fire.

Perhaps because Russia entered modern times later than the rest of Europe, its inhabitants observed pagan holdovers in their holiday celebrations well into the twentieth century. Christmastide in Russia lasted for an entire week, offering a respite from daily cares. Much like our Halloween, Christmas was a time of mischief and pranks, and anyone who failed to take proper care of his homestead became fair game for village pranksters, who might pile untended firewood on end to block a road, or throw water on a cottage gate to freeze it shut if a bucket had been left at the well. The most widespread pastime was mummery, which afforded a release— however brief—from public morality. Men dressed up as women, women as men. The mummers acted reckless in their disguise. Sporting coarse hair fashioned from hemp, and huge teeth cut from turnips, they raucously made their way through the villages. Often they donned shaggy furs to resemble bears, or horns to imitate devils, blackening their faces with soot or making them red with beet juice. Sometimes they covered their faces with scary animal masks crafted of birch bark, or stuck a large beet on their noses in mockery of drunkenness. This sort of mimetic behavior dates as far back as Paleolithic times, when hunters would dress in the skins, antlers, or feathers of the game they hoped to catch. In Russia, though, mummery retained its original superstitious meanings: by dressing up, the mummers could appropriate evil spirits for themselves, and thus drive them away. Rubbing soot onto their faces to represent the unclean spirits, they displayed the impurity literally outside of themselves. In this way the mummers could begin the new year free of devils and demons. Mummery was also part of a larger caroling tradition, the participants often carrying a large wooden Star of Bethlehem with a lighted candle in the center as they caroused through the streets. Reaching a house, they would stop to sing, dance, perform, and pretend to frighten small children. But as soon as their identities were discovered, the mummers had to remove their masks. Then, to compensate for their lost disguise, they received holiday treats, often small cakes in the same animal shapes their costumes imitated.

Caroling for treats was widespread throughout Europe, as were various other revelries. In medieval England, the Catholic Church actually condoned such lively entertainments as dancing, wrestling, and cockfighting, all of which took place in churchyards. But the sixteenth-century Reformation banned this merrymaking, and a period of tension between the popular need for release and official disapproval ensued. The Puritans outlawed Christmas altogether and even carried this mean spirit across the sea to America, where in Plymouth colony anyone caught feasting on Christmas Day was fined. Happily for future generations, the Restoration returned a semblance of gaiety to the Christmas season, but the holiday never quite regained its original, unrestrained vigor. Christmas as we celebrate it today derives largely from the practices made popular by Queen Victoria and her German-born husband, Albert, who set up a lavishly decorated tree, indulged in sugarplums, and invited carolers and dancers in for entertainment. Despite its relatively recent introduction into our lives, though, the Christmas tree aglow with lights also serves as a reminder of early forms of nature worship and of mankind's perennial passion for light.

Greens customarily have symbolized life during nature's dormancy, and branches of mistletoe, holly, and pine boughs complemented the Christmas tree, bringing further scents of the outdoors inside. In England, until the mid-nineteenth century, the Christmas decoration of choice was rosemary, because of its association with death and remembrance. At the Roman celebration of the Kalends of January, the goddess Strenia presided over gifts. Each year the Romans ceremoniously cut boughs from the plants at her grave to present as a new year's offering. These boughs, known as *strenae,* ultimately lent their name to the modern French *étrennes,* for the gifts exchanged at the new year, but originally they were intended to appease the spirit of plant life. Fire and light as the guiding metaphors of the winter season find expression in the second color of the season, red, represented by holly berries as well as by the robin's breast, harbinger of the sun. Red eventually found its way into American culture, too, in Rudolph the Reindeer's shiny nose.

For most European cultures, the yule log epitomized light during the Christmas season. In England, an entire bole or tree trunk was chosen well in advance of winter, then trimmed and laid on blocks to age. The ideal bole was one large enough to blaze almost continually from Christmas Eve until Candlemas (February 2). Most families, of course, had no access to such a large log; neither could they afford to buy one. But even a small log could yield a brand to set aside until Candlemas, when it would be ritually lit for the last time, extinguished, and then carefully stored for lighting the next season's log. This Yule log was believed to warm the spirits of the dead, but just as important the ritual of lighting ensured continuity and a sense of participation in an unbroken cycle of seasons. Newfoundlanders tried to keep their Yule logs burning until Twelfth Night, when they would ceremonially throw flaming chunks over their houses to protect them from fire in the coming year. The French burned their Yule log, the *Calendas,* from Christmas Eve until New Year's, the Roman Kalends. This log was preferably cut from a fruit tree to ensure the greatest luck and the most fruitful harvest. Old-time families from Provence carried the log three times around the kitchen before placing it on the hearth, then poured a glass of *vin cuit* over it to feed the ancestral spirits believed immanent in the fire. Once the log was lit, the family could sit down to Christmas Eve supper.

Yule logs were not limited to indoor fireplaces. In western England, a log called an "ashen faggot" was bound with withes or twigs and burned outside for public merriment. As each twig burned from the log, a new jug of hard cider was brought out for all to enjoy, leading to ever greater jollity and rowdiness. The brewing of alcoholic drinks at Christmas is a long-standing tradition, which likely originated in ritual drunkenness associated with sacrifice. No doubt the earliest brewed intoxicant was mead, with its main ingredient of honey promising fertility for the coming year. In *History of Food* Maguelonne Toussaint-Samat reveals another connection between intoxication and fire when she relates how the ancient Irish crowned their fallen kings in a vat of mead, then set their palaces on fire. Brewing is tamer today, but tipplers still enjoy their special sweet: heavy Yule beers that are heady with spices. Other inebriant beverages such as *glögg* (mulled wine) and eggnog contribute further to seasonal cheer.

Fire has found its way into all sorts of Christmas activities, some rather unlikely. "Snapdragon" was an amusing, if risky, game devised in the sixteenth century. Delicacies such as fruit were placed in a large bowl, then covered with lighted brandy. The players had to be extremely agile to dip their hands through the flames and snatch, or "snap," the treats without getting burned. Boys and girls alike played this game, but other, rowdier instances of playing with fire were reserved for men alone. In Westmoreland a torch-covered holly tree was paraded through town. At the end of the procession, the flaming tree was thrown to a waiting crowd of rivals who fought to gain possession of it. This sport recalls the Scottish New Year's eve celebrations (Hogmanay) when burning tar barrels were once carried through the streets. Onlookers vied to catch the flaming bits that fell from the barrels in the hope of protecting themselves from bad luck. At the far reaches of the villages the barrels were sent flying downhill, just as the Celts had set their burning wheels in motion so many centuries before. Old practices certainly die hard. If we are to believe popular anthropology, even U.S. Election Day bonfires (during the dark days of November) can be traced to this annual pagan event. And what would English plum pudding be without its wreath of flaming brandy?

Of all of the fiery customs, the one that has endured longest is the flaming wassail bowl. Wassailing is the age-old practice of wishing well, which gradually was carried over to Christmas celebrations. The word comes from *waes hael,* or "Be hale." Like other set formulas, *waes hael* demanded a particular response, in this case *Drinc hael* or "Drink and be well." The wassail bowl was filled with ale or cider and seasoned with nutmeg, then placed before a log fire. Apples were hung on strings over the bowl and roasted until the pulp fell in puffy heaps into the drink, giving the beverage its nickname of "Lamb's Wool." Originally wassailing was a sacred act designed to make the orchards fertile, most often carried out on the evening before Twelfth Day. The revelers lit fires as part of the wassailing ritual, and over time pagan and Christian symbolism became intertwined. Sometimes a ring of twelve fires was made to represent the twelve months of the year; at other times twelve small fires and one large one were lighted to signify Christ and the apostles.

Light was believed to increase the family's yield as well. In Brittany, before midnight mass on Christmas Eve, the family would gather around the hearth to share hot buckwheat crêpes, which they eagerly devoured after their day-long fast. The most stalwart family member, however, agreed to forgo immediate pleasure in order to stand watch outdoors and await the appearance of the first stars. When the ninth star appeared, he could finally come inside to join his family with the assurance that their wishes would come true. Many Breton families enjoyed a special *fouace en étoile,* a flat loaf formed into the shape of a star, in addition to the crêpes. *Le réveillon,* the Christmas Eve feast that breaks the Christmas fast, was highly ritualized in France and often involved the lighting of candles. Thirteen different desserts were served to recall Christ and the twelve apostles. Such delicacies as dried fruits, nougat, biscuits, puffy beignets, and *nougat noir* made with honey and almonds were washed down with the same *vin cuit* that had been poured on the Yule log.

Even in warm climates, where the winter nights are neither as long nor as dark as in the north, the use of fire is widespread at the solstice. Mexicans still enact *posadas,* processions depicting Mary and Joseph's search for a place to spend the night in Bethlethem. The processional route is illuminated with candles to help the pilgrims find their way. In the Southwest United States, *luminarias*—lighted candles inside paper bags—line sidewalks and streets to help light the way for the Christ Child. Like so many twinkling fairy lights, the *luminarias* have found their way into other regions of America. Grander in scale are the Christmas Eve bonfires set along the Mississippi River, which extend for twenty miles. Logs, sugarcanes, reeds, even old tires go up in flames, mimicking the old French tradition of *feux de joie* introduced to Louisiana by Marist priests. Louisianans have adapted this bonfire tradition to their own culture, however. Instead of partaking in *le réveillon* after midnight mass, they enjoy a spicy gumbo dinner.

Not surprisingly, the winter holiday season closes with a final image of light. February 2 is portentous in many cultures. According to the Christian church calendar, this is Candlemas, a feast honoring the purification of the Virgin Mary and the presentation of Christ at the Temple forty days after His birth. On this day the liturgical candles are blessed and inventoried to make sure enough remain for the rest of the winter. But like the other winter celebrations, Candlemas, too, has ancient roots. They can be traced to the major Celtic festival of Imbolc, which rejoiced in the appearance of snowdrops, the first flowers of spring. Folk customs mark February 2 in other ways. In the United States, on Groundhog Day, we eagerly await news of Punxsutawney Phil, whose shadow (or lack thereof) forecasts whether spring will be early or late, allowing us unwittingly to celebrate the return of the sun just as our forebears did. An old German method of weather forecasting was less whimsical. An onion was cut into twelve equal slices to make an "onion calendar." Each piece was then sprinkled with salt, and the wetness or dryness of the coming months could be predicted from the amount of moisture that appeared on each slice.

In all peasant cultures, life depended on a good harvest, but from year to year the quality of the harvest could not be assured. Food was often scarce. Thus people took it upon themselves to try to influence the reigning powers of the universe through incantations and rituals, most of which had to do with fertility and light. Even after Christianity was established, holiday celebrations continued to express jubilation at the rebirth of the sun. As Piero Camporesi points out in *The Magic Harvest,* this cosmic aspiration is reflected in the vertical shapes of many Christmas sweets. Just consider the pyramidal loaf of *pannetone* or the Swedish *julhög,* a soaring tower of baked goods topped with a bright red apple. The rhythms of the agricultural year allowed for indulgence during the winter season, when farmers could rest from tilling, sowing, and gathering. Excess was in fact encouraged: The very act of eating without measure symbolically guaranteed an abundant year. People countered their fear at nature's death with assertions of life, engaging in rituals and enjoying special foods that were not permitted at other times of the year. As they confronted their darkest fears in winter, people everywhere surrounded themselves with light. Bonfires, candles, and burning logs; wine ritually poured at the grapevine's root or cider spilled onto the apple tree; honey-soaked grain dishes and wassail bowls—all represent expressions of blessing and good cheer. Today these practices may seem quaint, or mainly of anthropological interest. But in our own quest for good health and harmony, we should not forget to indulge in the good life in winter. Let us regale ourselves and especially others, and thereby bring good fortune for the year to come.

Flaming Punch *(Krambambuli* or *Zhzhonka)*

Sugar Cone

Chickpea Fritters *(Panelle)*

Cheese Pennies

Potato Pancakes *(Latkes)*

Saffron Buns *(Lussekatter)*

Swedish Gingersnaps *(Pepparkakor)*

Danish Rice Pudding *(Ris à l'amande)*

Cherry Sauce

Sugarplums

Flaming Punch *(Krambambuli* or *Zhzhonka)*

The names of this flaming punch have always intrigued me. The Russian *zhzhonka,* from a verb meaning "to burn," makes onomatopoeic sense, with its prolonged *zh* mimicking the hiss of burning sugar. But *krambambuli* sounds like nonsense, or the Marx Brothers speaking a foreign language; so, even before tasting this delicious wine warmer, I set out to discover its origins. A cherry brandy from Danzig, *krambambuli* was quite popular among the smart set in eighteenth-century Germany. According to Uschi Fischer, an acquaintance from Bavaria, the name may derive from the dialect form *krampf*, which means "mixed up"; Uschi adds that the word sounds as though you're all mixed up from having drunk too much. This comic-sounding name also appealed to Gotthold Ephraim Lessing, who used it in his 1767 comedy *Minna von Barnhelm;* and a century later, *krambambuli* still figured prominently in German literature, although by then it referred to a mixed bowl of flaming wine and spirits. E.T.A. Hoffmann mentions flaming punch in many of his tales, while Marie von Ebner-Eschenbach wrote a famous story entitled "Krambambuli," the eponymous hero of which is a loyal dog named after the brandy his master enjoys.

I suspect that *krambambuli* became fashionable in Russia along with Hoffmann's stories, which were all the rage in the mid-nineteenth century. The Russians added exotic fruits such as pineapple or hothouse cherries to their punch to make it even more extravagant, but I prefer the unadorned German version offered here. Whether you call it *krambambuli* or *zhzhonka,* try this dramatic concoction at your next holiday party instead of plain champagne.

> 1 bottle (750 ml) dry white wine
> Rind of 1 orange, removed in a continuous spiral
> One 3-inch cinnamon stick
> 6 ounces sugar cubes, preferably Demerara, or 1 Sugar Cone (recipe follows; see Notes)
> 1 cup light rum
> ½ bottle (about 350 ml) dry champagne, at room temperature
> ½ cup freshly squeezed orange juice, at room temperature

In a medium saucepan heat the wine with the orange rind and cinnamon. Do not allow it to boil.

Use a large, flameproof bowl to serve the punch. Rest a metal grate (such as one used for grilling vegetables) on the punch bowl and arrange the sugar cubes close together in the center of the grate. Moisten them with ½ cup of the rum, allowing any excess rum to drip into the punch bowl.

Open the champagne and have the orange juice ready. Strain the warm wine into the punch bowl.

Heat the remaining ½ cup rum in a small pan. When it is warm, ignite, and pour the flaming rum slowly over the sugar cubes. Most of the sugar should melt into the punch bowl; push any remaining sugar through the grate with the back of a spoon. Remove the grate. Immediately pour in the orange juice and champagne and serve.

Makes 6 cups, serving 6 to 8.

NOTES: A metal strainer may be used to hold the sugar cubes instead of a grate. The flames will be more dramatic and longer-lasting if you use a sugar cone instead of cubes. Sugar cones are easy to make at home.

Sugar Cone

    1 cup sugar
    1 heaping teaspoon cornstarch
    1 tablespoon cold water

In a small bowl mix together the sugar and cornstarch. Stir in the water. Turn the sugar mass out onto a piece of wax paper and shape it into a cone that is about 3 inches high. Leave to dry for 24 hours.

To prepare *krambambuli* with a sugar cone, place the dried cone on a grate as described above and moisten it with about ¼ cup of rum (it absorbs the rum faster than cubes do). Heat the remaining ¾ cup rum and ignite. Proceed as directed above.

Chickpea Fritters *(Panelle)*

The ancient Romans enjoyed hot chickpea cakes sold on the streets and in taverns. Today, in Palermo, Sicily, *panelle* are still a popular street food. Although savored year round, they are traditional for December 13. Carol Field reports that on this day they are eaten plain, instead of in sandwiches, to honor Santa Lucia. Sicilian cooks spread *panelle* on special flat, wooden molds, but an oiled cutting board works just as well.

½ pound chickpea flour (about 2¾ cups)
4¼ cups cold water
1¾ teaspoons salt
Freshly ground black pepper
2 tablespoons minced parsley

Vegetable oil for frying

Rub a wooden cutting board with vegetable oil and set aside.

Place the flour in a large saucepan and gradually mix in the water, stirring vigorously to avoid lumps. Cook over medium heat until the mixture is very thick and begins to pull away from the sides of the pan, 12 to 15 minutes. Stir in the salt, pepper, and parsley.

Turn the mixture out onto the oiled board. Using the back of a wooden spoon that has been moistened with cold water, spread it into a 10 x 12-inch rectangle about ¼ inch thick. Leave to cool, then cut into 2 x 3-inch rectangles.

In a large skillet heat ½ inch of vegetable oil. Fry the *panelle* in the hot oil in batches for 2 to 3 minutes on each side, until golden. Drain on paper toweling and serve hot.

Serves 4 to 6.

NOTE: To serve as an appetizer, cut the *panelle* into small squares before frying.

Cheese Pennies

In some families, cheese dishes are traditional for Hanukkah. These tender golden biscuits are like so many pieces of savory *gelt,* the gold candy coins distributed to children during the holiday. They taste best when very fresh.

> 1 cup all-purpose flour
> ½ teaspoon baking powder
> 4 tablespoons cold unsalted butter, cut in pieces
> 1 cup grated sharp yellow Cheddar cheese
> ⅛ teaspoon cayenne
> ½ teaspoon salt
>   Freshly ground white pepper
> 6 to 8 tablespoons ice water

Preheat the oven to 400°F. Lightly grease a baking sheet.

In a medium bowl mix together the flour and baking powder. Cut in the butter until the mixture resembles fine meal. Stir in the cheese, cayenne, salt, and pepper. Add just enough water to make a soft dough. Do not overmix.

Roll the dough out ¼ inch thick on a floured surface. Cut into rounds with a 1½-inch cutter. Transfer the biscuits to the prepared sheet and bake for 10 minutes, until pale golden in color. Serve warm or at room temperature.

Makes 4 dozen biscuits.

Potato Pancakes *(Latkes)*

Sizzled in oil to commemorate the lamp that miraculously burned for eight days, *latkes* are the quintessential Hanukkah dish. Many modern recipes call for baking, instead of frying, the pancakes, but if the oil is hot, they won't absorb too much of it, and the flavor of fried *latkes* is hard to duplicate. Flour or matzo meal is usually added to thicken the batter, but I like to leave it moist so that the pancakes turn out crisp on the outside and creamy inside. *Latke* aficionados swear by their favorite method of preparing the potatoes, either grating them coarsely by hand or pureeing them until nearly smooth in a food processor. I like to grate the potatoes first by hand, then finish them off with a few pulses in the processor. The pancakes brown best in a heavy cast-iron pan; for a beautifully burnished finish, avoid nonstick or aluminum pans. Although controversy rages about how to make the perfect *latkes,* everyone agrees on one thing: you don't have to celebrate Hanukkah to enjoy these pancakes.

    1 large onion
   2½ pounds russet (baking) potatoes (4 large), peeled
    3 eggs, lightly beaten
    1 teaspoon salt
    2 tablespoons minced parsley

       Vegetable oil for frying
       Applesauce and sour cream (optional)

Peel and quarter the onion, then chop it finely in the bowl of a food processor fitted with the steel blade.

Grate the peeled potatoes on the largest blades of a four-sided grater, then transfer the grated potatoes to the food processor with the onion. Using the pulse motion, process a few times until some, but not all, of the coarsely grated pieces have been chopped.

Turn the potato-onion mixture out onto the center of a clean dish towel, and roll it up in the towel. Over a sink, wring out the excess liquid, then scrape the mixture into a large bowl. Beat in the eggs, salt, and parsley.

In one or two large skillets, preferably cast-iron, heat ⅛ to ¼ inch of vegetable oil.

With a soup spoon, scoop dollops of the potato mixture into the hot oil, pressing down slightly to flatten into pancakes 3 to 4 inches in diameter. Cook them on both sides over medium-high heat until crisp and brown.

Place the pancakes briefly on paper towels to drain, then serve hot with applesauce and sour cream, if desired.

Serves 4 as a main course; 6 as a side dish.

Saffron Buns (*Lussekatter*)

These decorative buns are served in Sweden on December 13, St. Lucia's Day. They can be formed into an almost endless variety of shapes, from the traditional *lussekatter* or "Lucia's Cats" resembling cats' eyes, to figure eights, crowns, plaited wreaths, hearts, sheaves, and my favorite "golden wagons" from the province of Småland. Some shapes, such as priest's locks, Christmas stars, crosses, and church doors, take their inspiration from the Church, rather than nature. But whatever their shape, these golden buns sparkling with pearl sugar are radiant on a bleak afternoon.

2½ teaspoons active dry yeast
6 tablespoons lukewarm water
¾ cup evaporated milk
¾ cup sugar
4 tablespoons unsalted butter, melted
2 eggs, at room temperature
½ teaspoon saffron threads, crumbled
¼ teaspoon salt
4 to 4½ cups all-purpose flour
Raisins

Pearl sugar and sliced almonds (optional)

Proof the yeast in the water for 10 minutes, until bubbly. Stir in the milk, sugar, butter, 1 lightly beaten egg, saffron, salt, and enough flour to make a soft dough. Turn out onto a floured surface and knead until the dough is smooth and elastic, about 10 minutes. Place the dough in a lightly greased bowl and turn to grease the top. Cover with plastic wrap and leave to rise until doubled in bulk, 1½ hours.

Punch down the dough and divide into eighteen pieces. Divide each piece of dough in half. Roll each half between your palms into a rope about 4 inches long. To make Lucia cats, place the two ropes together lengthwise, then turn each end in toward the center to make four coils. For golden wagons, lay one rope over the other to form an X. Turn the four ends in to form coils as for Lucia cats. Transfer the buns to two greased baking sheets and place a raisin in the center of each coil. Repeat with the remaining dough.

Cover the buns with a cloth and leave to rise until puffy, 30 to 40 minutes.

Preheat the oven to 425°F. Brush the buns with the remaining egg, lightly beaten and decorate with pearl sugar and sliced almonds, if desired. Bake until nicely browned, 12 to 15 minutes.

Makes 18 buns.

Swedish Gingersnaps *(Pepparkakor)*

Ilove making these cookies for the spicy smells that envelop me as I mix the dough, later to spread throughout the house as the cookies bake and linger in the air long after they are done. *Pepparkakor* are traditional for St. Lucia's Day in Sweden. Of all the varieties I learned to make when living in Stockholm, these crisp, peppery ones are my favorite. They may be fancifully decorated with icing sugar but are just as good plain.

1	cup vegetable shortening
1	cup firmly packed light brown sugar
3	tablespoons dark molasses
	Finely grated rind of 1 lemon
3	cups all-purpose flour
1¼	teaspoons baking soda
4	teaspoons ground cinnamon
2	teaspoons ground cloves
¼	teaspoon ground ginger
1¼	teaspoons ground cardamom (from about 24 pods)
¼	cup water

In a large bowl cream together the shortening and brown sugar. Mix in the molasses and lemon rind.

In a small bowl combine the flour, baking soda, and spices. Add half of these dry ingredients to the creamed mixture, then stir in the water. Add the remaining dry ingredients, mixing well.

Shape the dough into a ball and wrap in wax paper. Refrigerate for several hours or overnight.

Preheat the oven to 350°F.

Take a portion of the dough and roll it out ⅛ inch thick on a floured surface. Cut with cookie cutters into desired shapes, such as hearts, rounds, and stars. Repeat with the remaining dough. Bake the cookies on lightly greased sheets for 8 to 10 minutes, until they turn mahogany at the edges. (They will still be soft when removed from the oven but will crisp as they cool.)

Makes 6 dozen cookies.

Danish Rice Pudding *(Ris à l'amande)*

If the only rice pudding you have ever tasted is dense and thick, then this traditional Christmas Eve dessert will come as a revelation. Silky and light, it makes the perfect finale to a lavish meal. This version of *ris à l'amande* is the specialty of Jytte Brooks, an excellent cook originally from Viborg, Denmark. Jytte explains that rice porridge in Denmark dates back to the fifteenth century, when it was served warm with a lump of butter in the middle and sugar and cinnamon sprinkled on top. Milk or cream was offered on the side. Some Danes still serve the old-fashioned porridge as a first course on Christmas Eve. It is the stuff of fairy tales: Danish storybooks always depict a bowl of rice porridge next to the Christmas *nisser* or gnomes. Some porridge was always placed in the attic for the gnomes, to let them know that they were loved. As for the lighter and richer *ris à l'amande,* this Frenchified dessert did not appear until the nineteenth century, although today it is served more often than the traditional porridge.

Whether pudding or porridge, it must contain a hidden almond. And whoever finds the almond receives marzipan or chocolate as a reward. Often the finder tries to conceal the nut in his or her mouth until the pudding bowl is empty, just to add to the suspense and keep everyone guessing.

Jytte serves her luscious dessert with cherry sauce. In a departure from tradition, it may also be topped with good marmalade or jam.

> 2 cups water
> ¾ cup raw short-grain rice, such as arborio
> 2 cups milk
> ½ cup coarsely chopped blanched almonds
> 2 tablespoons pure vanilla extract (or seeds scraped from
>   1 vanilla bean)
> 3 to 4 tablespoons sugar
> 1½ cups heavy cream
> 1 whole blanched almond
>
> Cherry Sauce (recipe follows)

In a heavy saucepan bring the water to a boil. Add the rice and cook for 10 minutes. Pour in the milk and stir until the mixture returns to a boil. Cover the pan and simmer, stirring occasionally, for 30 to 40 minutes, until all of the liquid has been absorbed.

Stir in the chopped almonds, vanilla extract or bean, and sugar. Cover the pan and leave the pudding to cool completely. (It may be held in the refrigerator until the next day.)

Whip the cream until it forms soft peaks and gradually fold it into the pudding. Hide the whole almond in the pudding, then transfer to a dish and chill before serving. Pass the sauce separately.

Serves 6 to 8.

Cherry Sauce

One 16-ounce can pitted dark sweet cherries in syrup
  1 tablespoon cornstarch
  ¼ cup Cherry Heering or Cherry Kijafa

Reserve about 2 tablespoons of the cherry syrup. Pour the remaining syrup along with the cherries into a medium saucepan and bring to a simmer over low heat.

Dissolve the cornstarch in the reserved syrup and stir into the cherries. Cook for 2 to 3 minutes, until thickened. Stir in the cherry liqueur or wine. Serve the sauce warm over the cold pudding.

Sugarplums

These sweet morsels are a modern version of medieval comfits—fruits, seeds, or nuts preserved in sugar. The orange flower water lends a faintly exotic taste, making them quite addictive. Use the best dates you can find to keep these confections moist.

2 dozen Medjool or Deglet Noor dates
4 teaspoons unsalted butter, softened
6 tablespoons confectioners' sugar
¼ cup ground blanched almonds plus 2 dozen whole blanched almonds
½ teaspoon orange flower water
2 teaspoons granulated sugar

With a sharp knife slit the dates and remove the pits.

In a small bowl cream the butter with the confectioners' sugar. Stir in the ground almonds and the orange flower water, mixing well.

Use a demitasse spoon to place some almond filling in each date. Place a whole almond on the filling and gently press the sides of the date together. Some filling will be visible.

Roll the dates in the granulated sugar. They will keep for a few days, stored airtight between layers of wax paper.

Makes 2 dozen sugarplums.

Suggested Menus

A SUNDAY SUPPER

Mushroom and Barley Soup   (page 50)
Potato Pancakes *(Latkes)*   (page 289)
Cranberry Apple Pie   (page 258)

A SOUP SUPPER

Cabbage Pie Soup   (page 43)
Baked Apples with Cider   (page 254)

A COZY MEAL

Roasted Red Pepper and Cheese Pockets   (page 33)
Spanish Omelet *(Tortilla de patatas)*   (page 63)
Orange Rice Pudding   (page 230)

A WINTER VEGETABLE CELEBRATION

Fireplace-Roasted Rutabagas   (page 179)
Roasted Winter Vegetables   (page 162)
   or Winter Vegetable Stew   (page 164)
Popovers   (page 244)
Glazed Chestnuts with Oranges   (page 257)

A FIRESIDE ROAST

Hot Apple Toddy   (page 26)
   or Dean's Hot Buttered Rum   (page 25)
Roasted Chestnuts   (page 37)
Raclette   (page 67)

A SPICY SAMPLER
Turkish Lentil Soup   (page 49)
Hot and Spicy Bulgur   (page 103)
Potato *Köfte (Patates Köftesi)*   (page 154)
Sliced Oranges Sprinkled with Confectioners' Sugar

A LOW-FAT MENU
Sicilian Olives   (page 32)
Roasted Chestnut Soup   (page 47)
Pureed Beets with Wine   (page 141)
Mashed Potatoes and Celery Root   (page 155)
Poached Pears   (page 256)

A FORMAL DINNER
Pear and Brie Croustades   (page 35)
Butternut Squash and Apple Puree   (page 46)
Cornmeal Soufflé   (page 60)
Warm Mushroom Salad   (page 192)
Poached Pears with Sabayon Sauce   (page 256)

A PIQUANT DINNER
Roasted Potatoes with *Rouille*   (page 36)
Warm Beet Vinaigrette   (page 140)
Sautéed Mushrooms with Olives   (page 150)
Garlic Buns   (page 221)
Upside-Down Apple Tart *(La Tarte des Demoiselles Tatin)*   (page 260)

A MEAL IN MINUTES
Sicilian Olives   (page 32)
Welsh Rabbit   (page 65)
Assorted Dried Fruits

LIGHTING UP A DARK DAY
Flaming Punch *(Krambambuli* or *Zhzhonka)*   (page 285)
Almond Soup *(Sopa de Almendras)*   (page 48)
Mediterranean Orange Salad   (page 187)
Crusty White Bread
Apricot Diamonds   (page 267)

A TASTE OF TURKEY
Warm Hummus   (page 31)
Green Olive Turnovers *(Yeşil zeytinli börek)*   (page 89)
Lentils and Leeks   (page 108)

A CENTRAL ASIAN FEAST
Spicy Squash Turnovers *(Oshkovok somsa)*   (page 38)
Winter Holiday Pilaf *(Bairam plov)*   (page 112)
Assorted Fresh Apples

A RUSSIAN REPAST
Vegetarian *Borshch*   (page 218)
Mushroom Coulibiac   (page 90)
Turnips in Wine Sauce   (page 228)
Countess Tolstoy's Hot Apple Compote   (page 229)

A WINTER BUFFET
Jerusalem Artichoke Pickles   (page 10)
Georgian Vegetable Torte   (page 39)
Georgian Cheese Bread *(Khachapuri)*   (page 248)
Black Bean Chili   (page 105)

A LAVISH BRUNCH
Basque-Style Scrambled Eggs *(Pipérade)*   (page 64)
Roasted Red Pepper Tart   (page 97)
Spanish Escarole Salad   (page 188)
Crusty White Bread

A WEEKEND BREAKFAST
Old-Fashioned Oatmeal   (page 197)
Bran Muffins   (page 196)
    or Cinnamon Walnut Wreath   (page 237)
Freshly Squeezed Orange Juice
Preston County Buckwheat Pancakes   (page 132)
    with Maple Syrup

A WARMING LUNCH
Onion Pie   (page 93)
Garlicky Winter Greens   (page 146)
Lemon Marmalade Cake   (page 264)

A LATE-AFTERNOON TEA
Date and Nut Loaf   (page 240)
   or Buckwheat Honey Cake   (page 135)
Apricot Diamonds   (page 267)
Sugarplums   (page 295)

A ST. LUCY DAY FÊTE
Glögg   (page 24)
Saffron Buns *(Lussekatter)*   (page 290)
Swedish Gingersnaps *(Pepparkakor)*   (page 292)

INSIDE ON A SNOWY AFTERNOON
Mulled Cider   (page 20)
   or Hot Chocolate   (page 22)
Gingerbread with Hot Orange Sauce   (page 262)
Sugar-on-Snow   (page 270)

Bibliography

GENERAL

Allen, Brigid, editor. *Food: An Oxford Anthology*. Oxford: Oxford University Press, 1994.

Greene, Bert. *The Grains Cookbook*. New York: Workman Publishing, 1988.

Hechtlinger, Adelaide. *The Seasonal Hearth: The Woman at Home in Early America*. Woodstock, New York: The Overlook Press, 1977.

Moulin, Leo. *Les liturgies de la table: Une histoire culturelle du manger et du boire*. Anvers: Fonds Mercator, 1988.

Stone, Sally, and Martin Stone. *The Essential Root Vegetable Cookbook*. New York: Clarkson Potter Publishers, 1991.

THE WINTER PANTRY

Beard, James. *Delights & Prejudices*. New York: Simon and Schuster, 1964.

Beecher, Catharine E., and Harriet Beecher Stowe. *The American Woman's Home or, Principles of Domestic Science*. Hartford: The Stowe-Day Foundation, 1987.

The Cook's Room: A Celebration of the Heart of the Home. Edited by Alan Davidson. New York: HarperCollins Publishers, 1991.

Hayden, Dolores. *The Grand Domestic Revolution: A History of Feminist Designs for American Homes, Neighborhoods, and Cities*. Cambridge, Mass.: The MIT Press, 1981.

Home: A Place in the World. Edited by Arien Mack. New York: New York University Press, 1993.

Innes, Jocasta. *Notes from a Country Kitchen*. New York: William Morrow and Company, 1979.

Lifshey, Earl. *The Housewares Story: A History of the American Housewares Industry*. Chicago: National Housewares Manufacturers Association, 1973.

Lupton, Ellen, and J. Abbott Miller. *The Bathroom, the Kitchen, and the Aesthetics of Waste: A Process of Elimination*. Cambridge, Mass.: MIT List Visual Arts Center, 1992.

Paston-Williams, Sara. *The Art of Dining: A History of Cooking & Eating.* London: National Trust, 1993.

SHROVETIDE FESTIVITIES

Beauviala, Anne-Christine, and Nicole Vielfaure. *Fêtes, coutumes et gâteaux.* Le Puy-en-Velay et Paris: Christine Bonneton Editeur, 1984.

Belov, Vasilii. *Lad: Ocherki o narodnoi estetike.* Moscow: Molodaia gvardiia, 1982.

James, E. O. *Seasonal Feasts and Festivals.* London: Thames and Hudson, 1961.

Kovalev, N. I. *Rasskazy o russkoi kukhne.* Moscow: Ekonomika, 1984.

Kovalev, V. M., and N. P. Mogil'nyi. *Russkaia kukhnia: Traditsii i obychai.* Moscow: Sovetskaia Rossiia, 1990.

Massie, Suzanne. *Land of the Firebird: The Beauty of Old Russia.* New York: Simon and Schuster, 1980.

Wright, A. R. *British Calendar Customs: England.* Vol. II: Movable Festivals. Nendeln/Liechtenstein: Kraus Reprint Limited, 1968.

A WORLD OF BUCKWHEAT

The American Heritage Cookbook and Illustrated History of American Eating and Drinking. American Heritage Publishing, 1964.

Anderson, E. N. *The Food of China.* New Haven and London: Yale University Press, 1988.

Chamberlain, Lesley. *The Food and Cooking of Eastern Europe.* London: Penguin Books, 1989.

The Dictionary of American Regional English. Edited by Frederic G. Cassidy. Cambridge, Mass.: Belknap Press of Harvard University Press, 1985.

Dorje, Rinjing. *Food in Tibetan Life.* London: Prospect Books, 1985.

Dumas on Food. Selections from Le Grand Dictionnaire de Cuisine by Alexandre Dumas. Translated by Alan and Jane Davidson. London: Folio Society, 1978.

Escoffier, A. *Le Guide Culinaire.* Translated by H. L. Cracknell and R. J. Kaufmann. New York: Mayflower Books, 1982.

Food in Chinese Culture. Edited by K. C. Chang. New Haven and London: Yale University Press, 1977.

Grigson, Jane. *The World Atlas of Food.* London: Mitchell Beazley Publishers, 1974.

Lehner, Ernst, and Johanna Lehner. *Folklore & Odysseys of Food & Medicinal Plants*. New York: Farrar Straus Giroux, 1973.

Mariani, John. *The Dictionary of American Food and Drink*. New Haven and New York: Ticknor & Fields, 1983.

Mitchell, Richard S., and J. Kenneth Dean. *Polygonaceae (Buckwheat Family) of New York State*. New York State Museum Bulletin No. 431. Albany: University of the State of New York, 1978.

Rink, Oliver A. *Holland on the Hudson: An Economic and Social History of Dutch New York*. Ithaca and London: Cornell University Press, 1986.

Root, Waverley. *Food: An Authoritative and Visual History and Dictionary of the Foods of the World*. New York: Simon and Schuster, 1980.

The Sensible Cook: Dutch Foodways in the Old and the New World. Translated and edited by Peter G. Rose. Syracuse, N.Y.: Syracuse University Press, 1989.

Smith, R. E. F., and David Christian. *Bread & Salt: A Social and Economic History of Food and Drink in Russia*. Cambridge: Cambridge University Press, 1984.

Thomas Jefferson's Farm Book. Edited by Edwin Morris Betts. Charlottesville, Va.: University Press of Virginia, 1976.

Towle, George Makepeace. *American Society*. London: Chapman and Hall, 1870.

Twain, Mark (Samuel L. Clemens). *A Tramp Abroad*. Hartford, Conn.: American Publishing Company, 1889.

Willan, Anne. *La France Gastronomique*. New York: Arcade Publishing, 1991.

RUTABAGA STORIES

Eldridge, Judith. *Cabbage or Cauliflower?* Boston: David R. Godine, 1984.

Kaplan, Anne R., et al. *The Minnesota Ethnic Food Book*. St. Paul: Minnesota Historical Society Press, 1986.

Leach, Charles. *Early American Root Crops: The National Colonial Farm Research Report #9*. Accokeek, Md.: Accokeek Foundation, 1984.

Lovelock, Yann. *The Vegetable Book: An Unnatural History*. London: George Allen and Unwin, 1972.

Pierce, Lincoln C. *Vegetables: Characteristics, Production, and Marketing*. New York: John Wiley and Sons, 1987.

The Poetical Works of Percy Bysshe Shelley, Vol. II. Edited by Harry Buxton Forman. London: Reeves and Turner, 1882.

Rupp, Rebecca. *Blue Corn and Square Tomatoes.* Pownal, Vt.: Storey Communications, 1987.

Thomas, Edward. *Collected Poems.* New York: Thomas Seltzer, 1921.

TOLSTOY'S TABLE

Barkas, Janet. *The Vegetable Passion: A History of the Vegetarian State of Mind.* New York: Charles Scribner's Sons, 1975.

Classic Russian Cooking: Elena Molokhovets' A Gift to Young Housewives. Translated by Joyce Toomre. Bloomington, Ind.: Indiana University Press, 1992.

Frierson, Cathy A. *Peasant Icons: Representations of Rural People in Late Nineteenth-Century Russia.* New York: Oxford University Press, 1993.

Grabar', I. E. *Repin: Monografiia v dvukh tomakh.* Moscow: Nauka, 1964.

———, and I. S. Zil'bershtein. *Repin: Khudozhestvennoe nasledstvo.* Vols. I and II. M–L: izd. Akademii nauk SSSR, 1949.

Kirillina, E. *Repin v Penatakh,* Leningrad: Lenizdat, 1977.

Medkova, I. L. et al. *Vse o vegetarianstve.* Moscow: Ekonomika, 1992.

Molokhovets, Elena. *Podarok molodym khoziakiam ili sredstvo k umen'sheniiu raskhodov v domashnem khoziaistve.* St. Petersburg: Tipografiia N.N. Klobukova, 1901, rpt. Moscow: Polikom, 1991.

Povarennaia kniga S.A. Tolstoi. Tula: Priokskoe knizhnoe izd-vo, 1991.

Repin, I. I. *Dalekoe blizkoe.* Leningrad: Khudozhnik RSFSR, 1986.

Severova, N. B. *Povarennaia kniga dlia golodaiushchikh.* St. Petersburg: Tipografiia pervoi Sankt–Peterburgskoi trudovoi arteli, 1911.

Spencer, Colin. *The Heretic's Feast: A History of Vegetarianism.* London: Fourth Estate, 1993.

Valkenier, Elizabeth Kridl. *Ilya Repin and the World of Russian Art.* New York: Columbia University Press, 1990.

Zelenkova, Olga Konstantinovna. *Ia nikogo ne em: 365 vegetarianskikh meniu.* Edited by I. P. Tret'iakova. Moscow: Moskovskii rabochii, 1991.

———. *Nechto o vegetarianstve.* vyp. I. St. Petersburg, 1902; vyp. II, III, and IV, St. Petersburg, 1903.

Zhuravleva, Larisa. *Kniaginia Mariia Tenisheva.* Smolensk: Poligramma, 1994.

Burland, C. A. *Echoes of Magic: A Study of Seasonal Festivals through the Ages.* Totowa, N.J.: Rowman and Littlefield, 1972.

Farley, Marta Pisetska. *Festive Ukrainian Cooking.* Pittsburgh, Pa.: University of Pittsburgh Press, 1990.

Field, Carol. *Celebrating Italy.* New York: William Morrow and Company, 1990.

Hadfield, Miles, and John Hadfield. *The Twelve Days of Christmas.* Boston: Little, Brown and Company, 1961.

Henisch, Bridget Ann. *Cakes and Characters: An English Christmas Tradition.* London: Prospect Books, 1984.

Pushkin, Aleksandr. *Eugene Onegin.* Translated from the Russian, with a commentary by Vladimir Nabokov, 4 vols. New York: Bollingen Foundation, 1964.

Relph, Ingeborg, and Penny Stanway. *Christmas: A Cook's Tour.* Oxford: Lion Publishing, 1991.

Santino, Jack. *All Around the Year: Holidays & Celebrations in American Life.* Urbana, Ill., and Chicago: University of Illinois Press, 1994.

Schauss, Hayyim. *The Jewish Festivals: From Their Beginnings to Our Own Day.* Translated by Samuel Jaffe. Cincinnati: Union of American Hebrew Congregations, 1938.

Scullard, H. H. *Festivals and Ceremonies of the Roman Republic.* Ithaca, N.Y.: Cornell University Press, 1981.

Wright, A. R. *British Calendar Customs. England.* Vol. I: Fixed Festivals. Nendeln/Liechtenstein: Kraus Reprint Limited, 1968.

Index

cheese:
    baked in grape leaves, 34
    bread, Georgian (*khachapuri*),
      248–49
    buckwheat dumpling with (*struklja*),
      130–31
    cornmeal soufflé, 60–61
    grits soufflé, 61–62
    millet pancakes, 110
    onion pie, 93–94
    pancakes, sweet (*syrniki*), 201
    pear and Brie croustades, 35
    pennies, 288
    popovers, 244
    raclette, 67
    ring, puffed (*gougère*), 68–69
    and roasted red pepper pockets, 33
    and rutabaga soufflé, 177
    Stilton bread pudding, 62–63
    turnip and onion casserole, 161
    Welsh rabbit, 65–66
Chekhov, Anton, 72–73
chestnut(s):
    glazed, with oranges, 257–58
    and mushrooms, sautéed, 151
    soup, roasted, 47–48
    roasted, 37
chickpea(s):
    with chard, 106
    fritters, 287
    and onions, curried, 107
    Turkish lentil soup, 49–50
    warm hummus, 31
chili, black bean, 105
chocolate:
    hot, 22
    Russian lace, 269
chowder, parsnip, potato and spinach,
    52
chutney, cranberry, 12
cider, mulled, 20
cinnamon walnut wreath, 237–38

clementine and sweet potato pudding,
    95–96
Collins, Bill, 132
compote, Countess Tolstoy's hot apple,
    229
condiments:
    cranberry chutney, 12
    onion jam, 11
Cookbook for the Hungry, A (Nordman-
    Severova), 213
cookies:
    apricot diamonds, 267
    old-fashioned molasses, 268
    rusks, 241–42
    Swedish gingersnaps, 292
Cooper, James Fenimore, 117
cornmeal soufflé, 60–61
coulibiac, mushroom, 90–91
Countess Tolstoy's hot apple compote, 229
cranberry:
    apple pie, 258–59
    chutney, 12
    quaff, 21
crêpes, sweet buckwheat (*crêpes de blé
    noir*), 82–83
crescents, squash, 245
croustades, pear and Brie, 35
crudités, spicy winter, 8–9
curried chickpeas and onions, 107
curried potato casserole, 156

date and nut loaf, 240–41
Dead Souls (Gogol), 78
Dean's hot buttered rum, 25
desserts:
    apricot diamonds, 267
    baked apples with cider, 254–55
    bread pudding with custard sauce,
      265–66
    buckwheat honey cake, 135–36
    Countess Tolstoy's hot apple compote,
      229

turnovers:

    green olive (*yeşil zeytinli börek*), 89–90

    spicy squash, 38–39

Twain, Mark, 117

upside-down apple tart (*la tarte des demoiselles Tatin*), 260–61

vegetable(s):

    broth, roasted, 44–45

    roasted winter, 162–63

    roasted winter, with mustard sauce, 163

    salad, mixed (*vinegret*), 220–21

    spicy winter crudités, 8–9

    stew, winter, 164–65

    torte, Georgian, 39–40

vegetarian *borshch,* 218–19

vegetarianism, in Russia, 205–17

Vegetarian Pleasures (Lemlin), 60

Verigin, Peter, 205

Vesta, 1, 273

Vikings, 275

vinaigrette:

    mustard, for celery root and carrot salad, 190

    raspberry, for watercress and endive salad, 189

    salsify, 158

    sherry, for Spanish escarole salad, 188

    warm beet, 140

vinegret (mixed vegetable salad), 220–21

walnut cinnamon wreath, 237–38

Washington, George, and buckwheat farming, 124

watercress:

    and endive salad, 189

    and spinach puree, 69

Weaver, Ardath, 186, 240

Weaver, William Woys, 134

Welsh rabbit, 65–66

Whistler, James McNeill, 117

white bean and potato pie, 92–93

Williams, Howard, 205

wine:

    mulled (*glögg*), 24

    mulled (*Glühwein*), 25

    pureed beets with, 141

    sauce, turnips in, 228

winter festivities, 71–78, 273–84

    see also Shrovetide

"Winter Evening, The" (Cowper), 18

wreath, cinnamon walnut, 237–38

yellow pea soup, 54

yeşil zeytinli börek (green olive turnovers), 89–90

Zelenkov, Aleksandr and Olga, 208

zhzhonka (flaming punch), 285–86